GEORGE AND LAURA

GEORGE
AND
LAURA

PORTRAIT OF AN AMERICAN MARRIAGE

Christopher Andersen

WILLIAM MORROW
An Imprint of HarperCollins*Publishers*

Grateful acknowledgment is made to the following for permission to
reprint the photographs in this book:

AFP/Corbis: 43, 49, 52, 54, 55, 61
AP Wide World: 34, 35, 36, 37, 48, 50, 56, 57, 58
Associated Press, The White House: 59
Corbis: 33, 46, 47, 60
George Bush Presidential Library: 2, 3, 4, 5, 6, 7, 11, 12, 13, 22, 23, 24, 25,
26, 27, 28, 29, 30, 31, 32
Kraft Brooks/Corbis Sygma: 38, 39, 40, 42, 44
Liss Steve/Corbis Sygma: 41
Phillips Academy, Andover: 8, 9, 10
Randolph D. Rubin Photography Collection: 17, 18
Reuters NewMedia Inc./Corbis: 1, 45, 51, 53
The Jenna Welch Collection: 14, 15, 16, 19, 20, 21

Designed by Oksana Kushnir

ISBN 0-06-621370-3

Printed in the U.S.A.

To my sister, Valerie

The best decision I ever made
was asking Laura to marry me.
I'm not sure the best decision
she ever made was saying yes.
But I'm glad she did . . .

—*George W. Bush*

PREFACE

They would be called upon to lead a nation through one of its darkest hours. Yet there seemed little to indicate that either was equal to the task. He had been the floundering, hard-drinking scion of one of America's most influential families. She was the former teacher and school librarian with the enigmatic smile that belied a tragic secret of her own. Together, George W. Bush and his wife Laura would overcome their own private demons and capture the White House after the most hotly contested presidential race in modern political history—a race that would ultimately be settled in the United States Supreme Court, and then by a vote of just 5–4. Incredibly, that mind-spinning constitutional crisis was only a prelude to the surreal events of September 11, 2001.

After eight years of almost unremitting scandal that had climaxed with the impeachment of the President, a Clinton-weary America was ready for someone to restore a sense of morality to the White House. Ostensibly, the Bushes seemed to be the antithesis of their predecessors, unencumbered by rumors of marital infidelity or financial improprieties.

Yet similarities between the two couples abounded. All were baby

boomers, weaned on *Captain Kangaroo, Davy Crockett,* and *I Love
Lucy.* All came of age listening to the Beach Boys, the Beatles, and
the Supremes—and to the news bulletins alerting the world that
John F. Kennedy, then Martin Luther King Jr., then Robert F.
Kennedy had been assassinated. All enrolled in college during the
tumultuous sixties, and for the most part watched from the relative
comfort of their dorms as the nation was torn apart by the war in
Vietnam.

Shaped by the same forces and sharing the same ideals, Bill and
Hillary Clinton knew what they wanted from the beginning. While
still in their early twenties, they pooled their impressive talents and
embarked on a remarkable political journey that would take them to
the pinnacle of power. By contrast, Laura had watched as her husband, despite his own formidable political legacy, stumbled from one
failed dream to the next. He, too, would manage to reach the zenith,
after only six years in the national spotlight.

In many ways, the Bushes' struggles, heartaches, and triumphs
mirrored those of a generation. Each had experienced grief early
on—W. over the death of his beloved little sister; Laura over a tragic
death she herself had caused. As a couple, they coped with crushing
political defeat, business setbacks, substance abuse, a life-threatening
pregnancy, the inevitable soul-trying pressures of child-rearing—and,
ultimately, the doubts and fears of a nation under siege.

In the months following the terrorist attacks on the World Trade
Center and the Pentagon, the President and his First Lady were more
visible than ever—though not necessarily in sharper focus. He
became the embodiment of America's fighting spirit, and she took on
the role of First Comforter with seemingly effortless grace. But the
true nature of their relationship remained a mystery.

Certainly the uncomplicated, folksy facade had little to do with
reality. Like so many of the presidents and first ladies before them, as
individuals each was a mind-spinning tangle of contradictions. He
was the dutiful son who reveled in embarrassing his family with his
frat-boy antics, the binger-turned-teetotaler, the Ivy League graduate *cum* Good Ole Boy with a penchant for cringe-inducing malaprops, the proverbial black sheep who stumbled upon his true calling
at age forty-eight and wound up in the White House. She was the
prim librarian who chain-smoked Kent cigarettes and played the

field until age thirty-one, when she married after a whirlwind courtship. Polite to a fault, she nevertheless delighted in her husband's often outrageous behavior. Most important, the seemingly mild-mannered Laura Bush had succeeded through sheer force of will in accomplishing what Jackie Kennedy and Hillary Clinton could not: Seeing the self-destructive streak in her husband, she did something about it, and in the process saved the man she loved from himself.

Not since Franklin Delano Roosevelt has a president faced a surprise attack delivered against American citizens on American soil. Not since Eleanor Roosevelt has a first lady been called upon to be her husband's strongest ally in a time of national crisis. Now, as George and Laura Bush step into history, it is important to understand the forces that shaped them as individuals, and the crucibles—both private and public—that put their marriage to the test. For in the end, whether played out in the White House or on a ranch in Texas, theirs is an intriguing, inspiring, and uniquely American love story.

George and Laura love each other, but just as important, they are *proud* of each other.

—*Nancy Weiss,*
longtime friend

It's a pretty overwhelming job, but they handle it, they handle it . . .

—*Jenna Welch,*
Laura's mother

1

September 11, 2001
A Tuesday

He rolled out of bed just before 6 A.M. at Sarasota's Colony tennis resort, pulled on shorts and an old T-shirt, then laced up his favorite pair of frayed-at-the-edges, broken-in-to-perfection running shoes. Thirty minutes later, in the half-light of dawn, the President of the United States was pounding around the palm-lined perimeter of one of Longboat Key's most exclusive golf courses, trailed by puffing Secret Service agents.

Richard Keil, White House correspondent for Bloomberg News and a former All-American distance runner, chatted with the President while they ran. "He was clipping along, and talking very comfortably," Keil recalled. "If you're not in real good shape and running that fast, you can't carry on a conversation." Running, George W. Bush explained, was his way to "cope with the stress of this job."

This morning the President would cover just four and a half miles—two laps around the course in just over thirty-two minutes. Then it was back to his hotel suite and a quick shower before changing into the gray suit, blue shirt, and burgundy tie that had been spread out on the bed for him by an aide. Before he left, the President was given his daily intelligence briefing. The heightened threat of terrorism was mentioned this morning, as it had been nearly every morning since George W. Bush took office.

Nine hundred miles to the north, Laura Bush also started the day early. In her husband's absence, the job of taking Spot the English springer spaniel and their frisky black Scottish terrier Barney for their morning walk had fallen to the First Lady. Afterward, Laura returned to the second-floor family quarters for a quick breakfast with her in-laws. George H. W. Bush and his wife Barbara had spent the night at the White House and were about to board a private jet bound for a speaking engagement in Minnesota.

Laura had always had an easy, comfortable relationship with the ex-president and his first lady, but now they rightly sensed their daughter-in-law was preoccupied. This morning, the former school-teacher was going to appear before Senator Edward Kennedy's Senate Committee on Health, Education, Labor, and Pensions to plead for more federal funding of early childhood education. She took even greater care than usual in picking out just the right wardrobe for the occasion: tailored red suit, a three-strand pearl necklace, matching pearl earrings.

Laura kissed her in-laws good-bye, checked her purse for the essentials ("lipstick, hairbrush, Altoids"), then headed for the White House limousine waiting to take her to Capitol Hill. It was, she said to no one in particular as she stepped out into the brilliant September sunshine, "a beautiful day, just beautiful." But as she walked the few steps toward the car, a member of her Secret Service detail took her aside to tell her he was getting some disturbing news over his earpiece. Something terrible had just happened in New York . . .

The presidential motorcade was making the twenty-minute trip from the Colony to Emma E. Booker Elementary School when Press Secretary Ari Fleischer's pager went off. There were early reports that a plane had crashed into one of the Twin Towers of New York's World Trade Center just minutes before, at 8:48 A.M. President Bush had emerged from his car and was shaking hands with local officials standing outside the school when Chief of Staff Andrew Card sidled up to him with the news.

A terrible accident, Bush thought to himself as he walked into the gray-carpeted second grade classroom and, smiling broadly, took a seat to the immediate left of the teacher. Scrawled on the blackboard behind him was the slogan "Reading Makes a Country Great!" Less than twenty-four hours before, the President had been cheered at Jacksonville's Justina Elementary School as he declared "war on illiteracy." Sarasota was the second stop on a whirlwind tour of the Southeast to promote his administration's "Putting Reading First" initiative, and to muster support for an education bill that had stalled in Congress.

The eighteen students seated in two rows before him had just begun to take turns reading aloud a story about a goat when Card reappeared. He walked to the head of the classroom, leaned down, and whispered in the President's right ear. "A second plane has just hit the World Trade Center," he said. "America is under attack."

The President, sitting with his legs crossed and his hands folded in his lap, was intensely aware of the television cameras that were recording his every expression. "I have nobody to talk to," he thought to himself as he tried to absorb it all in an instant. "My God, I'm Commander-in-Chief and the country has just come under attack!"

There was no way he could conceal his feelings of shock and dismay at the horrible news. There was a fleeting look of panic in the President's eyes as Card stepped back. "It was a surreal moment," Card later said. "It was immediately obvious that it was neither an accident nor a coincidence."

But without all the facts at hand, George Bush had no intention of upsetting the schoolchildren who had come to read for him. The rest of the children's story about the goat did not register with him at all, but the President, raising his eyebrows and nodding, interrupted the second graders to praise them. "Really good readers, whew!" Bush told the class. "This must be sixth grade."

At the end of each chapter, the students read the line "more to come," and at one point the President asked them if they knew what that meant. "Something is happening!" several excitedly replied in unison. Something is happening . . .

After six minutes of patiently listening to the children and trying to mask his growing anxiety, President Bush abruptly left. It was 9:12 A.M.

At this moment the West Wing of the White House was gripped by panic. Secret Service agents burst into the office of Vice President Dick Cheney and lifted him up by his arms, legs, and by his belt. "They literally propelled him out of his office," said one staffer. The agents then rushed the Vice President along with his wife Lynne Cheney, National Security Adviser Condoleezza Rice, and a few others down to the Presidential Emergency Operations Center (PEOC), a bunkerlike warren of rooms beneath the White House designed to withstand a nuclear blast.

American Airlines flight 77 was bearing down on the White House, they were told. In the Old Executive Office Building next door, flak-jacketed members of the bomb squad were running through the hallways yelling "Get out! Get out! This is real!"

"What a weird, freak accident," Laura had thought when she first heard the news of a plane crashing into the north tower of the World Trade Center. But when she arrived at Capitol Hill, Senator Kennedy met her at the door of the conference room with news of the second plane. They immediately agreed to postpone the planned Senate hearing, and Kennedy promptly escorted her to his office.

For a moment Laura was transported back to that time in November 1963 when, like every other seventeen-year-old in America, she sat in stunned silence as grainy coverage of JFK's murder in Dallas flickered across the nation's black-and-white TV screens. "It was a very strange, almost ironic time—since what I remembered as the most traumatic time in my childhood was the assassination of Senator Kennedy's brother, when I was a senior in high school," she later said. "Words can't describe the depth of feeling that I had, being with President Kennedy's brother as our nation's heart was broken with another tragedy."

While Secret Service agents and senior staff scrambled to get more details over cell phones and earpieces, Laura sat, silent and motionless, watching the unfolding horror on a television set perched in one corner of Kennedy's office. "Nothing," she thought, "is ever going to be the same."

Back in Florida, her husband was also glued to a television—a small portable that had been rolled into a special staging room set up for the presidential party at Emma E. Booker Elementary School. Both towers were now engulfed in smoke and flame, and there was panic in the streets of lower Manhattan. "Goddamn whoever did this," said the President, his face red with rage. "Goddamn them."

He sat down at a laminate-topped cafeteria table with folding legs and picked up a "Stu-Three"—one of the bulbous black phones that provide the President with a secure line wherever he travels. Bush's first call was to Vice President Dick Cheney, already monitoring events from the subterranean PEOC beneath the White House. The second call was to FBI Director Robert Mueller. Already there was speculation that these attacks were the handiwork of fugitive Arab terrorist Osama bin Laden. After a second conversation with Cheney, the President hung up the oversized "Stu-Three" and turned to his aides. "We're at war," he said. "That's what we're paid for, boys. We are going to take care of this. When we find out who did this, they are not going to like me as president. Somebody is going to pay."

Minutes later, Bush walked briskly into the school library packed with scores of students, parents, and local officials who had waited for two hours to catch a glimpse of their president. They were unprepared for what he was about to say as he stepped up to a podium hung with the presidential seal. "Ladies and gentlemen, this is a difficult moment for America," he told the hushed crowd. "We have had a national tragedy. Two airplanes have crashed into the World Trade Center, in an apparent terrorist attack on our country. I am going to conduct a full-scale investigation and hunt down and find those folks who committed this act. Terrorism against our nation will not stand."

The President asked for a brief moment of silence and then, clearly on the verge of tears, lowered his head in prayer. Then he abruptly grabbed his notes from the podium and rushed out the door, leaving behind a visibly stricken audience. "I'm gonna leave," he told his aides. "Going back to Washington."

While the presidential motorcade was racing up North Washington Boulevard toward Sarasota-Bradenton Airport and Air Force One, Laura and Senator Kennedy agreed they should offer some words of reassurance to the American public. "Our hearts and our prayers go out to the victims of this act of terrorism," she told the reporters who had initially come to cover her Senate testimony. Of special concern to the former school librarian was the effect all this would have on America's youngest citizens. "Parents need to reassure children everywhere in our country," she said firmly, "that they're safe."

Along with the rest of the nation, Ted Kennedy was impressed with the First Lady's calm demeanor. "You take the measure of a person at a time like that," he later said. "She is steady, assured, elegant."

But what of her own nineteen-year-old twin daughters, Jenna and Barbara? At Yale, sophomore Barbara heard the news when her clock radio woke her up at 9 A.M. Jenna, in her second year at the University of Texas, was still fast asleep when a Secret Service agent knocked on her dormitory room door a few minutes after 8 A.M. Central Time. When Mom tried to contact both girls, she was told they had both already been hustled off to what the Secret Service called "secure locations." Within minutes, the First Lady was spirited to a secure location of her own—a windowless room in a nondescript federal building on the outskirts of Washington.

Even before Air Force One had taken off from Sarasota-Bradenton, there was more terrible news. At 9:43 A.M. a third passenger jet—American Airlines flight 77—crashed into the Pentagon, presumably killing hundreds. One air traffic controller who was tracking the plane that morning theorized that American flight 77 was indeed aiming for the White House, but that on that particularly brilliant day the sun was at such an angle that it might have blinded the hijackers, making it difficult for them to spot their target. The Pentagon was impossible to miss.

Ten minutes later, Air Force One was rolling down the runway. As the plane took off, a somber Bush asked where his wife and children were and what precautions were being taken to protect them. Satisfied that his daughters were out of harm's way in Austin and New Haven, he told his aides to get the First Lady on the line.

"Oh, Bushie," she said when she heard the sound of her husband's voice. "How horrible. How terrible . . ."

"Are you okay, Bushie?" he asked. Bushie was their pet name for each other.

"Yes, I'm okay," she replied. "Somewhere safe . . . The girls are safe . . . Don't you worry about us. We'll be fine."

"I'll be home soon," he told her before hanging up. Later he would say that his wife "couldn't have been more calm, resolved, almost placid—which was a very reassuring thing."

Laura knew her husband wasn't the only one in the family who needed to hear her soothing words. When she finally reached her daughters, they were both on the verge of hysteria. "Freaked out, the girls are," the President later said of his daughters. "Wife's okay. She understands we're at war. Got a war mentality."

Perhaps. But once she was finished being strong for everyone else, Laura placed a call to her mother, Jenna Welch, back home in Midland, Texas. "She thinks I called to reassure her that I was okay," Laura later said, "but the fact is I called to hear her voice . . . I think that's what happened all over the country. People called their mothers or their children to talk to them and make sure they were safe and to reassure each other."

"I think it's a very natural thing for a girl to do," Laura's mom agreed, "to call her mother at a time like that. It's one way to sort of get a grip on reality, by talking to the one person who knows you better than anyone."

Tensions eased for one fleeting moment, when the President jokingly asked if Barney, his mischievous Scottie, was also in a "secure place."

"He's probably nipping at the heels of Osama bin Laden right now," cracked Andy Card.

The President's wan smile vanished, however, when Condoleeza Rice informed him that someone had called the Emergency Operations Center at the White House and said simply, "Air Force One is next." What made the threat credible—and terrifying— was that the caller not only knew how to phone into the nerve center beneath the White House, he knew the code name for Air Force One. "To get put through into the secure facility," Rice said, "and hear the code name for Air Force One, there's something headed for Air Force One—I don't think you can underestimate that." Bush was bluntly told, Air Force One "is in grave danger."

For the first time in history, the Federal Aviation Administration was ordering all commercial airliners to land at the nearest airport.

But accomplishing that would take time, and with hundreds of planes still in the air, there was no way of knowing which, if any, had been hijacked by terrorists.

Meantime, passengers aboard Air Force One, particularly the journalists who were traveling with the President, were instructed not to use their cell phones. Doing so, they were told, might reveal the plane's whereabouts to terrorists.

In his airborne conference room, the President was now working the phones. In rapid succession, he called Vice President Cheney and Secretary of Defense Donald Rumsfeld, then was briefed by Rice.

All the while, Bush kept one eye on the conference room television monitor. Along with the rest of his countrymen, he watched in utter disbelief as the south tower of the World Trade Center, its steel infrastructure fatally compromised by the impact of the plane and thousands of gallons of flaming jet fuel, began to collapse. The massive white 110-story, 1,350-foot-tall skyscraper appeared to virtually dissolve from the top down, and was gone in a matter of ten surreal seconds. Five minutes later, at 10:10 A.M., another hijacked plane—United flight 93—plowed into a field in Pennsylvania's Somerset County southeast of Pittsburgh.

Passengers were pressed back in their leather seats as Air Force One climbed swiftly now—to a more secure forty thousand feet. The Secret Service "made it clear they wanted to get us up quickly," Bush adviser Karl Rove said, "and they wanted to get us to a high altitude, because of the specific threat made to Air Force One." Flying off each wingtip were two fighter jets. Wherever Air Force One was headed, this escort would ensure that it got there safely.

Rumors ran rampant: Of another plane headed toward Washington, approaching from the south. Of more hijacked planes forced down around the country. Of a bomb at the State Department, and another at the White House. "There *is* a 'fog of war,'" Bush would later observe. "You have heard about it, and you have read about it. Well, there is one. We had all kinds of reports. Once I was able to focus on what the conditions were in the country, I was able to more clearly think about what we needed to do." But, he said, "the first thing we had to do was to make sure we understood what the heck was going on."

The one man whose counsel he leaned on heavily, Vice President Dick Cheney, urged his boss not to come to Washington. "You are a target, Mr. President. It's just too dangerous."

"How about Camp David?"

"No, Mr. President," Cheney insisted. "Our people tell me that's still too risky."

At 10:28 A.M. the President's eyes widened as he watched the World Trade Center's north tower plummet to earth, leaving a gaping hole in the Manhattan skyline. At her hiding place outside the capital, Laura leaned forward on the edge of her seat and placed her hand to her mouth. "Those poor people," she said, shaking her head. One of her aides, a young woman in her twenties, began to cry. "Horror" was the first word Laura would use to describe her feelings at that moment. "Unbelievable sadness as we watched those buildings fall, and you know, you knew what happened to all those people inside. Everyone had anxiety and uncertainty, not knowing if this would happen all over the country."

Beneath the White House, Cheney, Rice, and other senior advisers watched the horrific scene on television. "There was just a momentary pause in activity," one staffer recalled. "Just total silence. But no one talked about it, not even an 'Oh, God.' They just went back to work."

While Bush's advisers assessed the threat to the nation at large and the President in particular, there arose one overriding concern: Air Force One needed to refuel. Moreover, the Secret Service wanted to "downsize the package"—get rid of the reporters and other nonessential personnel.

Around 11:50 A.M., Air Force One touched down at Barksdale Air Force Base in northern Louisiana. This time there was no red carpet, no reception line. Instead, the plane was met by soldiers in full combat gear—flak jackets, green fatigues, helmets, and drawn M-16s. Humvees mounted with machine guns guarded the tarmac as the President's motorcade sped to a secure area within the General Dougherty Conference Center. There they were met by Lieutenant General Thomas Keck, commander of the Eighth Air Force, and the base commander, Colonel Floyd Carpenter. Both officers wore combat uniforms and sidearms. "And that's the moment where, if it wasn't real for you before," said Rove, "it's pretty damn real." A sign posted at the entrance to headquarters read Def Con Delta—the military's highest possible state of alert.

After conferring over the phone yet again with Cheney, Bush stepped up to another podium bearing the presidential seal. His eyes were red from crying. "Freedom itself," he told the nation, "was attacked this morning by a faceless coward."

Back on a "Stu-Three" phone with the Vice President, Bush now insisted that it was time for him to return to Washington. "I think I need to come back," he said.

"We still think it's unstable, Mr. President," Cheney replied. "We still have a number of planes in the air that are unaccounted for."

"But I want to meet with the National Security Council," Bush said.

With jet fighters patrolling the skies and fires still raging at the Pentagon, a state of emergency was declared in Washington at 1:15 P.M. Ten minutes later, Air Force One was airborne again, this time heading for Offutt Air Force Base in Nebraska—headquarters of the Strategic Air Command.

The Commander-in-Chief had agreed to confer with his National Security Council via phone from Offutt, but his patience was wearing thin. "I want to go home," he told Andy Card. "I want to go back to Washington now—as soon as possible."

"But, Mr. President," said a Secret Service agent, "there are still a dozen planes we can't . . ."

"Don't care," Bush said, cutting him off. "I don't want some tinhorn terrorist keeping the President of the United States out of Washington. People want to see their president, and they want to see him *now*."

But Cheney urged his boss to hold off on his return—at least for the time being. "Let's," Andy Card agreed, "let the dust settle."

Back in Washington, Laura wanted the same thing. She was mesmerized by what she was seeing on television, and disturbed by the swelling crescendo of criticism being leveled at her husband. Where was the President hiding? *Why* was he hiding? As Air Force One hopscotched from one air base to the next over the course of nine hours, the growing public perception was one of a president not fully in control.

In many ways, he wasn't. "Have you heard from my parents?" he asked, turning to an aide. The forty-third president learned that the forty-first president and the former first lady were somewhere over the Midwest heading toward Minnesota when their plane was told to land like all the others, but that was all. "Can you get my parents on the phone?" he asked. "I want to make sure they're all right."

But there were limitations, even for "Forty-one" and "Forty-three," as father and son sometimes called themselves. The President had only his father's cell phone number, and like millions of others trying to reach loved ones that day, he could not make a connection because the system was taxed beyond capacity.

When he finally did reach his dad, the President was overjoyed if still somewhat confused. "Where are you?" he asked.

"I'm in Milwaukee," the senior Bush answered.

"*Milwaukee?* What are you doing there?"

"This," his father answered, "is where you grounded me."

Even more than Cheney, the former president was worried about his son's safety. The elder Bush had also once headed the Central Intelligence Agency, and in that capacity he knew that his son was an obvious target. In a time of crisis like this, the safety of the president was of paramount importance.

In a voice cracking with emotion, Forty-one advised Forty-three to return to Washington as quickly as he could—but not before the Secret Service was satisfied that it was safe for him to do so. The President could hear his mother, Barbara Bush, talking in the background. "Just don't take any chances," Dad repeated. "It's important that you stay safe—that the Office of the President is protected."

"Don't worry," he reassured his father. "I've already told them that's what we're going to do."

Once on the ground at Offutt, another armored Humvee escorted the President's motorcade to the base command center. At 3:15, he convened his teleconference with the National Security Council. The terrorist acts amounted to "an attack on freedom," he told Cheney, Rice, and the others. "And we're going to go after it, and we're not going to lose focus. And we're going to minister to the country and deal with the horrors that people are experiencing and the consequences, and we're going to get through our period of mourning. But we're not going to lose focus and resolve on what happened here and what this means for the United States of America, its leadership role, to mobilize the world, now, to deal with this scourge."

By 4:15, the President had finished his teleconference with the National Security Council and rushed back to the plane. With machine gun–toting soldiers lining the runways, Air Force One taxied into position. All vehicles on the ground were ordered to stop immediately, but one white tanker truck loaded with aviation fuel pulled directly in their path. Then, in an instant, the truck lurched ahead as the driver stomped on the gas—narrowly avoiding a collision.

Air Force One was still climbing as the President placed a call to Laura. By this time, she had joined Dick Cheney and his wife Lynne in the emergency operations center beneath the White House. "I'm coming home," he told her.

"Thank God, Bushie," she said with a sigh. "Thank God."

The President made good on his promise at 7 P.M., and made his way straight down to the PEOC—and into the arms of his wife. The Vice President, his wife Lynne, and Secretary of State Colin Powell looked on as the Commander-in-Chief, his eyes brimming with tears, held the First Lady in a lingering embrace.

For Laura, everyone else in the room seemed to vanish. "I know the Cheneys were in the room," she later recalled. "It didn't seem like we were the only ones there. We hugged, of course. We were really glad to see each other, but also the enormity of what had happened in our country had really sunk in by then, and so we just comforted each other."

At 8:30 P.M., the President was behind his desk in the Oval Office and looking into a television camera. "None us of will ever forget this day," he told the nation, "yet we go forward to defend freedom and all that is good and just in our world." When it was over, Bush returned to the Emergency Operations Center to preside over his second National Security Council meeting. "We're going to win," he told his advisers. "We're going to do what it takes to win this war."

Once the meeting was over, the President took Laura by the hand and headed toward the elevator. But the Secret Service had something else in mind. "Mr. President," said one agent, pointing to a sleeper sofa in a corner of the conference room that had been brought downstairs for the First Couple, "we're staying down here in the basement."

"Oh, no, we're not," the President replied sternly. "I'm really tired. I've had a heck of a day and I'm going to sleep in my own bed!"

The agents capitulated, but with one caveat. "If we have any threats," the agent said, "we'll come and get you."

With Barney and Spot already snoozing nearby, George donned his pajamas and climbed into bed with Laura at 11 P.M. Within minutes, Laura was fast asleep. The President was finally beginning to doze off when suddenly he heard someone breathing heavily in the hallway just outside his bedroom door.

"Mr. President! Mr. President!" a Secret Service agent said, bursting into the room. "There's an unidentified aircraft heading toward the White House! I think we're under attack, Mr. President! We need to go back in the bunker."

The President slid out of bed, grabbed Barney and Spot, and took Laura's hand as they headed for the door. The First Lady did not have time to put in her contact lenses. "I'm blind," she conceded, so the President had to lead her out of their room, and down the cavernous Center Hall of the family living quarters toward the elevator. Clutching her husband's right arm, Laura shuffled along in her nightgown and fluffy slippers. "This is so embarrassing," she said. The President held Barney in his left arm, with Spot trailing behind. "Kitty," he said of the family cat, "was left behind to defend herself."

In the elevator on the way down, Bush turned to his wife. "Probably a false alarm," he said. "Yep," she agreed.

Once they arrived in the basement, George and Laura were rushed to the conference room. The First Lady, leaning heavily on the President, could scarcely remain awake. "She was *so* tired," he remembered. As a White House orderly began making up the sofa bed ("The bed I refused to sleep in," Bush said), the President looked around the room. "Where's the phone?" he demanded. "What the heck is going on? Attacked again?"

At that moment, an enlisted man burst into the room. "Mr. President, good news! It's one of our own!"

George and Laura turned and looked knowingly at each other. Then they laughed. Trudging back upstairs, they got back into bed and turned out the light. "We will get whoever did this," he said in the dark. "We will win."

"I know we will," Laura said. "I know we will . . ."

To understand Laura and me, you must understand Midland. All that we are, all the things we believe in, come from that one place.

—*George*

His personality comes from Barbara. They both love to needle and they both love to talk.

—*Laura*

Without her, he would not be where he is.

—*Paul Burka,*
journalist and friend

He is clearly the wild son—even today.

—*Karl Rove, adviser*

When I was young and irresponsible, I was young and irresponsible.

—*George*

2

To all outward appearances, they seemed as starkly different as two people could possibly be. She was serenely calm; he lived life at a frenzied pace. She was softspoken; he was loud—even he would concede sometimes obnoxiously so. She was reserved, scrupulously polite, self-effacing; he was unremittingly in-your-face, leaning into strangers until he was nose-to-nose with them, hugging them, touching them, flagrantly violating their personal space.

Laura would say George made her laugh. George would say she was a good listener and it was a good thing, too, because he liked to talk. But what drew them together was not so much their differences as their bedrock similarities. Both grew up in the oil-rich, dust-blown West Texas town of Midland—and both grew up desperately trying to please the parents who loved them.

In George W.'s case, the family pressures to succeed were obvious. His predecessor in the White House, Bill Clinton, never knew his biological father—or for that matter could even be absolutely certain who his natural father was. "W.," on the other hand, grew up in the looming shadow of his namesake. Moreover, George W. was heir to a legacy of power and privilege that reached back to fourteenth-century England. According to *Burke's Peerage,* W. was a fourteenth cousin of the Queen Mother once removed and a fourteenth cousin twice removed from the Queen herself—as well as a distant relative of the late Princess Diana, Winston Churchill, and George Washington. Through his mother, Barbara Pierce Bush, he was also a direct descendant of the fourteenth president of the United States, Franklin Pierce.

Not that the Bushes ever trumpeted their blueblood lineage or their influence; lacking the hauteur of the Roosevelts and the Rockefellers or the cockiness of the Kennedys, they invariably came down on the side of discretion. The foundations of what *Time* magazine would later call "The Quiet Dynasty" were actually laid at the dawn of the twentieth century. Like subsequent generations of Bushes, New Yorker Samuel Prescott Bush journeyed west to make his fortune, settling in Ohio and rising to become president of the Buckeye Steel Casting Company in 1905—a position he held for twenty years. A firm believer in corporate paternalism—employee housing and unemployment compensation were of particular concern—Samuel became a close adviser to President Herbert Hoover at the start of the Depression.

Samuel's son, Prescott Sheldon, grew up on the sprawling Bush family estate near Columbus, and—like most male offspring of the monied classes at the time—was packed off at age thirteen to one of the elite prep schools that dotted the New England landscape. After graduating from tony St. George's in Newport, Rhode Island, Prescott went on to Yale University. There the six-foot-four-inch, movie-star-handsome Prescott would excel at virtually everything he tried: academics, football, baseball, golf—a bass, he was even president of the Yale Glee Club.

Prescott graduated from Yale just as the United States entered World War I, and in 1918 boarded a troop ship bound for Europe. After seeing action as an artillery officer in France, he returned home to size up his business options.

His first shrewd move was to marry Dorothy Walker, whose father George Herbert Walker had founded the prestigious private investment firm of Brown Brothers Harriman, then Wall Street's largest. Prescott, who would soon be taken on as a partner at Brown

Brothers Harriman, was an outstanding golfer, and in this he found a kindred spirit in his father-in-law. A onetime president of the U.S. Golf Association, Walker would go on to establish the Walker Cup, one of the sport's most coveted trophies.

Slim, athletic Dorothy Walker—future mother of one president and grandmother of another—grew up in a Gatsbyesque world of stately Fifth Avenue mansions, private railroad cars, and turreted summer "cottages" that rivaled the chateaux of the Loire. In addition to their in-town Sutton Place address, the Walkers owned a palatial Long Island estate, and Duncannon, a ten-thousand-acre South Carolina plantation. Yet it was their more modest vacation home perched on the rockbound coast of Maine at Kennebunkport that would serve as a magnet for succeeding generations—not to mention a Republican answer to the Kennedys' fabled Hyannisport compound. From the time she was a girl, W.'s "Ganny Bush" could count any number of Morgans, Drexels, Vanderbilts, Astors, Harrimans, and Mellons among her friends.

While most Americans endured untold economic hardship during the Depression, Prescott and Dorothy Bush raised their brood of five—Prescott Jr., George, Jonathan, William ("Bucky"), and Nancy—in a rambling Greenwich, Connecticut, mansion with a broad veranda, a porte cochere, and a large household staff. To the Bush children, this was the norm. "We never felt that Dad had any wealth at all," Jonathan Bush said. "We had a cook and a maid and a chauffeur, but other kids had a lot more."

Like their dynastic counterparts Joe and Rose Kennedy, Prescott and Dorothy were fiercely competitive—and determined that their children be no less so. Above all else, the Bushes instilled in their progeny the drive to win—at checkers, Scrabble, Parcheesi, Monopoly, running, golf, tennis, football, baseball, horseshoes, volleyball, badminton, dominoes, virtually any conceivable competitive endeavor.

Even more than his grandfather, W.'s grandmother Dorothy, herself a champion tennis player, clung to the notion that life was essentially a series of contests from which only one winner could emerge. She kept the family Ping-Pong table in the mansion's tiled foyer, and would on a moment's notice take on anyone who challenged her to a match. More important, the Ping-Pong table was the first thing her children saw when the chauffeur drove them home from Greenwich Country Day School and they walked into the house—a symbol of the family's fighting spirit and a constant reminder of what was expected of every Bush.

Unlike the win-at-all-cost approach of Joe Kennedy, however, Dorothy Walker Bush put a premium on sportsmanship. Her rules were simple: No cheating, no bragging, no quitting—and no cruelty. Always play to win, she counseled her children, but be kind—and never look down on anyone. "You must never make someone feel bad because you are beating them," she told her son George. "And you must never whine if you lose."

For his part Prescott, who commuted by train every day to his offices at 1 Wall Street, was cast in the role of stern and forbidding patriarch. He expected jackets and ties to be worn at dinner, and for even the youngest at the table to know which fork to use. Later, when Prescott was appointed to fill a vacant seat in the U.S. Senate, he instructed everyone—including members of his own family—to address him as "Senator."

The Bush family dynamic was fairly typical for the time— particularly among upper-class WASP families in the Northeast. Open displays of affection, even among family members in private, were generally frowned upon. Discipline was strictly enforced, and no back talk was tolerated. Like his brothers and his sister, George Herbert Walker Bush—future president and father of a president— grew to adulthood wanting nothing more than to please the father he idolized. "You see, Senior was never a child," a family friend said. "He grew up always doing what Prescott expected. He never rebelled; he was always a responsible little man-child."

From an early age, the elder George would be known as "Poppy"—a nickname derived from the man he was named after, his maternal grandfather George Herbert Walker. Dorothy's younger brothers called their father "Pops," and his namesake— their nephew—"Little Pops." That quickly became "Poppy."

For all intents and purposes, Poppy never made a misstep when it came to impressing his formidable father. Shipped off to Phillips Academy in Andover, Massachusetts, the lanky, six-foot-two-inch Poppy quickly distinguished himself as both athlete and scholar at the elite prep school. He was captain of the baseball and soccer teams, and at various times secretary of the Student Council, treasurer of the Student Council, and Senior Class President. In addition to winning the prestigious Johns Hopkins Prize, Poppy would be proclaimed "Best All-Around Fellow" by his peers.

While home for the holidays during his senior year, he went to a Christmas dance at Greenwich's exclusive Round Hill Country Club and was introduced to a lively sixteen-year-old brunette in a festive red and green dress. Her name was Barbara Pierce.

Born in Manhattan and raised in upscale Rye, New York, Barbara was the daughter of McCall's Publishing President and Chairman of the Board Marvin Pierce. Along with her big sister Martha, Barbara had been sent to one of the country's leading finishing schools— Ashley Hall in Charleston, South Carolina. Poppy asked her to his senior prom, and not long after brought her to Kennebunkport to meet the family. There she quickly learned that Dorothy Bush was indeed "*the* most competitive living human."

Still, Barbara clicked instantly with everyone in the Bush tribe— especially Prescott Bush Jr., who liked to tease his little brother's girlfriend by calling her "Barsil," the name of one of the family's draft horses. Soon all the Bushes were calling Barbara "Bar"—a diminutive form not of her own name, but of Barsil. Such good-natured ribbing aside, Barbara was smitten. Within the year, she was engaged to Poppy—the first man she had ever even kissed.

On graduation day at Andover that year, Secretary of War Henry Stimson was on hand to pass out diplomas. Poppy knew that he would be expected to follow his father into Yale, but like other eighteen-year-old Americans he was not about to pass up a chance to get into the war. In what would become part of Andover lore, the school's "Best All-Around Fellow" approached Stimson and declared, "I don't want to go to Yale right now. I want to fight for my country."

Not long after Poppy shipped out for duty in the Pacific, Barbara enrolled at Smith, the elite women's college in Northampton, Massachusetts. When she dodged invitations to go out on blind dates with boys from nearby Amherst, a college gossip spread the rumor that Barbara was a lesbian. "I was shocked by all of this," the future first lady said. "What a protected life I had lived."

Poppy, meantime, was racking up an impressive record as a combat pilot flying off the aircraft carrier USS *San Jacinto* in the South Pacific. The most memorable of his fifty-eight missions occurred on September 2, 1944, when his Grumman TBF Avenger—which he named *Barbara*—bombed a radio transmitter on Chichi Jima, one of the Bonin Islands southeast of Japan. Homing in on the target, Bush felt a jolt as his plane was struck by enemy antiaircraft fire. Bush continued his dive, dropped his payload, and destroyed the tower before leveling off over water and ordering his two fellow crew members to bail out.

Bush then jumped, but after he hit the water his parachute became tangled in the tail assembly. Yanked toward the tail, he suffered a gash in his forehead when it struck the plane's horizontal stabilizer.

Miraculously, Poppy was spotted by an American submarine, the *Finback,* and plucked from the water. His ordnance officer and radio gunner were not so lucky. One man's chute had failed to open, the other went down with the plane. Back home, Barbara and the Bush family would have to wait three days before learning of Poppy's fate. For his heroism under fire, he was awarded the Distinguished Flying Cross.

Four months later, Barbara Pierce dropped out of Smith College to marry Poppy at the First Presbyterian Church in Rye. Several hours later they were in New York's Radio City Music Hall listening to Judy Garland sing a new holiday song, "Have Yourself a Merry Little Christmas," from the film *Meet Me in St. Louis.* That night they boarded a sleeper car at Penn Station and headed off to Sea Island, Georgia, for their honeymoon.

As soon as he was discharged from the service at war's end in 1945, Poppy enrolled at Yale under the GI Bill. The young war veteran rushed to complete his degree in economics in just two and a half years—distinguishing himself in the process as president of his fraternity (Delta Kappa Epsilon), captain of the baseball team, a member of the Skull & Bones and Torch Honor societies, a principal fund-raiser for the fledgling United Negro College Fund, and winner of the Gordon Brown student leadership prize.

While Poppy started assembling what would become one of the most impressive résumés in the history of American politics, the

newlyweds and their black poodle Turbo moved into a tiny apartment just two doors from a funeral parlor on New Haven's Chapel
Street. Their bathroom, which they shared with other tenants, was
down the hall.

The Bushes' landlord loved dogs, but not children. When Bar discovered in the middle of her husband's first year at Yale that she was
pregnant, they were told in no uncertain terms to start searching for
another apartment. They moved into a small house at 281 Edwards
Street, and on the night of July 5, 1946, Bar awakened with labor
pains. She was rushed to New Haven Hospital and checked into the
maternity ward at 12:30 A.M. July 6. Poppy's mother met them there.

After nearly seven hours of labor, Dorothy Walker Bush took
matters into her own hands. She gave her daughter-in-law a stiff
dose of castor oil that, in addition to strengthening the contractions,
had the predictable effect. "That baby came all right," Barbara later
said of George Walker Bush's rather messy delivery, "I'm tempted to
say covered with glory."

A few months later, "Georgie" moved with his parents into their
last New Haven address, 37 Hillhouse Avenue. There were nine
families and eleven children living at 37 Hillhouse, right next door
to the imposing Victorian residence of Yale President Charles Sey-
mour. Despite the distractions, Poppy managed to graduate Phi Beta
Kappa in 1948.

With a wife and infant son to support, he might easily have signed
on with his father or at another Wall Street firm. But shortly after
being shot down in the Pacific, Poppy had experienced an epiphany
of sorts. He did not want a button-down life juggling balance sheets
and portfolios; he wanted to be involved in producing a product he
could see and feel—something tangible.

At first, George was so impressed by Louis Bromfield's book *The
Farm* that he actually weighed the possibility of moving to the Midwest and becoming a farmer. Once it became apparent that farming
was, in his own words, "high-risk, no-yield," Poppy reluctantly
started applying for a position in New York.

Throughout that spring before graduation, Georgie's dad applied
for job after job. After being turned down by Proctor & Gamble,
Bush was offered a position by Neil Mallon, an old college buddy of

Prescott Bush's and a longtime family friend. Prescott had worked behind the scenes through "Uncle Neil" to secure a trainee's job for his son at the International Derrick and Equipment Company (Ideco) in Texas. Ideco was a subsidiary of the Bush-controlled and Neil Mallon–run Dresser Industries, one of the world's leading manufacturers of drill bits and portable oil rigs. Not only would young Mr. Bush be a Dresser trainee learning every aspect of the oil business in Texas, Uncle Neil assured him, he would be Dresser Industry's *only* trainee. The catch: He would have to move with his wife and son to remote, sizzling, sand-blasted Odessa, Texas.

Instantly seduced, as he later put it, by the "romance and adventure of searching for black gold," Bush accepted. The day after graduation he packed up his shiny new fire engine–red Studebaker—a gift from Mom and Dad—and with a three-thousand-dollar stake (another gift from Mom and Dad) drove solo cross-country to Odessa.

Barbara was "not exactly thrilled" with the prospect of pulling up stakes yet again and moving to one of the remotest corners of the country. *Odessa?* Russia, yes, she observed, "but who ever heard of Odessa, Texas?" Nevertheless, one week after Poppy departed, she and two-year-old Georgie made the bouncy twelve-hour flight aboard an unpressurized propellor-driven plane to their new home—stepping down the gangway and into what Barbara would call with characteristic understatement "a new and very hot world."

Cradled in the heart of the oil-rich Permian Basin—a subterranean sea of oil covering 100,000 square miles—Odessa was a gritty blue-collar boomtown inhabited primarily by the roughnecks and roustabouts who first dug the wells and then manned the rigs that kept them pumping. The Bushes moved into a two-room duplex apartment on Seventh Street where the first Texas neighbors of the two future presidents were mother-and-daughter prostitutes who lived next door. Georgie and his parents shared the only bathroom with the two women, whose paying customers trooped in and out at all hours of the day and night and sometimes wandered into the Bushes' apartment by mistake.

The Bushes were lucky to have a bathroom at all; most of their neighbors made do with outhouses. Since they also had the only refrigerator on the block, the new arrivals felt doubly blessed. Besides, housing was so scarce in Odessa that some newly arrived laborers were forced to settle for living in barns, tents, and in some cases chicken coops.

The lack of adequate shelter was of particular concern in a place that seemed so singularly unforgiving. In contrast to the lush natural greenery of the Northeast, the terrain in this part of Texas was vast, flat, treeless, motionless. Motionless, that is, except for the tornadoes and sandstorms that occasionally swept in. Whole neighborhoods seemed to vanish in an instant, enveloped in a stinging, swirling tsunami of grit. "There were times," said Bush friend Earle Craig Jr., "when you simply could not see across the street."

Even when the air was perfectly still, dirt crept stealthily into homes, offices, and schools. People installed storm windows not to keep out the rain, but to keep out the sand. As soon as they arrived at school in the morning, the first thing youngsters in this part of Texas did was brush off the fine layer of sand that covered every desk.

Then there were the rattlesnakes, and the scorpions and tarantulas the size of a child's fist. On the rare occasions when it rained, there would sometimes be an invasion of frogs that Georgie would later liken to "the biblical plague." The tumbleweeds cheerfully bounced along the landscape, blowing into people's backyards and sometimes wedging themselves under cars. Making the best of the situation, some enterprising West Texans painted the tumbleweeds gold, covered them in glitter, and used them as Christmas decorations.

At least Poppy was learning the business, as Uncle Neil had promised, from the ground up. He spent twelve-hour days painting pump jacks and sweeping out the warehouses where Ideco stored its equipment. It was also during this time that the family got its first taste of West Texas racism when Poppy casually invited a member of the National Association for the Advancement of Colored People for dinner. The young black civil rights worker appreciated the gesture, but was wise enough not to accept. When word of the proffered invitation got around, the Bushes were warned never to try something like that again—"unless," as one neighbor put it succinctly, "you folks don't mind bein' tarred and feathered and run out of town on a rail."

Georgie and his parents spent only a few sweltering months in Odessa before Poppy was dispatched by Uncle Neil Mallon to continue his education in the oil business at various Dresser-held operations in California. His main job was to travel from rig to rig hawking Ideco-made drill bits.

It was a lonely time for the little boy and his mother, who tagged along with Dad over the next year as he bounced from Huntington Park to Bakersfield to a motel in Richard Nixon's hometown of Whittier to Ventura's Pierpoint Inn. By the time they moved into another one-bedroom apartment, this time in the Los Angeles suburb of Compton, Bar was pregnant again.

His wife was in her seventh month and, as she herself put it, "enormous," when Poppy came home from work early with terrible news: Back in Rye, New York, Marvin Pierce had lost control of his car and slammed into a stone wall, instantly killing Barbara's mother—Georgie's grandmother—and seriously injuring himself. From his hospital bed, Barbara's father insisted that his daughter not risk endangering her unborn child by making the arduous journey back to New York for the funeral.

At age three, Georgie was a happy and rambunctious boy who quickly and easily adjusted to his constantly changing surroundings. He was also old enough to recognize the cumulus of grief that hung over his family. Now he saw his mother cry for the first time. Sadly, it would not be the last.

Two months after the crash that killed her mother, Barbara Bush gave birth to a daughter on December 20, 1949, and named the baby Pauline Robinson Bush in memory of her mother. They called her Robin, and brought her home to meet her big brother on Christmas Day. For a little boy accustomed to being alone in a world full of adults, Robin was "the best Christmas gift I ever had."

Robin was three months old when the family was transferred back to Texas—this time to the decidedly more staid bedroom community of Midland, twenty-five miles east of Odessa on U.S. 20. Texas's answer to Promontory Point, Utah, Midland was the spot where the Southern Pacific and Texas Pacific railroads met midway between Fort Worth and El Paso. The town was, in fact, originally called Midway until it was learned that there was another, older Texas city of the same name. No matter. Because of its convenient location, Midland became the hub of the West Texas oil boom. Here, in the hotels, banks, and office buildings that sprang up around the railroad station, weather-beaten wildcatters and pallid-faced money-men from places like New York and Boston met to hammer out the deals on which fortunes would be made and lost and made again.

More than a quarter century after the fabled Santa Rita No. 1 gusher first put the Permian Basin on the map in 1923, there were still rich new fields of oil and natural gas to tap into deep under the earth, fantastic new fortunes to be made. (Nor was the boom about to end any time soon; by the time W. was inaugurated President in 2001, the Permian Basin was second only to Alaska—the entire state—in the amount of oil and natural gas it had produced.)

"You raise hell in Odessa," the old West Texas adage went, "but you raise a family in Midland." If the foot soldiers of the oil business lived in Odessa, then white-collar Midland was home to its colonels and generals. To be sure, a few of these were grizzled West Texans. Most, however, were college-educated carpetbaggers—the geolo-gists, engineers, and financiers who came to stake their claim. A gilded few, like Poppy, were the baby-faced progeny of Wall Street bankers and financiers. What the "Yalies," as locals dubbed them, lacked in hands-on experience they made up for in access to operat-ing capital. "Cash was the lifeblood of Midland," said a director of one of the town's banks, "and you needed to pour a lot of it into the ground before you could ever hope of seeing a profit. When these kids rolled into town from back East with Daddy's checkbook, well, let's just say everybody wanted to be their new best friend."

As soon as they arrived, the Bushes moved into a motel aptly named George's Court. Every day Poppy would get up at dawn, get behind the wheel of his red Studebaker, and strike out in search of wildcatters who might be interested in buying one of his Ideco drill bits. He was now peppering his language with "yep"s and the occa-sional drawn-out "y'awl," but certain Yalie habits died hard. When he stepped outside of his motel room to buy milk for Robin wear-ing Bermuda shorts, truck drivers blared their horns and leaned out the windows of their rigs to whistle at him. Poppy dashed back in and changed. In 1950s Midland, he had just learned, real men did not wear shorts.

Before long, the Bushes joined the swelling ranks of postwar homeowners. With the help of an FHA loan, they purchased a single-story 847-square-foot wood-frame tract house with a carport on the north edge of town for $7,500. The bungalow at 405 East Maple Avenue was only one of scores of virtually identical houses that were painted in eye-popping shades of red, blue, green, and pink. Fittingly, the neighborhood was called Easter Egg Row.

"Yuppieland West" was the way Poppy would later describe Midland in the 1950s. With good reason. Big George, as W.'s dad now came to be called, quickly banded together with his Yankee brethren. They lived on streets named after Ivy League colleges—Harvard, Princeton, Yale—in functional, low-slung houses. They wore their Brooks Brothers suits to church on Sundays, played golf at the Midland Country Club, and swapped tall tales at the Petroleum Club. They even became accustomed to the periodic wail of a train whistle—not-so-mute testimony to the fact that Midland was also a center for shipping cattle.

Over the next decade, Midland's population would nearly triple, and office towers would rise twenty stories and more above the hot, flat expanse of sagebrush and sand. "Tall City of the Plains" is the way one brochure described Midland, although proud town fathers preferred the more grandiose "Headquarters City of the Vast Permian Basin Empire."

Yet the Midland young George W. Bush would remember was a slice of small-town America, and his Norman Rockwell childhood there would be unlike anything his father or his father's father had experienced. On Easter Egg Row, Poppy and his ebullient, dark-haired wife were just like any young suburban family at the time with two small kids. "We were young and eager to do new things," said the Bushes' Easter Egg Row neighbor John Ashmun, "trying to make our way in a part of the country that was completely foreign to us. All we had was each other's company."

Not surprisingly, not all the socializing that went on was of a particularly wholesome nature. "It wasn't all *Ozzie and Harriet,* believe me," a former Easter Egg Row resident recalled. "A lot of the people who moved out there weren't prepared for the heat, or the dirt, or the isolation. A lot of the women whose husbands were out working all day just felt trapped, lonely. So there was a lot of drinking, and a lot of people cheating on their spouses." According to another Midlander, several Bush acquaintances were involved in a popular suburban pastime of the Eisenhower era: wife-swapping.

Georgie's parents carefully avoided becoming embroiled in any such "high jinks," as one local put it, preferring instead to hurl themselves into community work. Both taught Sunday School at First Presbyterian Church, where Poppy quickly became a deacon and by age thirty-one rose to become a church elder—the youngest ever.

Bar joined the Midland Service League, and volunteered at the Little Theater, the Community Chest, and Midland Memorial Hospital. Dad, meantime, was a director of the Midland Chamber of Commerce, chairman of the Midland County Cancer Unit, a United Way board member, and an organizer of the Commercial Bank and Trust Company. In a region of the country where the Republican Party was virtually nonexistent, Big George took on the daunting task of trying to convert his fellow Midlanders to the GOP.

After work, they'd all get together at one of the houses on Maple Street in their sport shirts and khakis and grill up some hamburgers in the backyard. Like the rest of the wives, Bar Bush wore pedal pushers and often went barefoot. While the men talked oil in one corner and the women traded war stories about their children in another, Georgie and his little friends "ran wild," Ashmun recalled. On weekends, the well-lubricated dads got a little wild, too, playing touch football, with the "Lubbock Leftovers" squaring off against the "Midland Misfits" in what they coyly dubbed the Martini Bowl. Bar and Georgie were always there, cheering Big George on from the sidelines. "You would always see Georgie, who was about four at the time, holding on to Robin's pram," remembered another expatriate New Englander, Earle Craig Jr., "and his mother pushing the pram along."

It was during a backyard cookout that Poppy began tossing around the idea of striking out on his own with John Overbey, a University of Texas–educated oil and gas lease broker who lived across the unpaved street. With Uncle Neil's blessing, Poppy left Dresser Industries in 1950 to form the Bush-Overbey Oil Development Company—but not before securing $350,000 in start-up capital with help from his maternal "Uncle Herbie," George Herbert

Walker Jr. Dad Prescott Bush kicked in $50,000, as did one of his Brown Brothers Harriman clients, *Washington Post* publisher Eugene Meyer. Meyer also convinced his son-in-law, Phil Graham, to invest $50,000. Graham was married to Meyer's daughter, future *Washington Post* publisher Katharine Graham.

That same year, Prescott Bush ran for senator from Connecticut and lost by a stunningly narrow margin. In a preview of what would happen to his grandson a half-century later, ballot boxes were impounded to prevent tampering as the ballots were counted. Out of more than 860,000 votes cast, the moderately conservative Prescott lost to incumbent Democrat Bill Benton by a scant 1,102 votes.

Two years later, Prescott got a second chance when Connecticut's other senator, Brien McMahon, died in office. A special election was held to fill McMahon's seat and this time, riding the Eisenhower wave that swept Republicans into office in 1952, Prescott trounced his Democratic opponent, Abraham Ribicoff.

Before his father Prescott's victory, Big George had never mentioned pursuing a career in politics. To be sure, he had already tried to convert his fellow oilmen to the GOP, although Democrats had had a lock on this part of Texas since before the Depression. But running for office? If he had had such ambitions, Big George had never shared them—not even with his wife.

That all changed with the first of several trips the Senator would make to Midland. People in this desolate part of the Lone Star State were not accustomed to having a bona fide United States senator in their midst—especially not one whose regal bearing and stentorian delivery hearkened back to another era. It was not long before Big George, who had labored assiduously to build an impressive network of business associates and cronies in the region, was being cornered and asked if he, too, might toss his Stetson into the ring.

Big George shrugged off the notion of a political career for himself. "How am I supposed to run for office," he told one woman who needled him good-naturedly at a cocktail party, "when the oil business takes up all my time?"

Certainly, the Senator's visits to Midland only served to enhance his son's stature there, and Barbara tried to make sure that Georgie was on his best behavior when "Gampy Bush" arrived in town. No

less was expected of the boy when he and his parents joined the rest
of the large Walker-Bush clan for holidays and summers at Kennebunkport, or at the Senator's winter estate on Jupiter Island, Florida.
In contrast to laid-back Kennebunkport, names like Vanderbilt, Mel-
lon, Ford, and Whitney were sprinkled along the shores of fifteen-
mile-long Jupiter Island like so much diamond dust. Then there
were the visits to his great-grandfather's cavernous apartment on
Sutton Place in New York, and the Prescott Bushes' mansion in
Greenwich . . .

Of all his rich and powerful relatives, Georgie found the Senator
easily the most intimidating. The boy was not alone. Even within
the family, "scary" was the word most frequently used to describe
Prescott Bush's Vesuvian temper. His grandson would learn that
early on, when at age five he made the mistake of running up to his
grandparents' dog Plucky and yanking the animal's tail. His mother,
Barbara, was in a nearby room when she heard Grandpa Bush erupt
into a purple-veined, window-rattling rage. Rather than come to
little Georgie's rescue, she decided to stay put. "You're on your own,
kid," Bar Bush said to herself.

"My grandfather's reaction was so swift and forceful," George W.
later said without going into the gory details, "that I never did it
again." While the incident became part of the Prescott Bush lore, W.
would blanch every time it was repeated for laughs at family gather-
ings. "For a chastened little boy," he said, "it was far from funny."

For the most part, Georgie's childhood revolved around pedaling
his Schwinn along the dust-blown streets of middle-class Midland.
But there would also be early memories of sailing off the Maine
coast, and of being chauffeured from Manhattan to Greenwich in
one of his great-grandfather's two Rolls-Royces. From the beginning Georgie was made keenly aware of his Yankee heritage, and of
the family ties that bound him to another world—an Old Money
world of opulence, privilege, entitlement, and influence firmly
rooted in the Northeast.

At Kennebunkport, Georgie's uncles—Prescott Jr., Jonathan, and
William "Bucky" Bush—would sit in gaping wonder as Big George
regaled them with stories straight out of Edna Ferber's *Giant*. Even
the Senator let loose his booming laugh when Poppy described the
nouveau-riche-as-Croesus wildcatters who swathed their bouffant-

coifed wives in sable and dropped small fortunes at Dallas's Moorish-themed Adolphus Hotel, where the black waiters were outfitted in billowing satin harem pants and bejeweled turbans.

The more outlandish the tales of wretched West Texas excess, the more Big George wanted his part of it. For the next several years, Bush hurled himself into his fledgling business, spending days and weeks at a time on the road trying to secure the mineral rights to lands that had not yet drawn the attention of the big oil companies. Back home in Midland, Bar had her hands full caring for Robin and her rambunctious big brother. Georgie, not yet in kindergarten, was already proving to be a handful—loud, quick-tempered, and defiant. He threw tantrums, broke things, and bullied the other kids. At first Big George seemed slightly bemused by it all. His son seemed so . . . Texan. "Georgie has grown to be a near-man," he wrote home to Prescott Bush. "He talks dirty once in a while and occasionally swears, aged four and a half."

As was the case with many families with absentee dads, it fell to Mom to play the part of resident disciplinarian. "Oh, I believed in spanking, believe me," Barbara said, "and Georgie got more than his share. But if you asked him now, he'd probably say he deserved it every time."

In 1952, about the same time that the locals started calling their boy "Junior," the Bushes moved into a three-bedroom house at 1412 West Ohio Avenue. At 1,492 square feet the clapboard house with a fireplace, bay window, and covered front porch was nearly twice as big as their house on Easter Egg Row.

The Bush family would be needing the extra space. On February 11, 1953, George and Bar drove the green Oldsmobile to Midland Hospital where she gave birth again to another boy, John Ellis Bush. They quickly used his initials to form the name by which he would always be known: Jeb.

At about the same time, Big George was also giving birth—to yet another new oil venture. Educated at Amherst, the University of Texas, and Harvard Business School, brothers J. Hugh Liedtke and William C. Liedtke practiced law in offices directly across the street from Bush-Overbey. The Liedtkes were already well known as the architects of some of the region's major partnerships by the time they asked Big George to go into business with them. They had all just seen the Elia Kazan film *Viva Zapata!*, which starred Marlon Brando as the fiery south-of-the-border revolutionary who championed the cause of redistributing Mexico's land among the peasants. In an odd twist of logic, they decided to name their new company the Zapata Petroleum Corporation, with Hugh Liedtke as president and Big George as vice president.

Zapata's guiding concept was daring if not entirely revolutionary. The partners raised $800,000—mostly from the Bush-Walker clan— and wagered it all on a single roll of the dice. They spent the entire amount on drilling beneath a dry patch of prairie just east of Midland called the West Jameson Field, where Hugh Liedtke (later dubbed the "boy genius of West Texas oil") was convinced there were vast underground lakes of black gold just waiting to be discovered.

It turned out Liedtke was right. Zapata drilled and drilled, and never came up dry—something virtually unheard of in Texas. By year's end Zapata would boast seventy-one West Jameson wells pumping 1,250 barrels of oil per day. Ultimately, West Jameson would be dotted with 130 wells pumping millions of dollars directly into the pockets of Zapata's executives and investors.

With her husband poised to make his first real killing and a squalling new addition to their tight-knit little family, Barbara felt doubly blessed. "Life," she later mused of this time, "seemed almost too good to be true."

Then, one early spring morning, Barbara was cradling three-week-old Jeb in her arms when she realized her daughter was still in bed. When Robin finally did toddle into their kitchen, the blond, blue-eyed little girl looked pale and lethargic. "I don't know what to do this morning," Robin sighed to her mother. "I may go out and lie on the grass and watch the cars go by, or I might just stay in bed."

Barbara decided that that didn't "sound like a normal three-year-old" at all. Although she assumed Robin was merely suffering from an advanced case of "spring fever," Mom decided to play it safe and make an appointment with the family's pediatrician, Dorothy Wyvell.

Dr. Wyvell examined Robin—no one had really noticed the bruising on her legs before—and then took a sample of the little girl's blood. Wyvell told Barbara that she would be calling later that day with the test results. "This time, you might want to leave Robin at home," she suggested, "but bring your husband."

That day Big George was in the next county going over land records when Barbara called him with the news that something might be seriously wrong with Robin. He rushed to be at Bar's side when the doctor delivered the terrifying news: their daughter had leukemia.

It was the first time the Bushes had ever heard of the disease, and they sat patiently while Dr. Wyvell explained what leukemia was. Not only was the disease incurable, but she had never seen a white blood count so high as in Robin's case. There was no point in telling anyone that Robin was ill, the doctor said. Instead, she advised the child's stunned parents to take Robin home and make her final days as comfortable and happy as possible. She would survive, Dr. Wyvell predicted, no more than three weeks—a month at the outside.

Big George wasted no time phoning his uncle John Walker, a noted surgeon-turned-investment banker who now served as president of Memorial Sloan-Kettering Hospital in New York. At the time, Memorial Sloan-Kettering was already regarded as the world's leading cancer treatment center. Dr. Walker was no more optimistic about Robin's chances than Dr. Wyvell, but he agreed that they should do everything they could to keep the child alive as long as possible while researchers worked feverishly to find a cure.

That night, friends and neighbors flocked to the Bushes' house on West Ohio Street, offering to do whatever they could to help out. When the visitors left, Big George and Barbara sat Georgie down and told him that his little sister was sick. They would be taking her to New York where there were special doctors who would help Robin get better. They did not tell Georgie that his sister was seriously ill, much less that she was not likely to recover. "We were too afraid to tell him his little sister was dying. We didn't want to worry him," Barbara said. "We hated that, but we felt it would be too big a burden for such a little fellow . . ."

The next morning, the Bushes flew to New York and moved into his grandparents' Sutton Place apartment, just nine blocks from Memorial Sloan-Kettering. So Barbara could be by their daughter's side as she underwent painful bone marrow transplants and massive transfusions, Dorothy Bush dispatched one of her own son's childhood nurses, Marion Fraser, to take care of Georgie and Jeb in Texas.

Poppy, now immersed in the formidable task of getting Zapata off and running, shuttled between Midland and Manhattan. Regardless of what business needed tending to, Bush dropped everything to spend every weekend with his wife and daughter.

For her part, Barbara never allowed herself to cry—and forbade anyone to show emotion in Robin's presence. Tears would only frighten the little girl, Georgie's mom reasoned, and what the family needed to do was focus on beating the leukemia. Big George was another matter. He never let Robin see him cry, but there were times when, in front of close friends and family, he was overcome with emotion and had to excuse himself from the room.

Over the next seven months, Robin was more often than not confined to her hospital room at Memorial Sloan-Kettering while she underwent treatments. When the little girl felt strong enough, she was allowed to spend time at home in Midland or joined the extended family for its annual summer revels at Kennebunkport.

Georgie had always been close to his sister, even protective toward her. But now what little time they spent together was closely monitored. Georgie was admonished not to engage in any roughhousing or horseplay with Robin; they did not tell him why—that even the slightest bump or bruise could result in serious hemorrhaging. "We had to watch them very closely," Barbara recalled.

"Georgie was a handful, even at seven," one neighbor said of the little boy they called "Bushtail." But "not when it came to Robin. He was always very gentle with her, very patient. Not that she was ever any trouble at all. Even before she was sick, Robin seemed incredibly mature for her age—an old soul. Georgie was always the hyperactive one." At times when he was being scolded by their mother for sassing back, Robin would simply roll her eyes and shake her head. "It was sort of like, 'Now what's he done?' "

By the fall of 1953, however, Robin was too sick to leave the hospital. The drugs that had been used to keep her alive were now having horrible side effects. She was bleeding internally. Poppy boarded the red-eye for New York, but by the time he arrived at the hospital Robin had slipped into a coma. On October 11, 1953, Big George and Barbara stood at their little girl's bedside as she died peacefully in her sleep. Barbara took Robin's comb from the night table, then sat on the edge of the bed and gently combed her daughter's hair.

Then they held their daughter in their arms one last time. "I never felt the presence of God more strongly," Barbara would later say, "than at that moment."

Within hours, news of Robin's death reached the Bushes' friends back in Midland. "We all knew Robin was ill, of course, but looking back it seems none of us really appreciated how serious it was," Earle Craig said. "We are all about the same age, with young children. It was just such a shock to us all. Everyone who knew the Bush family was deeply upset."

The next day, the Bushes drove north to Rye, New York, to play golf with Barbara's father. Hitting the links less than twelve hours after Robin's death may have seemed callous, but as Barbara later explained in her memoirs, the Bushes were "numb." However stoic she might have seemed, Barbara was showing the strain in other ways. At twenty-eight, her hair was already beginning to turn white.

The next morning, Big George and Barbara and family held a brief memorial service in Greenwich, but there would be no funeral. Instead, the Bushes donated Robin's body to the hospital for medical research. It would be three months before they learned that the final cause of death was liver failure.

As soon as the memorial service was over, Big George and Barbara raced for the airport and flew home to Midland. They had kept Georgie in the dark about Robin's condition, and now it was important that they be the first to break the terrible news to him.

It would be the defining moment in George W. Bush's life—one that would forever alter his nature and, by extension, change the course of history. Seven-year-old Georgie and one of his second grade classmates at Sam Houston Elementary School had been assigned the task of carrying a phonograph back to the principal's office. As they lugged the equipment down a covered walkway, Georgie spotted his parents' green Oldsmobile pulling up in front of the school.

For a split second, Georgie was certain he saw his sister's tiny blond head poking up from the backseat. He put the record player down and ran back to his classroom. "My mom, dad, and sister are home," he told his teacher. "Can I go see them?" Already alerted to the fact that the Bushes would be picking up their son for the rest of the day, Georgie's teacher nodded.

Georgie bolted back outside. "Hey, Mom! Dad!" he yelled as he ran toward the car, still expecting to see his sister. As he got closer, Georgie realized that he hadn't really seen his sister at all. "Where's Robin?" he asked.

Big George and Barbara knelt down beside their son and told him what had happened. Georgie was uncomprehending. He had known only that Robin was sick; no one had prepared him for the possibility that she might die. That his little sister was not coming home— ever—was simply too much to absorb. So was the fact that his parents had known all along that she was dying. "But why didn't you tell me she was so sick?" he asked repeatedly. "Why didn't you tell me she could die?"

"Well," Mom replied, "it wouldn't have made a difference . . ."

Nearly a half century later, George W. would recall those few minutes as "the starkest memory of my childhood, a sharp pain in the midst of an otherwise happy blur."

Now Georgie watched helplessly as his mother unraveled emotionally. All the anguish and grief that she had kept bottled up for seven months now rose to the surface, overwhelming her. Time and time again over the next six months, Poppy held his wife as she cried herself to sleep. "We awakened night after night in great physical pain," she recalled of their shared heartache. "It hurt that much."

For Georgie, there was nothing to do but find ways to make his parents laugh—or simply break the tension. When Big George and a few friends took Georgie along to a Friday night Midland Bulldogs football game, the boy turned to his dad and blurted, "Gee, I wish I were Robin."

Poppy's friends squirmed uncomfortably in their seats. "What do you mean, Georgie?" his father asked patiently.

"I bet she can see the game better from there," Georgie responded as he strained to see the field, "than we can here."

Another time, Georgie asked his father if Robin had been buried lying down or standing up. Once again, the adults in the room stiffened.

"I'm not really sure, Georgie," Dad replied. "Why do you want to know?"

"We've been learning in class about how the earth rotates," the boy replied, "and I just wondered if Robin spent part of the time standing on her head. Wouldn't that be neat?"

Georgie would remember none of this, only that he felt an immense sense of sadness that fall and winter of 1953. Mom was clinging to his baby brother Jebby, and Georgie worried about her—so much so that he seldom left her side. One afternoon after school, Barbara heard a knock at the door. It was one of the boys from the neighborhood, asking if Georgie could come over and play.

"No, I can't," she overheard Georgie say. "I can't leave my mom alone. She needs me."

That, Barbara said, "started my cure. I realized I was too much of a burden for a seven-year-old boy to carry." Later, George W. conceded, "she kind of smothered me, and then recognized it was the wrong thing to do."

Still, Robin's death left Georgie profoundly shaken. "You have to remember that children grieve," Barbara said. "He felt cheated." Georgie could not fathom how his parents could hide from him the fact that his beloved Robin was dying. Georgie tried to conceal his tears from his parents, but he suffered from nightmares for years afterward. "He would wake up screaming in the middle of the night, and his mother would come running to comfort him," a friend said. "Everyone else in the family had had months to deal with the tragedy, but it was dropped on the poor kid all at once."

Georgie's best friend at the time, Randall Roden, was sleeping over one night when he was awakened by one of Georgie's bad dreams. "It was one of the most realistic experiences I have ever had about death," Roden remembered, "and I am certain it had a profound effect on him because it had a profound effect on me."

The anxieties surfaced again when, just as suddenly, the infant brother of his pal Joe O'Neill succumbed to pneumonia. "Unless you've experienced the death of a sibling as a child," O'Neill said, "it's difficult to comprehend how frightening it can be. It's a feeling you never forget, and it's a feeling that colors the rest of your life." Nevertheless, George W. would later insist that the tragedy did not leave him traumatized, only determined "never to take life for granted."

Big George could not conceal the fact that he missed having a little girl in the house, a sentiment he expressed with heart-tugging eloquence in a letter to his mother a few years later. "We need some soft blond hair to offset those crewcuts," he wrote. "We need a doll house to stand firm against our forts and rackets and thousand baseball cards . . . We need a girl . . . We had one once—she'd fight and cry and play and make her way just like the rest. But there was about her a certain softness . . . Her peace made me feel strong, and so very important."

Barbara knew what she must do. "I'm going to keep trying," she confessed to friend, "until I get another girl." She would, eventually. In the meantime, however, Georgie and Jebby would be getting two new brothers in rapid succession: Neil Mallon in 1955 and Marvin Pierce in 1956. Then, in 1959, Dorothy Walker ("Doro") finally arrived.

Yet Robin's death had forever radically altered the family dynamic, opening a seven-year gap between George and his younger siblings, all bunched within two or three years of each other. That, coupled with his newfound responsibilities as self-appointed family morale-booster, put even more distance between Georgie and the rest of the Bush children—leaving him, in the words of one observer, "a quasi-only child."

Not surprisingly Georgie, like most big brothers, did not mind using Jebby as a punching bag on occasion. Nor did he hesitate to bark orders at his younger siblings. But when it came to choosing friends and confidants, Georgie turned outside the family to neighborhood kids, classmates, and, when he got older, roommates.

Many of those friendships were forged in the backyards and on the playing fields of Midland. Six months after Robin's death, Georgie invited Randall Roden to spend time with him at his grandparents' Georgetown town house. While Prescott Bush deliberated on the floor of the Senate, Georgie's grandmother took the boys to see the Washington Monument, the Lincoln Memorial, the Capitol building, and the White House.

It was on this first visit to Washington that the Senator introduced Georgie to a man who, if at all possible, looked even larger than his grandfather. "Lyndon, I've got one of your constituents here," Prescott Bush said. "Georgie, I would like you to meet Lyndon Baines Johnson, your United States senator." Just how removed from Texas the boys actually were was brought home when, while dining at the Georgetown residence, the Senator watched as Georgie's friend drank from the finger bowl.

Back on home turf in Midland, it was understood that everyone watched out for everyone else's children. One summer afternoon, Georgie ran out into the street without looking and suddenly he could hear a woman yelling at him. One of the other moms had seen him from her kitchen window and was now running to tell him to never, ever, race into the street without looking again. Anyone who tried to smoke behind a garage or a shed ran the risk of being spotted by one of the moms, who might then call in the much-feared football coach Thermon "Tugboat" Jones to offer some stern words of advice. In this regard, Tugboat was a godsend for Barbara Bush. She was in no position to lecture Georgie about the evils of smoking, since she taken up the habit after Robin's diagnosis. By this time, she was going through two packs of Newports a day.

Fully aware that for all intents and purposes their every movement was being monitored, Georgie and his friends essentially had the run of the town. They climbed fences, raced their bikes, ran through sprinklers, played marbles, and on Saturday afternoons pedaled downtown to catch a kiddie matinee (usually a Buck Rogers or Flash Gordon serial followed by a western) at the Ritz movie theater. Friday nights their fathers took them to cheer "Wahoo" McDaniel and the other players on the championship Midland High School football team. (The son of a Choctaw Indian, McDaniel went on to play with several professional football teams and became a fixture on the pro wrestling circuit.)

When no adults were around, Georgie and his friend Bill Sallee would climb up onto the goalposts or the stadium lights and "swing up there like a couple of monkeys," Sallee said. "If anybody'd have slipped, they'd have killed themselves."

Some activities were less wholesome than others. While all the neighborhood kids showed up each spring for milk and cookies at the home of the local ASPCA volunteer, the elderly woman's plea for kindness to animals fell on deaf ears. Behind the Bush house there was a gully that filled with water as soon as it rained, resulting in the "biblical plague" of frogs Georgie would recall decades later. With Georgie as their ringleader, the boys would take pot-shots at the frogs with their BB guns. Other times, Georgie and his friends would put a firecracker in a frog's mouth, then hurl it like a grenade so the frog exploded in midair. Allowed Georgie's boyhood friend Terry Throckmorton, "We were terrible to animals. Terrible."

No single pastime was a more important part of Georgie's life than baseball. His lifelong passion for the sport began at Sam Houston Elementary School, where Principal John Bizilo would doff his suit coat and hit balls for young Bush and his friends to field. Although smaller than his contemporaries, Georgie was an indefatigable player; he played catcher for one of the town's Little League teams, the Cubs, and was good enough one season to be selected as one of Midland's Little League All-Stars. His ambition: to be another Willie Mays. "All George ever wanted to be was a major league baseball player," Throckmorton said. "That's all he ever talked about."

The real baseball star in the family was still away for weeks at a stretch, guiding Zapata's transition into risky offshore drilling ventures. During Georgie's Little League career, his mother was a constant presence; his father did not attend a single Cubs game. But Big George would join in whenever his son got a few friends together for an impromptu game. "If Mr. Bush was standing in the outfield when someone hit a fly ball," recalled Georgie's friend Joe O'Neill, "he could put his glove behind him at belt level, drop his head forward, and catch the ball behind his back." As soon as Big George left, the boys would try the feat themselves—and invariably wind up getting hit in the back of the head with a baseball. "We all had scabs on the backs of our heads," O'Neill said, "from trying to catch the fly balls like Mr. Bush did."

There was no doubt that, even then, Dad's approval meant everything to Georgie. One of Georgie's proudest moments was the day his father stopped their game of catch and declared, "Son, you've arrived. I can throw it to you as hard as I want to."

Even off the field, Georgie managed to indulge his love of the game, committing volumes of baseball statistics to memory. He was also a canny trader of baseball cards. To boost the value of his collection, nine-year-old Georgie began sending cards to the players themselves, asking for their autographs and enclosing return postage. Boasting signed cards from Mickey Mantle, Willie Mays, Roger Maris, Whitey Ford, and scores of others, Georgie's became one of the finest baseball card collections in the state.

As idyllic as George W. Bush's childhood might have seemed, it was also colored by the fact that there wasn't any color. Midland, like all of Texas, was strictly segregated. Blacks went to their own schools, not to Sam Houston Elementary. There were separate waiting rooms for them at the courthouse and at the bus station, and wherever there were drinking fountains they were clearly marked "Whites Only" or "Colored." Blacks did not eat at the local coffee shop, much less at the Midland Country Club, and they still sat at the back of the bus. They could go to the local movie house, but only so long as they sat in the balcony.

Racial slurs were matter-of-fact in mid-1950s Midland, as they were throughout the state. "We used every awful word to describe blacks in those days," concedes one of Bush's closest friends. "That was how we were all raised."

Not Georgie, who made the mistake of using the word "nigger" while playing with his friend Mike Proctor in the Bush family living room. Barbara grabbed her son by the ear, hauled him into the bathroom, and washed his mouth out with soap. "His family was probably the only one around that didn't use racial slurs," Proctor said. "I probably didn't realize it was wrong until I saw that."

As a student of baseball, young Bush had few equals. But as a student, he was decidedly mediocre. His parents may have spearheaded a fund-raising drive to build the first school library at Sam Houston Elementary, but their eldest child spent scant time reading books. *Sports Illustrated*—Georgie bicycled to a friend's house just to get a peek at the inaugural August 16, 1954, issue—was another matter.

If he failed to impress his teachers at Sam Houston Elementary School and San Jacinto Junior High with his academic prowess, Georgie made his mark in other ways. "I have always lived in the moment," he would later concede, acknowledging that Robin's death had left him with the philosophy that life—or at least its rules of conduct—should "not be taken too seriously."

Since his antics at home had proven so effective in lifting his mother's sagging spirits, Georgie took it upon himself to spread his particular brand of mirth wherever he went. Much to his school-mates' delight, he was the quintessential class clown who squirmed in his seat, passed notes in class, made rude noises with his armpits, tossed baseballs and footballs through the open window of the class-room, and mimicked the teacher when her back was turned.

Fourth-grade music teacher Frances Childress was writing on the blackboard when the children began giggling behind her. She turned to see Georgie mugging for his classmates; he had taken a pen and drawn a beard and sideburns on his face.

Mrs. Childress clasped Georgie by the arm and dragged him off to the principal's office. "Just look at him," she told John Bizilo. "He's been making a disturbance in class."

To make matters worse, Georgie's mother would later report, "he sort of swaggered in, obviously making light of the fact that he was in trouble."

Bizilo took the quarter-inch-thick paddle that sat ominously on his desk and ordered Georgie to bend over. Then the principal administered three swift swats on the boy's derriere. "When I hit him he cried," Bizilo said. "Oh, did he cry! He hollered as if I'd shot him. But he learned his lesson."

Hardly. Georgie strutted and swaggered, smoked cigars (when he wasn't pilfering Mom's Newports), and swore like one of the rough-necks who worked his father's wells. When he went to church on Sundays, all the other boys would say "Good morning, Mrs. Wither-spoon" to the Sunday School teacher. Georgie, on the other hand, would shout, "Hiya, little lady. Lookin' sexy!" Instructed to behave himself when the Texas Bushes visited the grandparents in Maine, Georgie did nothing of the sort. Instead, he got in trouble for light-ing up a cigarette in the dining room of Kennebunkport's Nonan-tum Hotel. He was twelve.

At home, Georgie's victims tended to be willing ones. He would periodically assemble his brothers and command, "Okay, you little wieners, line up." Then he would shoot them in the back with his air rifle, and they would fall writhing on the floor in mock agony. Then, of course, they would all line up to be shot in the back again—it was that much fun, that much of an honor, just to be around their notoriously mischievous big brother.

Georgie had "a lot of personality," his mother would try to

explain. He was "a wonderful, incorrigible child who spent many afternoons sitting in his room, waiting for his father to come home to speak to him about his latest transgression."

One of those days when Big George was traveling out of state on business, Barbara called him up and said, "I'm desperate. I don't know what to do. Your son's in trouble again. He just hit a ball through the neighbor's upstairs window."

"My gosh, what a great hit!" Big George replied. "Did you get the ball back?"

In truth, Poppy hardly knew what to make of his son's boisterous behavior. "Georgie aggravates the hell out of me at times," Big George wrote to his father-in-law at one point. "But then at times I am so proud of him I could die."

"It's not that W. rebelled," explained a classmate, "he just was wilder than the old man expected—it was rowdiness. Not doing well in school when you could, being class funnyman—those were huge detours from the code."

Although Barbara was given the challenging task of reining in her insubordinate eldest boy, she clearly took pleasure—and perhaps some pride—in his rebellious streak. After all, among Midland wives, the chain-smoking, martini-drinking Mrs. Bush was known both for her candor, her irreverence, and her often caustic wit. "Bar is a wonderful woman," said a native Texan who befriended her in Midland, "but you sure didn't want to get on her bad side even back then. She is a very strong personality, and she has never had any trouble speaking her mind."

Georgie was always very much his mother's son. "We're pretty much alike, people tell us," W. would later say. "I don't mind a battle. She doesn't mind a battle. I've got my father's eyes and my mother's mouth."

Barbara saw in Georgie a kindred spirit—and a worthy adversary. Over the years, their verbal jousting would become the stuff of family legend. "We fight all the time," Barbara later laughed. "We're so alike in that way. He does things to needle me, always." Georgie, she liked to say, is "the son who pulls no punches and tells it like he *thinks* it is."

"I don't think George W. would ever be sarcastic or sassy with his father," said Georgie's cousin John Ellis. But as for Mom: "Bar will say to George W. something like 'Oh, don't be ridiculous,' and they're off to the races."

Sarcasm aside, Barbara leaned heavily on her eldest son. Like so many women of her generation who stayed home while their husbands struck out to make their fortunes in the wider world, Georgie's mom often felt trapped. "This was a period, for me, of long days and short years," she would recall. "Of diapers, running noses, earaches, more Little League games than you could believe possible, tonsils, and those unscheduled races to the hospital emergency room . . . of feeling that I'd never, ever be able to have fun again; and coping with the feeling that George Bush, in his excitement of starting a small company and traveling . . . was having a lot of fun."

With Dad on the road, Georgie pitched in with chores, played with his brothers, even tried to help Neil—who was eventually diagnosed with dyslexia—learn to read. "I wonder how I ever would have made it without my oldest son," Barbara conceded. "I probably put more responsibility on him than I should have, especially for a boy his age. But who else could I turn to with his father gone so much in those days? He was my Rock of Gibraltar, plain and simple, and because of that we have a very special relationship."

"She fostered, nurtured, and brought me up," George W. agreed. "She was the front line of discipline. She was the sarge." His father, W. went on, "was more the goals and ideals setter, the ultimate enforcer. But Mother was the immediate enforcer." It was a role that suited her well. "My mother's always been a very outspoken person who vents very well—she'll just let it rip if she's got something on her mind. Once it's over, you know exactly where you stand and that's it," he added. Whether she was pulling him down the hall by his earlobe or cheering him on at Little League, Barbara was simply "the one who was there. Because of this," explained W., "there will always be a special bond between us."

If Mom handled misdemeanors, then it was left to the "ultimate enforcer" to prosecute felonies. "I would scream and carry on," Barbara said. "The way George scolded was by silence or by saying, 'I'm disappointed in you.' And they would almost faint." Georgie would become particularly upset at the mere suggestion that he might have failed his father. "He could be made to feel," Georgie's brother Marvin said, "that he had committed the worst crime in history."

Dad's long absences on behalf of Zapata had paid off handsomely. The Bushes had always been able to rely on neighbors or on Anna Williams, Zapata's secretary, to baby-sit. Now they employed two African-American maids—Julia May Cooper and Otha Fitzgerald— whose duties included watching after the children whenever Mom and Dad were called back to Connecticut or Kennebunkport. "Not very many people in Midland had one maid," a neighbor recalled, "much less two. And there were no blacks in town then—I mean none—so the Bushes' maids were definitely noticed. But you got the sense that for the Bushes having servants around to do your bidding was just the norm. Barbara treated them both just like members of the family, but George really made them toe the line."

When Georgie was nine, the family relocated once more—this time to a house that reflected Big George's newfound status as a bona fide millionaire. The Bushes' new, three-thousand-square-foot brick ranch house at 2703 Sentinel Drive boasted a two-car garage and a pool with a cabana. It was surrounded by some of Midland's most expensive homes, many with circular drives and virtually all with manicured-to-perfection emerald-green lawns. The broad, gently winding streets were shaded by oak, pine, pecan, and maple trees, and neighborhood gardens bloomed with daisies, black-eyed Susans, sunflowers, bluebonnets, lavender, purple sage, and yellow roses. Moreover, the Bushes' new house backed onto Cowden Park Athletic Field, where neighborhood kids gathered to play baseball and soccer.

In the 1950s, swimming pools were only for the fortunate few— even in prosperous Midland. Georgie was not above lording his good fortune over the other kids. He went to school wearing swim trunks under his pants and bragged about it to his classmates. But the gambit backfired: A few doors down from the Bush house, Peggy Porter's parents also put in a pool. Peggy was one of the cutest girls at Sam Houston Elementary, and soon the neighborhood kids were flocking to the Porter house—and not to the Bushes'.

Yet Georgie undeniably had a following. In his first foray into politics, he ran against Jack Hanks Jr. for seventh grade class president. Just four years later at the American Legion Boys Nation in Washington, Hanks would run for vice president and end up trouncing another up-and-comer named Bill Clinton. (The next day, cameras would record what would become an historic moment when future President Clinton, then sixteen, shook the hand of JFK.)

But in the seventh grade contest for class president, Georgie Bush proved a tougher opponent than Bill Clinton; Hanks went down in defeat. Even Peggy Porter voted for Georgie—"because he was cuter," Porter said, "and in the seventh grade that's what counted."

As the 1950s drew to a close, Midland could claim to be the richest community per capita in the nation. Of the town's sixty thousand residents, an estimated one in one hundred were millionaires, and this at a time when the average annual income in the United States was under seven thousand dollars.

But it was not enough for Poppy. The first of the Ivy League carpetbaggers to really make it big, he was also among the first to recognize that oil production in West Texas had plateaued. Now he turned his attention eastward, to the vast reserves of oil along the Gulf Coast. In his new capacity as chief executive officer of Zapata-Offshore, Poppy raised enough capital to purchase five new rigs, each costing six million dollars and weighing nine million pounds. Zapata-Offshore would begin drilling in the Gulf, and eventually expand its operations around the world.

In 1959, satisfied that he could rightly claim to be a self-made man, Big George packed up his family and relocated to Houston. "I'll never forget the day we moved," Georgie later said. "I was shocked. I was a small-town boy moving to the big city. I learned to adjust, but it was hard. I had enough adventure in me, though, to also be excited about the move."

What's more, they were moving into what Georgie disparagingly called "our fancy new house." The Bushes had actually designed the "fancy" new house at 5525 Briar Drive themselves. Situated at the end of a long drive on a little over 1.2 wooded acres, the two-story brick home had a pool—larger than the one they had in Midland. There was also enough room in the backyard for a small baseball diamond. But before Georgie was allowed to go out and use it, he spent an hour each Saturday sitting in the study as his mother drilled him with vocabulary flash cards. The goal: to learn twenty-five new words a week.

By way of a little character-building, that summer before he started at his new school in Houston, Bar sent her oldest boy to

Camp Longhorn in the Texas hill country. Catering to Texas's most affluent families, Longhorn prided itself on its ability to toughen up the most mollycoddled of campers with mile-long swims across Inks Lake. Longhorn's slogan—"Aterwaytogo!"—was shouted by camp counselors and visiting parents, as well as by the children themselves when anything remotely positive happened.

It was in Houston that thirteen-year-old Georgie made the transition from public to private education, enrolling at Houston's exclusive Kinkaid School. The new arrival threw himself into sports, and if nothing else impressed his teachers with his unbridled enthusiasm for "just about everything. He was," said one of his teachers, "a real joiner."

Yet he also recognized from the outset that Houston and Midland were light years apart. After baseball practice one afternoon, Georgie was waiting for the bus when another student yelled, "Hey, you want a ride home, Bush?"

Georgie spun around to see another eighth grader behind the wheel of a GTO. "A GTO—in the eighth grade!" he recalled. "I remember saying, 'No thanks, man.' It was just a different world."

But the newcomer, brimming with enthusiasm and possessed of a certain good-ole-boy charm, would have no problem fitting right in. That vital component of Georgie's personality came as much from his gregarious, network-building mother as it did from his admired but seldom-seen dad. "Even when we were growing up in Houston," Jeb said, "Dad wasn't at home at night to play catch. Mom was always the one to hand out the goodies and the discipline. In a sense, it was a matriarchal family."

At times, Barbara was on the verge of throwing up her hands in defeat when it came to reining in Georgie. More than once, he and a friend were invited to play along with Mom when she went golfing at their country club in Houston. Invariably hitting a lousy shot off the first tee, Georgie would begin swearing—and the words would escalate in both volume and shock value as the game proceeded. A few holes later, Georgie would yell "Fuck!" just one too many times, and Mom would dispatch him to sit out the rest of the game in the car. It was what he intended all along. "You know," his friend Doug Hannah said, "he's one of those guys who, if things don't start off well, he wants to take his ball and go home. When his mother sent him packing, at least that way he couldn't lose."

Barbara worried about her son's lack of sportsmanship. During one of those games when she ejected Georgie from the course, his mother turned to Hannah and said, "That boy is going to have optical rectosis."

"'Optical rectosis'?" Hannah asked.

"A shitty outlook on life," Barbara replied.

It turned out, Hannah would discover over the years, that "optical rectosis" was one of Bar Bush's favorite phrases. "And she'd say it with this chuckle," Hannah remembered. "There was no harshness in the discipline. It was obvious she found George's antics fairly amusing."

The verbal tug-of-war between steel-willed mother and headstrong son would to a great extent shape Georgie's personality. But not to the exclusion of his father. Whenever the "Old Man" was around, Georgie paid keen attention to the masterful way he worked a room. Whether Big George was playing host to business associates, raising money for the United Way, or trying to lure potential fat-cat contributors away from the Democrats and over to his beloved GOP, the process was pretty much the same: start at one end of the room and work your way to the other, shaking hands, smiling, engaging in small talk, looking everyone straight in the eye, making sure that no one felt slighted or ignored. Never forget a name, Big George taught his son, and once you've committed a person's name to memory, use it as often as possible in conversation.

Big George was so methodical in his approach that he began keeping a card file on virtually every person with whom he came in contact. On each three-by-five index card was the individual's name, address, phone number, and business or party affiliation—as well as the names and ages of family members, and any other bits of personal information that might be gleaned.

At age thirteen, Georgie had not yet reached the card file stage. But he had already proven to be even more talented than his father when it came to putting names to faces. The boy went several steps further to put his own spin on the process. To begin with, he was far more tactile than previous generations of Bushes. Whenever possible, he would put his arm around someone's shoulder, or at the very least touch the other person's arm as they talked. He also bestowed nicknames on just about everyone he met: One hulking classmate became Rodan, after the monster in the cheesy Japanese horror movies. One lanky student was christened "Stretch," another who excelled academically seemed perfectly pleased at being dubbed "Brain."

Since "George Bush" was already taken, Georgie would also acquire several monikers over the decades—including Bushtail, Bombastic Bushkin, Bushman, Bush Boy, The Lip, George W., W., Dubya, Shrub, Junior (the nickname by which he would be known most of his adult life), and his future wife's favorite, "Bushie."

After two years at Kinkaid, Georgie had hoped to enroll at the local public high school, or one of the Houston prep schools that his classmates would be attending. He was not prepared for what his parents had in mind. "Congratulations, Georgie," his mother said one day. "You've been accepted at Andover. It will be a wonderful experience for you." She did not tell Georgie that their first choice, St. John's in Houston, had already rejected him.

"Man, you must have done something really *terrible*," his friends teased when they learned their ringleader was being shipped off to a school halfway across the country. Certainly Georgie dreaded the idea. "Andover was cold and distant and difficult," George W. later said. "In every way, it was a long way from home . . . forlorn is the best word to describe my sense of the place and my initial attitude."

Founded by Samuel Phillips in 1778, Phillips Academy has the distinction of being the oldest incorporated school in the United States. Situated twenty miles north of Boston and made up of 170 buildings spread across 450 landscaped acres, Andover (as Phillips Academy is more commonly called) boasted among its alumni the diverse likes of Oliver Wendell Holmes, Samuel Morse, and Jack Lemmon.

When George W. arrived in the autumn of 1961 as a tenth grader, then-all-male Andover was widely regarded as the most prestigious prep school in the nation—America's answer to England's Eton. Along with twenty-one other boys, George W. roomed at America House on Main Street. Samuel Francis Smith wrote the lyrics to "My Country, 'tis of Thee" in his room at America House in 1832. George W.'s rooms were on the opposite end of the campus from Rabbit Pond, into which an incorrigible Humphrey Bogart once tossed a teacher before he was booted out of school.

Despite his exposure to such Old Money bastions as Greenwich, Kennebunkport, and New York's Sutton Place, George W. felt as if he had been cast adrift in hostile waters. Not only were there no women for miles, but the winters were as harsh as the strictly enforced dress code. Andover students were required to wear coats and ties to class, and to attend chapel five days a week. From the moment they got up at 7:15 in the morning to their 10 P.M. curfew, every aspect of life at Andover was mapped out with the military precision befitting an institution patterned after West Point. Much to Georgie's horror, only seven minutes were allowed between each class. His new school was "very different from the happy chaos in the Bush household," Bush remembered. "It was a shock to my system."

Georgie was not the only newcomer to the school who found life there barely tolerable. "It was a shocking experience," said Clay Johnson, one of a handful of Texans in George's class at Andover. Johnson was so desperately unhappy that he told Bush he was looking for a way to be kicked out without disgracing his family. "It was far away from home and rigorous, and scary and demanding. The buildings looked different, and the days were shorter. We went from being at the top of our classes academically to struggling to catch up. We were so much less prepared than kids coming from Massachusetts or New York. We were in way over our heads in a foreign land."

Just how far over their heads became glaringly apparent when Andover Headmaster John Kemper appeared on the cover of *Time* magazine alongside the headline "Excellence and Intensity in U.S. Prep Schools." *Time* anointed Andover as the toughest of the lot. "I remember reading that," said Georgie's buddy Clay Johnson, "and thinking, 'Oh my God, I'm at the hardest school in the country!' I mean, I thought it was hard, but I didn't realize it was *that* hard."

To be sure, for the first time in his life, George W. found himself academically challenged—to put it mildly. Bush was so far behind that, after lights-out at 10 P.M., he spread out on the floor so he could study by the sliver of light coming under the door from the hallway.

It did little good. For his first paper at Andover, Bush chose to write about the impact Robin's death had had on him. His mother's valiant efforts to expand Georgie's vocabulary were apparently for naught. In an effort to impress his professors, he thumbed through *Roget's Thesaurus* looking for a synonym for "tears," as in the tears he shed over his little sister. In the end, he wrote, "*Lacerates* ran down my cheeks."

When the paper came back, Georgie was crestfallen to see a big "0" scrawled at the top in red ink, along with "Disgraceful!" and "See me"—all written with such force that they made an impression all the way through to the back of his blue exam book.

"He had this fear," Johnson said of his classmate, "that generation after generation had gone to Andover, and he would fail after three weeks." Terrified that he might disappoint his overachieving dad, George W. buckled down. Over the next three years, he would never excel as a student. But he would, through sheer determination, manage to squeak by.

Not that Georgie was willing to wilt in his father's colossal shadow. He, too, would make his mark at Andover, though in ways that would almost certainly have made previous generations of Bushes cringe.

The mischief-making George W. made a conscious decision to curry favor with both students and faculty by appointing himself class clown. His mission was, as he put it, "to instill a sense of frivolity" in an otherwise "cold, dark, serious" place.

Whatever the pressures he was facing, young Bush never allowed his spirits to flag. At the first sign of snow, it was Georgie who ran giddily out into the quad, trying to gather up enough flakes to form a snowball. He frequently challenged the stringent dress code, wearing sneakers without socks, horribly wrinkled shirts, and even the occasional army jacket. In the Commons, Andover's baronial dining hall, he led other students in a contest to see who could use a knife to fling a pat of butter at the wall with enough force to make it stick.

During his first year at Andover, the ceaselessly cheerful Georgie played junior varsity baseball and junior varsity basketball, where he made a running joke out of the fact that he seldom left the bench. On those rare occasions when he was summoned to play, what

Georgie lacked in talent he made up for in zeal. "He threw himself into everything he did," said his basketball coach. "You had to admire the guy . . ."

There were moments, however, when Georgie proved to be a shade too feisty. During one basketball game, he became so enraged over a referee's call that he hurled the ball at an opposing player—a stunt that resulted in Georgie being ejected from the game.

Georgie gravitated toward the athletes, many of whom, like him, came from outside the New York–Boston sphere. That did not make him a jock per se. Bush may have played on teams, but he was, observed classmate Peter Schandorff, "less of a jock and more of a jock hanger-on-er."

What Bush undeniably was—though his classmates were often hard-pressed to explain why—was cool. Like the others at the cool-guy table in the Commons, he comported himself with a bravado that implied he knew more about drinking, driving, women—more about *grown-up life*—than the rest of the student body. Unlike the others, Georgie could not boast of being a star athlete or student government leader. "He was very much a Big Man on Campus, definitely," said one of his classmates. "But it was hard to figure out why. It wasn't as if he had actually *done* anything exceptional, except hang out with the cool group and make fun of those who weren't in it."

Georgie did, in fact, assiduously court those Andover students who had already made names for themselves on the playing field— people like footballer John ("Moondoggie") Kidde, hockey standout Doug Brown, and Mack Thompson, a star wrestler and tennis player from Fort Worth. Those fortunate enough to be brought into Georgie's inner circle were invited to spend time with the rest of the Bush clan at Kennebunkport, or with the Pierces in Rye, where the top prep school teams competed against each other during Rye Tennis Week.

"Inclusive," classmate Robert Marshall observed, "is about the last word I would have used to describe George at Andover." Concurred another student, Matthew J. McClure: "If you were not cool, then George ignored you. When the people who are cool ignore you, it's unpleasant, and that was my experience."

Even back then there was simmering resentment concerning what many came to regard as George W.'s condescending smirk. "Maybe he was arrogant," said a classmate. "Or maybe he was just shy." Georgie's pals agreed that his purse-lipped smile seemed to send out all the wrong signals. "George's smile was really very self-deprecating," said one. "Most of the time the joke was on Bush, and that's the way he wanted it—whatever it took to get a laugh and to lighten things up a little, even if it was at his own expense."

Those who had experienced rejection firsthand from their peers at Andover found young Bush to be surprisingly congenial. "A guy from Puerto Rico was sort of unusual at Andover, but it didn't bother him," said Jose R. Gonzalez, one of only a handful of Hispanics at the school in the early 1960s. He was one of several classmates Georgie invited to spend Thanksgiving at his grandparents' house in Connecticut. It was only then, Gonzalez said, "that we figured out that our host was a United States senator. George never mentioned it."

Of the 240 students in Bush's class at Andover, only three were black—and one was the son of the Somali prime minister. Conway Dowling, a black student from Virginia, remembered Bush and his Texas friends as being much friendlier toward him than most of the northerners on campus. "At least with respect to African-American guys in the class," Dowling said, "he got along very well with them."

At sixteen, Georgie was already honing his political skills by "taking pains to get along with everybody. He was," said classmate Thomas Eastland, "building coalitions throughout." Another classmate, Doug Brown, said George had a "kind of easy charm—a charismatic charm that was humor-based. He could make people laugh and feel good about themselves."

Like the other cool guys, Georgie dated a cute girl from one of the surrounding all-female schools. Fifteen-year-old Debbie Taylor was his girlfriend at the time, and she remembered him as "more assertive and certainly more outgoing than some other guys. I thought he was kind of studly." She and Georgie shared a favorite song, one that suited the image he would make painstaking attempts to cultivate: "He's a Rebel" by the Crystals.

Sex remained something of a mystery to George, although he and his friends did pick up some tips from the Somali prime minister's son, whose father had five wives. Certainly Big George was no help. "Dad was shy," young Bush said. "We never had 'the talk.' He never told me to wear a 'raincoat' [condom] or anything."

Having charmed his way into his prep school's social elite, Georgie turned his sights on winning over the student body as a whole. It was as Head Cheerleader that George W. Bush was able to take center stage as Andover's self-appointed mirthmaker.

He would later pledge to "lift the spirit of America." But for now, Georgie was content putting on skits and pulling off stunts designed to lift the spirits of his schoolmates. At his first football pep rally, Bush dashed into the gym and hammed it up in full Beatles attire. Other times, he donned a squashed fishing hat and put the other eight sweater-clad male cheerleaders through their paces, shouting slogans and wisecracks through a giant megaphone emblazoned with the letter A. "I think that funky hat tells you a lot about George," said fellow cheerleader Sandy Greene. "The tradition of Andover cheerleaders was very clean-cut, with our letter sweaters and khaki pants. I suppose that old fishing hat was George's way of embracing tradition without taking it too seriously."

Already keenly aware of the value of a photo op, Georgie posed for the Andover *Phillipian* straddling a tree branch with the rest of the squad, feigning a nap in study hall, and taking a phone call from a booth crammed with his fellow cheerleaders. In his most outlandish stunt, Georgie and the other cheerleaders performed at one school assembly wearing short white skirts, bras, tight sweaters, and curly blond wigs—all designed to poke fun at a rival school's team.

Soon, there was concern on the part of the school administration that Georgie was *too* good at this job; the cheerleaders were becoming a bigger draw than the football team. When Dean of Students G. Grenville Benedict asked Georgie to abandon the skits, the *Phillipian* ran an editorial demanding that Bush be allowed to continue his "antics." Not to worry. Dean Benedict soon became one of Georgie's biggest fans, praising him for bolstering morale at the school more than anyone in recent memory.

As much as he relished his Head Cheerleader status at Andover, he never mentioned it to any of the folks back home in football-crazed Texas. "They wouldn't really know what to make of a male cheerleader," he confessed.

While Georgie mugged his way through campus life, there were serious moments as well. He claimed that a teaching legend at Andover, Tom Lyons, was so passionate about American history that he sparked Bush's own lifelong interest in the subject. Bush seemed equally impressed by the inspiring circumstances of the professor's own life. A twenty-year-old football star at Brown University when he contracted polio, Lyons would spend the rest of his life on crutches. "The polio crippled his body," George W. later wrote, "but never hindered his enthusiasm for his subject or his profession." It was because of Lyons, George W. said, that he would pick history as his major in college.

Nevertheless, at the time Georgie seemed oddly oblivious to the important world and national events swirling around him. The Berlin Wall, racial unrest in the South, and the Cuban Missile Crisis all happened during his time at Andover. "If he had any interest whatsoever in what was going on in the world," one classmate said of Georgie's first three years at Andover, "I didn't see it. Most of us were scared shitless by the Cuban Missile Crisis. People were emptying out supermarkets and crawling into their bomb shelters, everybody was so convinced there was going to be a nuclear war. But George just kept clowning around, trying to raise everybody's spirits. Either he felt it was his job to keep things upbeat, or he just didn't get it."

Georgie's apathetic attitude toward the great political issues of the day seemed even more inexplicable given his own family's involvement. In 1962, Prescott Bush, crippled by severe arthritis and suffering from exhaustion, decided not to run for reelection. At precisely the same time in Houston, Georgie's dad made his first plunge into politics, running for chairman of the Harris County Republican Party—and winning. Once Georgie's grandfather officially left the Senate in 1963—the start of Georgie's senior year at Andover—the torch was officially passed to the next generation as Big George announced his decision to run for the U.S. Senate in Texas.

For Georgie's dad, the Senate race seemed perfectly timed. Incumbent Democrat Ralph Yarborough was up for reelection, and he seemed particularly vulnerable. An ongoing feud between the state's liberal senator and its conservative Democratic Governor John Connally was splitting the party down the middle, threatening to hand Texas to the GOP in 1964.

Big George was in the thick of a primary battle for the GOP Senate nomination when JFK arrived with his wife Jackie in Dallas on November 22, 1963. The President's fence-mending trip to Texas was designed to ensure Yarborough's reelection and keep Texas's electoral votes in the Democratic column.

Barbara and her husband were campaigning in Tyler, Texas, when word crackled over the airwaves that JFK had been assassinated. The Bushes flew back to Dallas in a private plane, circling Love Field just as Air Force One took off carrying the newly sworn-in President Lyndon Baines Johnson, Jackie, and the body of the slain president.

Georgie's reaction to JFK's assassination seemed oddly out of sync with his peers—particularly given his own ties to Texas and his dad's political activities there. "Everybody was devastated, stunned, and, frankly, afraid," one classmate said. "People were worried that things could spiral out of control. It was the height of the Cold War, the Cuban Missile Crisis had been just the year before, and World War III always seemed a possibility." But Georgie "just did not seem that upset by JFK's assassination. He just didn't. A few of us commented at the time how it was that he could just keep breezing right along the way he always did when the rest of us were staggering around in a daze like the rest of the country."

The Lip, as he was now called, did care about the attacks leveled at his father during the primary battle. Big George was vilified by the other Republican hopefuls as a carpetbagger and "Nelson Rockefeller liberal." Barbara, meantime, was pilloried as a Cape Cod heiress. She wrote to her father pointing out that she had never set foot on Cape Cod, but that he should write back immediately if she was an heiress.

At about the time of the Kennedy assassination, George W. and his roommate Moondoggie (John Kidde) had been appointed proctors of a tenth grade dorm—a high honor bestowed on only a few seniors. The Lip went home to Houston for the holidays, and when he returned he brought with him a copy of Barry Goldwater's *The Conscience of a Conservative*. Mom and Dad thought that if Big George was going to run for the Senate, everybody in the family ought to know something about the party's standard-bearer. When he saw it on Georgie's desk, Kidde recalls saying, " 'What the hell is this?' George seemed honestly interested in the book. He said his parents had asked him to read it. I remember him telling me what Goldwater stood for."

Meanwhile, there was little doubt at Andover what Georgie stood for: fun. In April 1964, he stood up at the weekly assembly wearing a top hat and announced the formation of an intramural stickball league with himself as "High Commissioner." Over the next twenty minutes he ad-libbed the rules of the league in what amounted to a stand-up comedy routine. According to Kidde, Bush had not rehearsed the monologue. "He got some chuckles, and he just kept going. He was making it up as he went along. And he started talking about rules, and it was very funny. It was a riot."

A modified form of New York stickball, Andover stickball was played on a field with broomsticks and a tennis ball. The High Commissioner picked the team names based on what would get a laugh. One team was the Nads, and their cheer was "Go Nads!" Then there were the Beavers, the Stimson Steamers (a cheeky reference to both Andover alumnus Henry Stimson and what happens to dog droppings on a crisp spring morning), and the Crotch Rots. Players emblazoned their own colorful nicknames on their white jerseys. Vermin, Root, Zitney, and McScuz were among the stickball stars.

The tongue-in-cheek tournament, over which Georgie presided with great fanfare, poked fun at the serious business of Andover athletics. For the final grand championship game, which Georgie was to umpire personally, the High Commissioner was carried out onto the field on his classmates' shoulders. Virtually the entire student body turned out to watch the Steamers beat the Beavers 3–0.

Student David Mason saw Georgie's stickball league, which became the school's largest student-organized activity, as "a way to send up Andover and let off some of the inevitable senior-year springtime steam. To George's eternal credit, it did this without getting anyone expelled." Added the Beavers' "Zitney" (Peter Pfeifle): "Stickball was the thing, and Bush was stickball."

As absurd as it was, the stickball league both underscored his political talents and bolstered his confidence. Now Georgie knew without a doubt, said his friend Randall Roden, "that he could get people to do things." The High Commissioner went so far as to bestow yet another nickname on himself. He insisted on being called "Tweeds" Bush, after the notoriously corrupt Tammany Hall kingpin Boss Tweed.

George had proven to himself that, like his father, he too had leadership potential—albeit of a different, less distinguished sort. He had always felt the pressure to follow his grandfather and father into Yale, but Dean Benedict suggested that he apply elsewhere, "just in case."

The dean had good cause to feel that Georgie might not make the grade. He had never once made the honor roll, and his College Boards—640 in math and a verbal score of 566—were more than respectable but not up to the average scores of other students being admitted to Yale that year: 718 math and 668 verbal. A somewhat chastened Georgie applied to the University of Texas as his "safe" school, but wound up getting into Yale anyway. "It didn't hurt," said one of his former teachers, "that his grandfather *and* father—one a former senator and the other running for the office—were both Yale men. And not just Yalies, but stars—the kind of students the professors still talked admiringly about decades later."

Before he enrolled at Yale, however, Georgie returned to Texas to spend the summer working on his dad's Senate campaign. One of his jobs was to prepare a series of briefing books on each of Texas's 254 counties. Each book contained the names and phone numbers of local campaign leaders as well as summaries on the main industries, agricultural products, business, labor, and civic movers and shakers in each county.

In what amounted to a crash course in grassroots politics, the candidate's eighteen-year-old son also posted campaign signs along the highway and handed out campaign literature door-to-door. On one occasion, he drove a van full of BUSH FOR SENATOR signs to the state GOP convention in Dallas. He made use of his cheerleading talents by organizing rallies across the state. While Abilene's Black Mountain Valley Boys played country music from the back of a flatbed truck, Georgie and his dad's team of campaign workers known as the "Bush Belles" warmed up the crowd for the candidate's arrival.

Each time his father stood up to give a speech, Georgie unabashedly led the applause.

Georgie would make several trips that fall between Texas and New Haven, where for the next four years he would room with his two Andover buddies Clay Johnson and Rob Dieter. Like Andover, Yale was an all-male bastion of power and privilege. The university would not start admitting women until 1969, the year following George W.'s graduation. But the student body was undergoing a metamorphosis nonetheless. No longer were virtually all those being admitted the prep school–educated sons of button-down WASP alumni. Public school graduates were flooding into Yale's neo-Gothic dormitories and lecture halls in record numbers.

At the time, there was a social chasm between the preppies and the public school kids. George W., initially regarded as the quintessential East Coast rich kid preppy, was determined to bridge it. He sat down with a copy of the student directory and began memorizing names. According to his friend Roland Betts, within three months W. knew the names of every freshman "and actually knew fifty percent of the class."

"He would wander up to anybody, absolutely anybody, and stick his hand out and say, 'Hey, I'm George Bush,' and start talking," Betts said. "That's just his nature. He's not pretentious, not exploitive. George is a very disarmingly charming person." Betts estimated that by the time he graduated, Bush personally knew at least one thousand of the university's roughly four thousand undergraduates.

In November, W. and his grandfather flew back to Texas to spend election day with the family. At 7:01 P.M., just as the Bushes were pulling up to Houston's Shamrock Hotel in hopes of celebrating a Republican victory, the news came over the car radio that Ralph Yarborough had defeated George Bush.

Big George waded into the crowd of supporters who jammed the balloon-filled ballroom, shaking hands and thanking everyone for their hard work. George W. struggled to contain his emotions while his dad made a characteristically dignified concession speech. Afterward, George W. broke down and wept as startled campaign workers looked on.

"That really hit him hard," a close friend observed. "The Bushes were not accustomed to losing, and this was the first time in his life

George ever saw his father have to swallow defeat. He desperately wanted everyone to like him, but even more he wanted everyone to like his dad. He did, and still does, worship the guy."

Once back in New Haven, George W. sought out Yale Chaplain William Sloan Coffin Jr. for some words of consolation. It did not concern him that the left-leaning Reverend Coffin was now one of the nation's most outspoken social activists. Perhaps W., never one to read the newspapers or pay particularly close attention to current events, was not aware that Coffin had lent the prestige of his vaunted position to the cause of nuclear disarmament, or that he was a vocal critic of U.S. foreign policy. Soon, as American involvement in Southeast Asia deepened, Coffin would emerge as a star of the antiwar movement.

What mattered to W. now, in 1964, was that Coffin had been tapped by Poppy in 1948 to join the secret, ultra-exclusive Skull & Bones Society. Spotting Coffin on campus, W. went up to him, stuck out his hand and introduced himself. "Oh, yes," Coffin said. "I know your father. Frankly, he was beaten by a better man."

W. was livid. Not only was Coffin's remark patently cruel ("He's supposedly the guy who was there to comfort students"), but young Bush saw it as a sign of eastern liberal arrogance. "What angered me was the way such people at Yale felt so intellectually superior and so righteous," he later said. "They thought they had all the answers. They thought they could create a government that could solve all our problems for us. These are the ones who felt so guilty that they had been given so many blessings in life—like an Andover or a Yale education—that they felt they should overcompensate by trying to give everyone else in life the same thing."

Coffin's comment struck George W. as something only a northeastern elitist would say. "Texas people are more polite," he said. "I don't think a Texan would do that to a son." The offending remark, which would fester for decades, made W. want to "get back to Texas and away from the snobs." In the meantime, he would make a concerted effort to take nothing seriously—not his studies and certainly not the issues of the day. Picking up where he left off at Andover, W. cultivated the image of a beer-guzzling, football-watching, babe-ogling slob.

"We are all messy," one Yalie of the time confessed, "but George took it to new depths. He never did his laundry. His clothes smelled.

He'd take whatever was rolled up in a ball on the floor and put it on. Technically he'd be wearing jacket and tie, but the tie was looped around his neck like a scarf, the jacket was stained and creased, and underneath it he wore a T-shirt with holes in it."

W.'s open, easygoing manner instantly made him one of Yale's most popular students. But his professors scarcely noticed him. Despite the fact that he was not only a history major but the scion of a family steeped in political tradition, W. squeaked by in his political science courses with scores in the low seventies. By the end of his freshman year, he was officially in the bottom fifth of his class.

No sooner had he arrived back in Houston to begin another summer of swimming, golfing, tennis, and drinking than George W. was confronted by his father. Big George had arranged a summer job for his eldest son—one that would provide exposure to the nitty-gritty of the oil business akin to what Poppy had first experienced in Odessa.

That June of 1965, George W. reported for work on a small inland oil rig run by Circle Drilling Company in Lake Charles, Louisiana. He was part of a fifteen-man crew made up of other college kids with connections, as well as tattooed, tobacco-spitting roughnecks. The work was grueling and the conditions horrendous, but to nineteen-year-old George W. the four hundred dollars he was paid each week seemed like a small fortune. After working on the rig seven days straight, George would head off with his paycheck in hand and drive from one sawdust-on-the-floor dive to the next in search of a good time.

Eventually, George W. grew tired of the routine and wanted to spend more time with his platinum-edged pals back in Houston. One week before his commitment on the rig was up, W. packed up and left. After Big George got wind of what had happened, he summoned W. to Zapata's offices in downtown Houston.

"You agreed to work a certain amount of time and you didn't," Big George told his son. "I just want you to know that you have disappointed me."

Devastated, W. ran out of his father's office. But just two hours later Dad, never one to hold a grudge, called him up and invited him to a Houston Astros game. "And bring a friend," he added.

Yet the mild rebuke by his father left a lasting impression. "He wasn't screaming and he wasn't angry," W. said. "But he was disappointed. When you love a person and he loves you, those are the harshest words someone can utter."

Returning for his sophomore year in the fall of 1965, W. was assigned to Davenport College, one of the twelve residence halls scattered about the Yale campus. He would once again share his three-bedroom suite with his freshman roommates, Clay Johnson and Rob Dieter, although their social lives would revolve around the fraternity they were about to join, Delta Kappa Epsilon. All fraternities at the time engaged in some form of hazing, and "Deke" was no exception. Along with the other pledges, Bush and his friends were paddled, verbally abused, and given a variety of distasteful tasks to perform.

At one point all fifty pledges were brought to a room and, one by one, challenged to name the other fifty pledges in the room. As they went from pledge to pledge, none could name more than a half-dozen of the others standing right in front of them. Then they got to W., who without missing a beat named all fifty—a feat that had never before been accomplished.

"DKE was for jocks and jock wanna-bes," said one student. Of all the fraternities, it was the choice of the Big Men on Campus, boasting the loudest parties and the longest bar. Johnson remembered "lots of beer drinking and lots of television watching and lots of sports talk"—not to mention lots of sex talk, the cigar-smoking, and all-night poker games. "It was a very manly existence." Another fraternity brother described DKE in two words: Animal House, "and the George Bush part is played by John Belushi. With Bush it was always 'Toga! Toga!' In fact, George is the first person I ever heard come up with the idea of a toga party."

Just as he had done back in Midland when he was trying to cheer up his grief-stricken mother, and again at Andover, George W. made himself the designated purveyor of good times. It was W. who knew how to get tickets to sporting events, where to find the best parties with the prettiest girls, and how to smuggle booze "into just about anyplace," said a friend. Deke House was the "site of soul bands and dancing and dates," observed fraternity brother Don Ensenat. "There was a lot of alcohol."

Indeed, alcohol fueled fun times at Deke House, and W. was its principal supplier. Before a football game, young Bush would mix up a supply of screwdrivers in a garbage can. He was also an eager participant in Yale's "crew races," in which teams from a half-dozen fraternities competed in a beer-guzzling contest. Once, as he headed home from a party with friends, George W. suddenly collapsed on the pavement and began rolling down the street. Recalled his classmate Russ Walker, "He literally rolled back to the dorm."

DKE parties, often attended by women from neighboring colleges, were often rowdy affairs. It was not uncommon for revelers to come reeling out of Deke House to throw up or pass out on the lawn. "We drank heavily at DKE," allowed another frat brother, Gregory Gallico. "It was absolutely off the wall—appalling. I cannot for the life of me figure out how we all made it through."

As he did every year, George W. returned home to Houston for the Christmas holidays. It was then that he began dating Cathryn Lee Wolfman, a leggy, fresh-scrubbed coed who lived not far from the Bushes in Houston's exclusive Tanglewood district. Cathryn's stepfather was the owner of Wolfman's, one of Houston's best-known clothiers, and while Georgie was Head Cheerleader away at Andover, she was a more traditional pom-pom-waving Head Cheerleader at St. John's—as well as student body president.

Barbara Bush had dropped out of Smith College, and so, it turned out, did Cathy Wolfman. Her career at Smith was cut short when she was severely injured while tobogganing and flown home to Houston to recuperate. By the time George W. began asking her out, Cathryn was majoring in economics at Houston's Rice University. Like Georgie, Cathryn was ebullient, extremely popular, and a regular on the never-ending round robin of tennis matches and parties frequented by Houston's well-heeled preppy class. "Cathy was a terrific girl—beautiful, fun, just a great catch," Hannah said. "Everybody agreed that she and George made a great couple. They were very similar types."

Unlike young Bush, Cathy was well-read—she joined Rice's Elizabeth Baldwin Literary Society in her freshman year—studious, sensible, and possessed of a certain poise. "She was a very self-possessed young woman—very mature for her years," said a friend of both families. "George, of course, prided himself in being a bad boy. But Cathy always seemed to be having an awful lot of fun whenever they were together. He made her laugh the way he made everybody laugh. Maybe she lived vicariously through him a little."

Cathy was particularly impressed by George W.'s sentimental streak. "He was deeply sentimental, very emotional and completely family-oriented," she said. "He had been profoundly affected by his sister Robin's death, and he turned very solemn every time he spoke about her."

"We spent our summers together," Cathy Wolfman later said of her romance with George W. "We swam and went water-skiing in Galveston. We played tennis and bridge and, of course, we worked and got together with friends."

As their relationship turned more serious, the couple burned up the phone lines between Texas and Connecticut. Wolfman even paid several visits to New Haven. "If you were lucky, you'd see your girl-friend every other weekend," said Roland Betts. "She was around. I used to see her at Deke."

George W. was, Wolfman later recalled, "always a very passionate man—a good kisser, a real romantic guy, and a real gentleman. He was kind, caring, and sensitive. And he used to make me laugh all the time."

Big George made another stab at politics in the summer of 1966, campaigning for Congress virtually door-to-door in Houston's afflu-ent seventh district. This time, George W. had to divide his time between doing campaign chores for Dad and his summer job selling sporting goods at a Sears in Houston. He would later say this was his favorite summer job, recalling how on just his second day of work he rang up the highest volume of sales in the store. When one salesman asked him to leave the big-ticket items to the full-time staffers who needed the commissions, he voluntarily confined himself to selling Ping-Pong balls. Still, the Sears experience quickly wore thin, and W., unwilling to tone down his hyperactive social life, quit that job after just four weeks.

That fall, Big George became the first Republican ever elected to represent Houston's Harris County in Congress. At about the same time, George W. was also elected to office. By acclamation, he was chosen to serve as chapter president of Delta Kappa Epsilon.

With the holidays approaching, George W. and some friends struck out in the direction of downtown New Haven in search of

Christmas decorations. "I'm not saying whether I and a couple of others had a few glasses of Christmas cheer," he would later confess, "but we thought we needed a wreath for the Deke house." W. and his friends were indeed inebriated—and noisy enough to attract the attention of two police officers who happened to be driving by.

The cops jumped out of their patrol car and approached W. "What are you doing?" they demanded.

"We are liberating a Christmas tree wreath," he answered indignantly. "Don't you understand, the Delta Kappa Epsilon house is short a Christmas wreath?"

The police didn't understand, and he was arrested on the spot, hauled down to the police station, and charged with disorderly conduct. Later, a family friend interceded and the charges were eventually dropped.

Not long after his first brush with the law, George W. returned to Houston and headed for Neiman-Marcus with a considerable amount of cash in his pocket. There, with his old friend Doug Hannah looking on in mock horror, young Bush bought a one-carat diamond engagement ring. "I was astonished," Hannah said. "To see a friend of mine at that age taking a step like that—it just didn't seem realistic."

Always a stickler for tradition, George W. approached Cathryn Wolfman's stepfather and asked him for her hand in marriage. Then he got down on one knee and proposed to her. On New Year's Day 1967, the engagement was announced in the *Houston Chronicle* with the headline "Congressman's Son to Marry Rice Co-ed." An accompanying photograph showed the happy couple on the floor in front of the fireplace—he in buttoned-up suit and striped tie, she in a sleeveless dress, her long blond hair falling over her right shoulder.

"Cathy, we are so deeply pleased and thrilled that you will be part of our family," Big George wrote Wolfman. "Life has been good to us and you marrying our George proves it, for in you he is getting a very special wife and in you we are getting a very special daughter-in-law."

"I was really close to George's mom," Cathy later said. "The whole family was very warm, very welcoming. But Barbara and I got on exceptionally well—probably because she was so much like her son."

George W. had followed his father's footsteps to Andover and Yale, and now he was getting engaged at age twenty, just like Poppy. "I was impressed," Hannah said. "But the whole thing seemed ill-conceived to me."

In yet another attempt to emulate his dad, W. went back to Yale hoping that he would be finally invited to join the Skull & Bones Society—the sine qua non of secret societies at Yale. Since its founding in 1832, Skull & Bones counted as members the illustrious likes of William Howard Taft, Dean Witter, Henry Luce, Averell Harriman, McGeorge Bundy, and William F. Buckley—not to mention both of W.'s grandfathers and his dad.

The bells of Yale's Harkness Tower pealed precisely at eight on the evening of April 28, 1967. George W. was standing in the courtyard outside Davenport College when a mysterious black-suited man carrying a briefcase roughly clapped his hand on Bush's shoulder. "Skull and Bones!" the man said. "Accept or reject."

"I accept," W. said without hesitating. Contrary to the long-held myth that he had been "tapped" by his father, it was a senior named David Alan Richards who did the honors. In the process, he acquired a new nickname: "Temporary," because he could not come up with a permanent secret name for himself.

For someone who professed to be virulently antisnob, it was hard to find a more exclusive group on campus. Skull & Bones picked only fifteen new members each year, and they were never permitted to even speak the words "Skull and Bones" in the presence of a nonmember. Their meetings took place in a windowless tomb on New Haven's High Street, where on occasion they were required to strip off their clothes, lie naked in a coffin, and share the most graphic details of their sex lives with their fellow Bonesmen.

But this was the sixties, and Skull & Bones as well as other all-male secret societies at Ivy League campuses were being denounced as outdated, exclusionary, and ultra-elitist. As the United States sank deeper and deeper into the quagmire of Vietnam, fewer and fewer students across the country were opting to pledge with a fraternity or a sorority. "We were facing the real possibility that we were going to be sent to die in Vietnam," said one Bush classmate. "The whole fun-and-games atmosphere at the fraternities just seemed so silly given all that was going on. It was no longer the cool thing to do."

W. started off 1967 thinking he would be getting married that June. Cathy Wolfman had already been to New York to pick out her wedding dress along with the bridesmaids' outfits, when George called to say he did not want to get married "just yet." They agreed to postpone their nuptials indefinitely, but Wolfman was "devastated. I loved him," she said. "I really did. I thought he was fabulous and I wanted to marry him." W. would remember things in much the same way. "I was crazy about her," he said, "but we decided not to get married in between my junior and senior year in college."

Back in Houston that summer, W. earned sixty dollars a week as a bookkeeper for Rauscher, Pierce Securities. He abruptly quit the job after a month, leaving plenty of time for making the rounds of parties at places like the Houston and River Oaks country clubs with Cathryn. Still, it was already becoming clear to their friends that marriage seemed more and more unlikely.

Speculation ran rampant that the patrician, Protestant-to-the-bone Bushes objected to their son marrying a Jewish woman and had worked behind the scenes to sabotage the wedding. But the Bushes had never shown the slightest hint of anti–Semitism. Moreover, Cathryn wasn't Jewish; Mr. Wolfman was her stepfather, and she had been raised as an Episcopalian.

Uncertain about the future of his relationship with Cathryn, W. returned to Yale for his fourth and final year only to find his beloved DKE embroiled in controversy. In November 1967 the *Yale Daily News* ran an exposé on hazing that had the entire school in an uproar. Claiming that fraternity pledging was often "a degrading, sadistic and obscene process," the article pointed to DKE as the campus's worst offender. Not only were pledges made to sit motionless for hours with their heads between their legs, but according to the school newspaper they were kicked and beaten until the grand finale—the moment when each pledge was "branded" just above the buttock with the fraternity's insignia. Accompanying the article was a photograph showing a scab in the shape of the Greek letter delta.

Pledges were indeed paddled, kicked, and yelled at for up to five hours before they were finally shown a large branding iron glowing red hot in the fireplace. Then they were told to turn around, and a much smaller brand made of a coat hanger was used to make the

wooden goalposts. A series of scuffles ensued, and when the Princeton police arrived at the scene they spotted George W. perched on
the crossbar, struggling to rip off a piece of one of the posts to take
home as a souvenir.

"I was leaving the field," said W.'s classmate H. Rey Stroube III,
"and when I looked back, George was standing in the middle of the
crossbars, helping to bring down the goalposts."

By the time W. was escorted to the campus police station, the
posts were mangled beyond repair. He was bluntly told to leave
town. "So I was once in Princeton, New Jersey," he said more than
three decades later, "and haven't been back since."

Around this time, it was later rumored, a soused W. climbed on
top of a bar, stripped off his clothes, and danced nude—an episode
that was purportedly captured on film. No one would substantiate
the existence of such a photograph, or any concrete evidence that
such an event actually took place. No one could dispute the fact,
however, that George W. would often stand up on a chair, a table, or
even a bar to lead his fraternity brothers in their revels. As for the
nude photo, George W. conceded that his own memory of those
days was sufficiently hazy for him not to be able to issue a blanket
denial. "I don't think there is one," he said tentatively. "I'm too
modest to have danced on a bar naked."

As he approached his graduation in the spring of 1968, George W.
remained determinedly indifferent to the major issues facing the
nation and the world. During his freshman and sophomore years, all
the political organizations at Yale from the Yale Political Union to
the Young Republicans to the Young Democrats to the Young
Communists experienced a spike in membership as racial tensions
increased and the Cold War heated up. George "was not involved in
any of that," Craig Johnson said. At various times during W.'s four
years there, congressmen, senators, and presidential hopefuls spoke at
Yale. The congressman's son attended not a single one of these
events. "They would have political people come and debate and give
speeches," Johnson said, "and to my knowledge he just was not
interested."

Ostensibly, George W. had little interest in anything that could
not be categorized as fun. "I don't remember any kind of heaviness
ruining my time at Yale," W. said, insisting that "there wasn't a lot of

actual mark. To add to the pledge's terror, the big branding iron w
plunged into water at the exact same moment to create a frighter
ing sizzle. "When they burned me," Franklin Levy recalled, "
jumped a mile."

The venerated *New York Times* quickly picked up the story, and
George W. Bush stepped forward to defend his fraternity's hazing
practices—especially the branding ritual. He argued that the branding was "insignificant," comparable to "only a cigarette burn" and
left "no scarring mark, physically or mentally." He went on to complain that he could not understand why "Yale has to be so haughty
not to allow this type of pledging to go on." In making his case,
George W. pointed out that back in his home state of Texas, cattle
prods were routinely used on fraternity pledges.

But some Deke members would denounce the branding ritual
championed by George W. "I got branded, and I didn't like it," said
Bradford Lee, who eventually became a professor at the Naval War
College in Newport, Rhode Island. Lee, who was a guard on Yale's
varsity football team, recalled that he was unprepared for what was
about to take place when he showed up for initiation after football
practice. "I was already tired—so groggy I wasn't exactly sensitive to
what they were up to. I wasn't very happy about it. It did burn. I
still have the mark on me." As a historian, Lee would come to view
the experience as something that "was not all that unusual given the
atmosphere on college campuses at the time." But, he would add, "I
sure wouldn't want it done to my kid."

Thirty-five years later, Professor Lee and President of the United
States George W. Bush still bear the branding scar on the small of
their backs. "I don't know what the big deal is," George W. said
with a shrug. "It's a hell of a lot better than the skull and bones tat-
too I was going to get. Luckily, my dad talked me out of it."

The following week, Yale banned hazing rituals of the sort
defended by W. and levied a hefty fine against DKE and another fraternity. The branding scandal was still smoldering when, just a few
days later, George had another run-in with the law. On November
18, 1967, George W. was in Princeton with his fraternity brothers
watching the Yale Bulldogs trounce the Princeton Tigers 29–7 for
the Ivy League football championship. After the game, he was part
of the mob that rushed the field and tried to tear down the vintage

protest at Yale in '68. I don't remember that. And I think most people—I just don't remember any great days of rage. I think those were mainly in the seventies." Many years later, George W. would actually describe the 1960s as a "fairly placid period."

To be sure, Yale did not erupt in protest until after W. graduated. But 1968 was rife with domestic turmoil, some of it occurring right at Yale's door. There had been race riots in New Haven between W.'s junior and senior years, and the assassination of Martin Luther King Jr. in April 1968 triggered more across the country. Just two months later, Robert F. Kennedy was gunned down in Los Angeles.

Throughout this period, the antiwar movement was growing increasingly vocal as American casualties in Vietnam mounted. When W. entered Yale, some 20,000 American combat troops were on the ground in Vietnam. By his senior year, that number was well on its way to the 1969 high of nearly 550,000. Each night, the bloody reality of the war was brought home to Americans via television. At the war's peak in 1968, the weekly death toll for American troops reached 543.

Campuses from Berkeley to Columbia were already being rocked by violent clashes between demonstrators and police. At Yale, there were teach-ins and protests and draft card burnings. A petition was circulated by a group of seniors declaring they would refuse to be drafted. Strobe Talbott, who would later serve as Deputy Secretary of State in the Clinton Administration, signed the petition; George W. Bush did not. And in one of the more celebrated cases of the time, Yale Chaplain (and George W. Bush nemesis) William Sloan Coffin Jr. was indicted for aiding draft resisters.

Although he rarely expressed his feelings about it—or even acknowledged that it was happening at all—George W. was in fact keenly aware of the social revolution that was swirling around him. Suddenly he was at odds with many of the students he had made a point of getting to know personally. For someone who cherished his place in the Walker-Bush clan and its bedrock establishment values, the rise of the counterculture was disorienting, even threatening. W. watched uncomprehending as his fellow sons of privilege professed to hate not only the war, the government, business, and the establishment, but also their own parents.

To make matters worse, George H. W. Bush had aligned himself with the GOP's conservative wing in the House, staunchly defending American involvement in Vietnam. Because the Texas congressman was one of Yale's most high-profile alumni, the senior Bush was condemned by student antiwar leaders and liberal faculty members alike.

"George's world must have been turned upside-down," a classmate said. "But if he was depressed or upset by it, he never let on for a minute. It was hard to imagine anyone at Yale in those days who was having more nonstop fun than George."

Yet W. was harboring deep-seated feelings of resentment toward the eastern liberal establishment—feelings that would surface after he returned to Texas. "I always felt that people on the East Coast tended to feel guilty about what they were given," he explained. "Like, 'I'm rich; they're poor.' Or, 'I went to Andover and got a great education, and they didn't.' I was never one to feel guilty. I feel lucky. People who feel guilty react like guilty people: 'I will solve the problem for you.' It's being motivated toward largesse for the wrong reasons. Everybody has been given free will, and everybody has a chance to succeed. If someone has failed economically, that does not mean that the rest of us should be judged differently."

Just four days after Robert F. Kennedy was gunned down at the Ambassador Hotel in Los Angeles, George W. donned cap and gown to receive his bachelor's degree in history. Congressman Bush was on hand to witness the event—one of the few times anyone could remember seeing him at Yale during his son's tenure there. Big George stayed for the entire two-hour-long ceremony—which included the bestowal of honorary degrees on future Secretary of State Cyrus Vance, the poet Robert Lowell, and Anna Freud—and then left as abruptly as he had appeared.

At the graduation ceremony an antiwar petition signed by 312 of the 955 graduating seniors—W. was not one of them—circulated among the students and family members in attendance. Young Bush did not oppose the war, but he was not about to be drafted into service, either. A trip to Canada was unthinkable for several reasons, not the least of which was the fact that such a move could deal a death blow to his father's dreams of the Senate and, ultimately, perhaps even the White House. One week before graduation, he had flown to Houston to talk to Lt. Colonel Walter "Buck" Staudt, commander of the 147th Fighter Group of the Texas Air National

Guard. He told Staudt that he wanted to become a fighter pilot because his father was.

At the time, belonging to the National Guard offered virtual assurance that the individual would not be sent to Vietnam. Of the more than one million National Guardsmen and reservists in units across the country, only fifteen thousand were ever called upon to fight in Southeast Asia. There was a long waiting list—nationwide one hundred thousand people were waiting to get into the National Guard—and over the years there was speculation that the Bush family pulled strings to make sure George W. was bumped to the head of the list. That hardly seemed necessary; there was already an inclination on the part of those in command to make room for the sons of the prosperous and powerful. When W. was sworn in to the Texas Air National Guard by Lt. Col. Staudt, he raised his hand alongside Lloyd Bentsen III, son of the Texas senator and future vice presidential candidate.

It would be several months before W. was scheduled to start basic training—plenty of time to try and get his marriage plans back on track. He and Cathy went so far as to talk about printing up wedding invitations, but it soon became clear that they were simply going through the motions. "It just wasn't working," Cathy recalled. "It just seemed we were taking each other for granted. We grew apart because we spent so much time apart. Our relationship gradually died . . . I think you are always disappointed with failed relationships."

But George tried to keep the relationship going. When he asked her to spend another summer with the family at Kennebunkport and she refused, he was dumbfounded. "I don't want to go to Maine, George," she told him. "And I don't think this is going to work out." She slipped the engagement ring off her finger and handed it to him. George, stricken, began to weep. "Then I started to cry," Cathy said. "If there was a dramatic moment in all this, that was it. But it was for the best . . ."

Their friends had expected Cathryn to bolt. "Once they postponed it I wasn't surprised that they didn't get married," said his pal Roland Betts. "It didn't have anything to do with him or with her, it just had to do with being young."

Nevertheless, George W. was, in the words of one friend, "crushed. He was not used to being rejected, and it meant that he would not be going off with the love of his life the way his dad did at twenty." Agreed Doug Hannah: "That came as close to undoing him as anything that ever happened to him. She was," Hannah told journalist Bill Minutaglio, "spectacular, and they would have been a very good pair."

Only a few weeks after graduating from Rice, Cathryn met and fell in love with a Harvard MBA named Roderick Young. They were married in May 1969, less than nine months after her breakup with George W. He pretended not to notice. "I went to basic training and that's really the last time I spent any time with her," he later said with a shrug. "She met some other guy and she went off and got married."

Cathryn did, however, confide in friends that she was not worried about George W.'s marriage prospects. "The girls are lined up for George," she said. "He can have any woman he wants—and he knows it. It might take some time, but he's going to find the right one for him. I'm sure of it."

Laura is so quiet. George is always bouncing off the walls.

—*Anne Johnson, friend*

The thing about him was that he made me laugh.

—*Laura*

She really smoothed his edges.

—*Joe O'Neill*

I think she must be unflappable.

—*Anne Armstrong*

3

P erched on the edge of her bed, Laura Welch took a deep drag on a Kent, tossed back her head, and then slowly exhaled a gray-white ribbon of smoke. The Beatles' "I Want to Hold Your Hand" was playing on the small record player she had brought from home. Two of Laura's closest friends, Peggy Weiss and Susan Nowlin, were stretched out on the bed alongside her, also smoking cigarettes as they bopped their heads in unison to the beat. When the song was over, Laura leapt to her feet, lifted up her right hand and then began moving it from side to side in a robotic motion. The Kent dangled from her mouth, and she squinted through the cumulus of smoke that seemed to have settled in the room at just about eye level.

"What on earth are you doing, Laura?" Nowlin asked incredulously.

"I need to practice my Miss America wave," she drawled in a molasses-thick accent that was equal parts Scarlett O'Hara and Mayberry RFD. "You just never know when it will come in handy." Her friends dissolved in laughter. (Years later, when they saw her fulfilling her duties as First Lady of the United States, Laura's friends would scream, "Look! She's doing her Miss America wave!")

While George W. Bush watched his marriage plans evaporate,

Laura Welch was spending a few last carefree days before graduating from Dallas's Southern Methodist University and confronting life in that terrifying realm known as "the real world." Their paths had crossed repeatedly over the years and would again—yet, incredibly, they remained utterly unaware of each other's existence.

Just as Big George had done, Laura's father Harold Bruce Welch was drawn to Midland in the late 1940s, hoping to find a way to somehow share in the riches that were gushing out of the earth at the rate of tens of thousands of barrels a day. Welch had grown up the son of a builder in Lubbock, another hardscrabble town 120 miles to the north.

As eager to join the military as George Herbert Walker Bush had been, Welch dropped out of Texas Tech to enlist in the Army in 1942—the same year he met Jenna Louise Hawkins—and wound up being assigned to the 104th Infantry Division. In 1944, during a two-week leave, Welch returned home to El Paso and married Jenna Hawkins at the Fort Bliss military chapel. "It was wartime," she later said. "A lot of people did that back then—living in the moment because you really were not sure if you would ever see that person again."

Jenna was the winsome only child of a strong-willed Arkansas-bred farm girl named Jessie Laura Hawkins. Laura's great-grandmother Eva Louise Lamaire Sherrard was forty-two when her husband committed suicide, leaving her with seven girls to raise on her own. Eva and her seven daughters worked the family's small dairy farm outside Little Rock, and Jessie wound up making deliveries to local grocery stores, first from a horse-drawn wagon, then in a Model T. "That's what I remember," Jenna would later recall, "riding around with my grandmother while she delivered milk in her Model T."

Jessie's route often crossed that of a young mailman named Harold Hawkins. Like Jessie, Hawkins had been raised by his mother after his dad died at forty-two. Jennie Hawkins, Laura's other maternal great-grandmother, was left to run the family grocery store in Little Rock and raise her five children alone.

In 1918, six months after their paths first crossed, Jessie Sherrard and Harold Hawkins were married. In keeping with the Hawkins family tradition of iron-willed women, Jessie, then twenty, took over Harold's mail route when he joined the Army during World War I. Jenna arrived the following year, on July 24, 1919. When Harold Hawkins moved his wife and baby daughter from Little Rock to Taylor, Texas, and then on to El Paso, Jessie brought with her a passion for all things natural. Throughout her childhood, Jenna and her mother spent countless hours talking about the flora and fauna of the region; by the time Jenna married Harold Bruce Welch in 1942 ("My mother was so happy I found my own Harold") she knew the names of virtually every species of bird, tree, plant, and wildflower native to the region.

Laura's father would dream of those West Texas wildflowers as he spent the harsh winter of 1945 with U.S. forces in Germany. For months Welch's unit, the 104th Infantry, had trudged through waist-deep snow and sought shelter at night in the ruins of bombed-out villages. In April 1945, Welch and his fellow soldiers in the 104th Timberwolf Division liberated hundreds of hollow-eyed prisoners from the Nordhausen concentration camp—a firsthand glimpse of Nazi-wrought horror that left an indelible mark on Harold's psyche.

Once back in El Paso, Welch went to work for the Universal CIT Credit Corporation, a firm that financed car dealerships. But he had always wanted to follow in his father's footsteps as a homebuilder, and in nearby Midland there was a critical shortage of housing for button-down oil company executives and grime-necked roustabouts alike.

Just five months after leaving the Army, Harold moved with his pregnant wife, Jenna, from El Paso to Midland in May 1946. As they approached their fourth anniversary, Jenna had already suffered several miscarriages. So when Harold drove Jenna to Western Clinic on November 4, 1946, they were both understandably nervous about the possible outcome.

At a time when having the father actually witness the delivery was unthinkable, Harold opted not to pace the waiting room floor with the rest of the expectant dads. Instead, he put in time at his downtown office and periodically walked the two blocks to the clinic on Colorado Street to check on his wife's progress.

When the CIT Credit Corporation offices closed at 5 P.M.,

Harold returned to the clinic to wait. An hour later, Jenna gave birth to a healthy, blue-eyed baby girl. They drew on Jessie's middle name and Grandma Welch's maiden name to come up with a name for the newborn: Laura Lane Welch.

For the next several years, Harold continued to work as district manager for CIT Credit Corporation while he learned what he could about the construction business in his spare time. With no formal training, he would sketch a floor plan and then turn it over to a draftsman. In 1950, he quit CIT Credit and teamed up with local contractor Lloyd Waynick to form Waynick and Welch Builders. Determined to stay at home and raise their daughter, Jenna nevertheless played a significant role in the business as Waynick and Welch's bookkeeper.

Taking on both roles would not be that difficult for Jenna, thanks largely to Laura's temperament. "She was an easy baby," Jenna said. "She never cried and she was hardly ever sick."

Over the next three decades, Laura's father would become one of Midland's premier developers, building more than two hundred homes in five separate subdivisions. "My father wanted to do something tangible," she later said. "It was very gratifying for him to drive down the street and be able to say 'I built that.'"

In business as well as his personal dealings, Harold Welch was as affable as Jenna was diffident. "Laura's dad was very gregarious, kind of loud, very much a people person," a neighbor said. "Her mom was very pleasant, but you could see that sometimes she sort of shrank in his presence. That generation wasn't very touchy-feely in public, but there was no question that they doted totally on Laura."

Indeed, Laura would say that she had always been keenly aware that her parents had yearned for more children. Over the course of her childhood, Laura would witness her parents endure one miscarriage or stillbirth after another—each bringing with it an added measure of bitterness, heartache, and desperation.

At one point, Jenna and Harold decided to adopt. They took Laura along when they visited the Gladney adoption home in Fort Worth, telling her that she was about to get a little brother or sister. In the end, they decided not to follow through with the adoption, but Laura was keenly sensitive to her parents' pain. "I was very aware that my parents wanted other children and were disappointed that they didn't have any," Laura said. So, she added, "I felt very obligated to my parents. I didn't want to upset them in any way." That was why, she explained to a friend, "I just wanted to be the best little girl I could possibly be. I just wanted them to be happy with our little family . . ."

Laura was almost four when another four-year-old named Georgie moved into town in 1950. The Bushes had actually moved only a dozen blocks north of the Welch home on Estes Avenue, and over the next several years would repeatedly cross paths without ever actually meeting each other.

"It is really odd, considering Midland's small size and how remote it was, that the Welches and the Bushes didn't know each other back then," said a friend of Laura's. "It just seemed that everybody knew everybody in those days." It seemed particularly strange when Harold Welch, who would build scores of homes occupied by the friends of George H. W. Bush, was also a well-known figure in the tight-knit community. While the Welches attended First Methodist and the Bushes went to First Presbyterian, afterward they all still trooped over to the Agnes Diner or sometimes the coffee shop at the six-story Scharbauer Hotel for Sunday breakfast. Back-to-back in separate booths, passing each other on the street, sitting in the same darkened movie theater year after year, it seemed nothing short of remarkable that the two families in general—and their children in particular—did not connect in those days.

The same year the Bushes moved to town, Jenna enrolled her daughter in Alyne Gray's Jack and Jill kindergarten. At the end of her first week, Laura proudly declared to her mother that she had learned the names of everyone in her class. Skeptical at first, Jenna listened as Laura rattled off the first name and the surname of each of the twenty-plus kids at Alyne Gray's Jack and Jill—as well as the names of the teaching staff.

That year, Jenna also signed Laura up for swimming lessons at Hogan Park, for the children's choir at First Methodist, and for ballet lessons at George Harston's popular dance studio in downtown Midland. Within days, she had memorized the names of the children she encountered there as well.

It was an uncanny ability, certainly, but hardly unique; Laura Welch would ultimately discover that another child living only blocks away was displaying a similar knack for committing names and faces to memory—a talent that would help them both form countless friendships and alliances in the years ahead.

While little Georgie Bush had only just begun to stir up trouble along Easter Egg Row, Laura was proving to be, as she once described herself self-mockingly to friends, "the best little girl in the whole wide world." From age three, Judy Jones Ryan and Laura were inseparable playmates. Jones gave Laura her first pet: "A kitten from my cat," Jones said. "I remember he had a real pug nose, kind of flat, and she would always push on his nose. It was a tabby, and she loved it and always loved cats from then on. Every time we would go to her house for Christmas Eve parties or brunch, she was always fooling with her cats."

"She liked to cook, as all little girls do," Jenna said. "She enjoyed making cookies, muffins and things, and she's pretty good at casseroles. But the main interest we've always shared is books." So much so that Laura named one of her cats "Dewey," after the Dewey Decimal System.

While Georgie Bush wreaked havoc across town at Sam Houston Elementary School, Laura Welch was a model student at James Bowie Elementary. From the age of seven, she knew exactly what she wanted to do with her life. Inspired by Charlene Gnagy, her second grade teacher at James Bowie, she declared that she intended to become a teacher.

One of Laura's favorite games was to play teacher at home, often with a friend. Using dolls as pupils, Laura and her friend would each set up a classroom in a separate bedroom of Laura's house, and then leave to chat in the hall.

"What are you doing standing in the hallway talking?" Laura's mom asked when she saw the girls. "Shouldn't you be teaching your students?"

"But, Mom," Laura protested, "this is what our teachers do!"

At the same time Georgie Bush was trying to come to grips with the sudden and—for him—totally unexpected death of his little sister, Robin, Laura Welch was just a bike ride away reciting the Brownie oath. Like nearly every other seven-year-old girl in Midland, Laura was a Brownie. Once a week she put on her uniform and, after school, walked the few blocks to Mrs. Smith's house for a troop meeting. Fellow Brownie Gwyne Smith recalled that her mother "spent one afternoon each week trying to mold a lively group of seven-year-olds into domestic young ladies . . . Laura was one of my mom's favorites because she listened quietly and followed directions well." Sally Brady Rock remembered "our little arts and crafts projects that we would do. Laura was always so good. She always made things well, and I didn't. She was more artistic."

Weekly sleepovers were also an integral part of growing up in Midland in the 1950s. Laura's house was a favorite destination because, Sally Brady Rock said, Laura's "bedroom was so pretty and her mother was so sweet."

Understandably, as an only child who was the epicenter of the Welch family universe, Laura was closely tethered to her parents. When she graduated to the Junior Girl Scouts at age eight, she went to her first summer camp in the Davis Mountains, two hundred miles southwest of Midland. She managed to stick it out for a full week before finally calling her parents and begging to come home.

The atmosphere in Midland was, as one baby boomer remembered it, "as close to being in a Norman Rockwell painting as you could get." Jenna taught Sunday School at First Methodist, and when she brought Laura and a friend to church for choir practice she would first drop them off at the Southern Maid Donut Shop on Illinois Avenue. "We would walk down the block to the church at the corner of Ohio and Main," Laura's friend Polly Chappell Davis said, "but only after we ate our favorite doughnuts." (The Methodist church, with its strong tradition of evangelical fervor coupled with social activism, played a critical role in shaping Laura's ideals. Another young Methodist girl growing up at the same time in Illinois—Hillary Rodham—would also say she was strongly influenced by the church.)

Although Laura was by any definition one of the best-liked seventh graders at San Jacinto Junior High School, apparently neither she nor George Bush exchanged a single word during the entire year they shared there. Before he departed for Houston the following year, Georgie was elected class president. But Laura would not recall George at all—or he her, though at times he would insist that he had some vague recollection of the pretty brunette with her nose always buried in a book.

Reading was, in fact, Laura's passion long before San Jacinto. In primary school she favored Laura Ingalls Wilder's Little House series—at first because she and the main character had the same first name—as well as *The Secret Garden* and the Bobbsey Twins. "I wasn't a great reader back then, but Laura was *always* reading," said her pal Gwyne Smith Bohren. When she wasn't at the school playground with Gwyne going in tandem down the slide, Laura invariably seemed to have her nose in a book.

Another favorite of Laura's was Louisa May Alcott's *Little Women*. During sleepovers at Laura's house, her friend Georgia Todd Temple recalled, the two girls would be "propped up in a big double bed, eating crackers while we read and reread Beth's death." The crackers "always wound up soggy, we cried so hard."

Doak Walker: Three-Time All-American was about as far away from *Little Women* as any book could possibly be, but it would have a profound impact on the course of Laura Welch's life. After reading about the legendary football hero, twelve-year-old Laura decided she wanted to attend the school that Walker credited with shaping his values—Southern Methodist University.

Reading was a passion Laura shared with her mother. Often when they were on long drives together—the three-hundred-mile drive to visit Laura's maternal grandparents in El Paso, for example, or the two-hour drive to see Grandma Welch in Lubbock—Laura read aloud while her mother drove. Later, when Laura was able to share in the driving, they took turns reading everything from Dostoevsky to Agatha Christie.

The time spent with her grandparents would make a lasting impression on Laura. Grandpa Hawkins, for example, was, in Laura's words, "a memorable character" who sometimes drank Texas Select bourbon in the mornings; her maternal grandmother would later die while tending the plants in her garden.

Now that she was a little older and considerably more independent, Laura took another stab at summer camp. This time she flourished at the Girl Scout camp in the Davis Mountains, and would later spend summers in the hill country town of Bandera, "Cowboy Capital of the World."

In much the same way that Georgie sought to make friends with some kids who might otherwise be frozen out, Laura was constantly making overtures to others. Cindy Schumann Klatt had attended a private school, St. Ann's, until the eighth grade, and then transferred to San Jacinto. Unlike many of her peers, Laura was sensitive to the fact that transferring to a new school can be an uncomfortable, even painful, experience for a child. "I was rather intimidated by the other kids," Cindy said. "My first memory of Laura is how friendly and concerned she was that those of us from St. Ann's were included in the activities around school."

Another newcomer to the school, Lucy McFarland Woodside, said that what she "most appreciated about Laura and our whole group of friends was they were all so accepting about someone who was new. And they treated me like I'd been there forever." Karen Thompson Trout was also a new arrival at San Jacinto. "She really was a very, very sweet girl," Trout said. "When I think of Laura and junior high, I think of what a sincere person she was, and how she treated people so nicely."

Midland's Robert E. Lee Freshman High School opened its doors for the first time in September 1961, and Laura was among the first pupils to attend it. Once again Laura, like the man she would marry, made friends easily. "We traveled in a particular crowd," said Regan Gammon, one of her closest friends. "But it was huge, inclusive— not cliquey."

At about the time Laura started high school, Harold Welch moved his family into one of the new homes he built on what had once been a cotton field. The single-story, three-bedroom beige brick house at 2500 Humble Avenue boasted a big kitchen, a den with a fireplace, and a living room with a vaulted ceiling and exposed wood beams. The lot, on the corner of Humble and Lanham avenues, was ringed by a knee-high brick retaining wall and shaded by pecan trees. The price: a then-substantial $25,000.

The house on Humble Avenue (named after an oil company, as were nearby Sinclair and Shell avenues) became a favorite meeting spot for Laura's friends. Jan Donnelly O'Neill remembered how "cute" Laura's parents were when she would drop by, spot them sitting in the kitchen, and simply rap on the window. She recalled "sitting down and having Cokes with Laura and her mom and dad. You just always laughed and had a good time. You always loved to hang out at their house."

Harold Bruce, as Laura's friends like to call her dad, was one of the main reasons. "My daddy loved to laugh," Laura recalled. "He loved animals. He was just one of those men who never met a dog he didn't like or a dog that didn't like him. He was funny and didn't take himself too seriously."

Laura took her high school studies seriously, easily racking up straight As on her report card. But that did not mean she neglected her social life. "She was a nice, very kind person," a friend said. "But that makes her sound boring, and she wasn't. She was also very outgoing, with a little mischievous streak . . . You know the song 'Girls Just Want to Have Fun'? Well, that was Laura, too." Regan Gammon recalled that her pal "liked to do what everybody else did in high school, which was talk on the phone and drive around."

The legal driving age for Texans in the early 1960s was fifteen, and Laura's parents often let their responsible daughter use one of the two family cars to drive her friends around. "There were at least five girls in the car every time we went out cruising," Peggy Weiss said. A favorite destination was the Agnes Diner, where Laura and her girlfriends got together several times a week to "talk about clothes and boys" over hamburgers and Cokes.

Laura and her friends also used cars to conceal the fact that they had taken up smoking—a habit that Laura would continue into her fifties. Kent was Laura's brand of choice, and she and her friends would lie down in the backseat and puff away while the designated driver would search for neighborhoods where the girls would not be recognized. "We were always afraid," Weiss said, "that somebody would spot us and tell our parents."

Between her sophomore and junior years at Lee High, Laura teamed up with several of her friends and headed south of the border to study Spanish in the Mexican city of Monterey. For six weeks, the wide-eyed girls from Midland went to Spanish language classes, visited the town's picturesque churches, and shopped in Monterey's teeming open-air markets. At night, Laura would return with her friends to their dormitory, where they would spend hours listening to Mexican pop songs on the radio and then try to translate the lyrics into English before dissolving in giggles.

As might have been expected, the time in Mexico was not without its unpleasant moments. Several of the students suffered stomach ailments, and at times the heat was, even by Midland standards, barely tolerable. But Laura remained resolutely upbeat. "She never said anything negative," one of her companions on the trip recalled. "That's just not her nature."

Laura had decided early on in life that she would never do anything to upset her parents, and that meant no complaining. "She just never whined the way some other kids do," her mother said. "I know it sounds unbelievable, but it's hard to think of a time that she ever talked back or griped about having to do something."

Nor could her classmates, who marveled even then at Laura's sometimes unsettling stoicism. In high school, Weiss stated flatly, Laura "never complained." Once when Weiss dropped in on her friend, Laura was in the backyard with her dog Marty. On closer inspection, Weiss realized that Laura was picking ticks off Marty and methodically placing them in a jar.

"Oh my gosh, Laura," Weiss said, "I would never do that, and if someone forced me to do it, I'd complain the whole time. Yuck! Laura, how can you stand it?"

Laura did not look up, but continued searching Marty for ticks. "It's not so bad," she said matter-of-factly.

As popular as she was among the girls at Lee High School, Laura's sunny disposition and wholesome good looks meant that she also seldom lacked for male company. She always showed up at high school football games to cheer on the Lee High Rebels, and invariably had a date for the dance that followed. "She was 'Lovely Laura,'" her friend Pam Nelson said. "Sounds corny, I guess, but that really was kind of her nickname."

Laura herself was no athlete, but she was drawn to the best-looking and most popular boys on the track and football teams. "She was a very pretty girl and smart as a tack," said Laura's friend Dan Harris. She was also more poised and more self-assured than most of her peers. "I think that appealed to all her boyfriends," Harris said. "She lived her own life her own way." As a result, "she dated a lot of guys but she was never seriously involved with anyone."

With one exception. No sport in Midland—or throughout the state of Texas, for that matter—was more important than high school football. At about the same time that Head Cheerleader Georgie Bush was dressing up in drag at Andover, the Lee High

Rebels put on cheerleader uniforms and shouted words of encouragement to girl players in the annual Powder Puff game against arch-rival Midland High. Laura, eager to be a part of Midland's football mania, was among those who donned a football uniform and ran out onto the field to do battle. The men in skirts and wigs, meanwhile, did high kicks and cheers.

It was at the Powder Puff game in her junior year that Laura met a young man who would play a significant role in her life—Michael D. Douglas. Dark-haired, athletic Douglas was both a track star and a member of the football team. Mike was also one of the pom-pom-waving Powder Puff cheerleaders, and at one point during the game he sidled up to one of the girls he had long been interested in, Judy Dykes. She was involved with someone else, however, and introduced Mike instead to her teammate Laura.

Born in Corpus Christi, Douglas had moved from the small Texas city of San Benito to Midland in 1950—the same year George W. Bush arrived in town. Like Laura, he was the center of his parents' world. Douglas excelled at practically everything he attempted, and made friends easily. By the time he entered Lee High School, the same year as Laura, Mike was already one of Midland's best-liked teenagers. "He was handsome and funny," his friend Dwayne Casbeer said. "He had a quality that drew people in." In his junior year, he was nominated as the school's most popular boy—an honor that nearly always went to a senior. By the spring of 1963, Laura and Mike had become one of Lee High's most high-profile couples.

The summer before her senior year, Laura, having long since conquered her aversion to being away from home, now signed on as a counselor at Camp Mystic, eighty miles northwest of San Antonio on the Guadalupe River. "It gave Laura the chance to work with kids," a friend said, "but even more it was the first time she earned any real money. She was really looking forward to enjoying her last year at Lee, and couldn't wait to start college. Laura was always full of fun and enthusiasm, but for the first time she could sort of see an exciting future spread out before her. It was as if nothing could go wrong."

Laura plunged into high school life with even more gusto than usual. She joined the Rebelee yearbook staff, the student council, and the 100 Club. Although not an athlete herself, Laura nonetheless made a point of going to every sports event and rooting for Lee to win.

One of the football stars she cheered for from the sidelines, Mike Douglas, was no longer seeing Laura. Things had cooled off over the summer, and now he was seriously involved with Laura's pal Regan. According to one friend, Douglas was "still carrying a torch for Laura, but she wanted to play the field."

Laura and Mike remained friends, and after a particularly fierce game between Lee and San Angelo High, she looked on proudly as Mike was presented with a sportsmanship trophy. By the end of October, they were among the favorites to be chosen Homecoming King and Queen. "Mike's mom and dad thought Laura was wonderful, and I know Mr. and Mrs. Welch felt the same way about Mike," Joe O'Neill said. "They were just clean-cut, all-American kids."

On November 4, 1963, Laura turned seventeen, and her parents celebrated by throwing a small party for their daughter at the house on Humble Avenue. Two days later, Laura asked her father if she could borrow the family car to drive to a party being thrown at the home of a friend. Even though it was a Wednesday, Laura's parents did not hesitate to hand her the keys to the Welches' brand-new Chevrolet sedan. "Don't worry," she told them. "I promise I'll be home by ten."

Laura picked up her friend Judy Dykes, the girl Mike Douglas originally had a crush on, and the two headed for the party with Laura behind the wheel. It was a dry, clear, cool night as their car sped east along Farm Road 868 just north of town. They were far enough from the prying eyes of adults to feel comfortable lighting up, so Laura and Judy laughed, smoked their Kents, and chatted excitedly about clothes and school and boys in general and Mike Douglas in particular. Elvis blared on the radio. As was the custom in Texas in 1963, Laura was not wearing a seat belt.

As she sped east, Laura could glance in any direction and see an endless expanse interrupted only by the occasional tree, oil well, or road sign. The thirty-foot telephone poles that lined the unremittingly straight two-lane highway loomed ahead like colossal crucifixes.

Laura and Judy were deep in conversation as they barreled north on Farm Road 868. The speed limit on the outskirts of town was sixty-five miles per hour; Laura was going fifty. Neither girl would remember exactly what they were talking about when Laura failed to notice the stop sign that stood in plain, totally unobstructed view at the intersection of Farm Road 868 and State Road 349. It was particularly important that she see the sign, for this was a two-way stop; there was no stop sign for cross-traffic.

Laura had no idea what was happening when, at 8:08 P.M., she ran the stop sign and plowed into the side of a car traveling east on State Road 349. But she would never forget the sound—a horrific, deafening roar of crunching steel, screeching tires, and shattering glass. Laura slammed on the brakes, but quickly lost control of the car. The two girls screamed as they lurched forward on impact, then pitched to the left as the car careened across the highway and into a shallow gully.

The sole occupant of the other car, proceeding at a fifty-five-mile-an-hour clip, had no reason to believe that Laura would fail to obey the sign. Struck on the right front passenger side just above the wheel, the Corvair did what seemed like a macabre, slow-motion pirouette in the intersection, spinning counterclockwise 270 degrees before veering off the pavement. Even before the car came to rest in a cloud of dust, its driver was dead. As a result of the violent side impact, the young man's neck snapped even before he was thrown from the car.

Within moments, the young man's father came upon on the scene; he happened to have been following his son, and witnessed the crash from a distance. "He saw the whole thing," Joe O'Neill said. "It was horrible." The young man's father held his head in his hands and wept as police and ambulance personnel lifted the seventeen-year-old's lifeless body onto a stretcher. The victim was taken to Midland Memorial Hospital, and pronounced dead on arrival.

Miraculously, Laura and Judy had suffered only a few scratches and bruises. A second ambulance took the girls to Midland Memorial, where their worried parents had rushed to meet them. "It hurt all of us very deeply," Jenna Welch recalled. "Laura is an only child. It was dreadful to think she might have been killed."

Laura and Judy had been too shaken up to pay much attention to the other car, and now they wanted to know how the other driver was doing. Laura was told the man had died. She was understandably crushed by the news, and broke down in the emergency room. Yet she had, for the time being at least, been spared the whole bizarre truth of what had happened.

The young man in the other car was her friend Mike Douglas. "Laura didn't know who she had killed at first," said Dwayne Casbeer. "Nobody could bring themselves to tell her it was Mike."

In the meantime, within hours, Midland was buzzing with the news. That same night Dan Harris was also cruising Midland with Laura's friend Beverly Grindley. "We heard about the accident on the car radio," Harris said, "and immediately contacted our other friends, all of whom knew both Mike and Laura."

"Laura's accident had a huge impact on the town," McCleskey said. "It was front-page news—everybody knew about it and everybody was shaken up." Agreed neighbor Jack Hickman, "It was as if two of Midland's favorites had been involved in an unthinkable act of fate." The heartbreaking task of telling Laura who had been killed fell to her parents. Laura was devastated, numb. Her father, Hickman said, "would have taken that hurt for her if he could."

Discharged from the hospital that night, she returned home and holed up in her room, unable to return to school or even talk to friends. "It was pitiful," Harris said. "It took the heart and life out of her. She kind of disappeared for a few weeks."

It seemed as if half of Midland turned out for Mike's funeral at St. Mark's Methodist Church that Saturday. "Mike was a superstar," Joe O'Neill said. "He was a terrific athlete, a top student, great-looking, incredibly nice—everybody loved him." Their friends kept scanning the crowd for Laura's face, but to no avail. Neither she nor her parents attended the service, opting to send flowers instead. Laura was still badly shaken by the accident, and worried that Michael's parents would resent her if she showed up at the funeral. "Won't they hate me?" she asked her mother. "I killed their son."

The crash that killed Mike Douglas was the ninth auto fatality in Midland that year—a town record. It also marked the second time in 1963 that someone had been killed at that same intersection. "It was sort of in the middle of nowhere," O'Neill recalled. "A lot of people went through that stop sign." There was no evidence that alcohol or drugs played a part in the crash (though no tests were done), and police determined that neither car had been speeding. As a result, the authorities labeled the collision a mishap and no charges were filed. Laura was not cited for careless driving, or even ticketed for running a stop sign.

"In the case of an auto fatality, it is almost unheard of for there not to be some sort of investigation," observed one Midland attorney who routinely handles traffic cases. "I have never heard of a case—not even back in the sixties—where a person broke a traffic law, killed someone in the process, and not a single action was taken, or apparently even contemplated. If it had happened today, there would probably also be a wrongful death suit. Laura's dad was a very successful builder, and it's obvious he had some clout in town. Everybody knew everybody back then, so I guess they just figured she'd suffered enough."

"The accident *destroyed* Laura," Joe O'Neill said. "It was the kind of traumatic event you don't get over right away." Years later, Laura would describe the accident as "crushing. It was crushing for the family involved and for me as well." For the next few weeks, she stayed at home, unable to return to face her teachers and fellow students. "The students were devastated," Lee High student counselor Annalon Gilbreath said. "Like all young kids they thought they were immortal. Laura spoke like she thought she was invulnerable. The accident broke her heart and made her realize life is full of as much tragedy as laughter."

When she was not crying inconsolably in her room, Laura sought counseling from her pastor at First Methodist as she tried to grapple with her sense of loss—and her sense of guilt. "I grieved a lot," she said decades later. "It was a horrible, horrible tragedy. It's a terrible feeling to be responsible for an accident. And it was horrible for all of us to lose him, especially since he was so young. But at some point I had to accept that death is a part of life, and as tragic as losing Mike was, there was nothing anyone could do to change that."

"Laura took it really hard," childhood friend Robert McCleskey said. "Nobody held it against her." Certainly not Regan, who despite losing her boyfriend spent hours comforting Laura and reassuring her that no one blamed her for Mike's death. "Regan's support during that time obviously meant a great deal to Laura," Joe O'Neill said. "It bonded them even closer together as friends."

Mike's parents also went out of their way to make it clear that they did not blame Laura for their son's death. "The Douglases were good people, kind people," said McCleskey, who had also been a close friend of Mike's. "They were fond of Laura and knew it was just a freak accident—the kind of thing that could happen to anybody."

The Douglases would dedicate a Civil War–style cannon as a monument to Mike on the grounds of Lee High, but the memories would prove overwhelming. The Douglas house on Solomon Lane "became a place of sadness and tears," Dan Harris recalled. "They never recovered. He had filled their house with so much energy and now that was suddenly snuffed out."

Within two years, Mike's parents would leave Midland for good. Mike's married sister remained behind in Midland, but nearly forty years later she was still grieving. "If you even mention Mike's name," O'Neill said, "she just breaks down."

In the meantime, less than two weeks after Mike's funeral, Lee High and the rest of the world would be consumed by another tragedy in the state of Texas. On November 22, 1963, Laura watched Walter Cronkite choke back tears as he confirmed that President John Fitzgerald Kennedy had been shot to death by a sniper in the streets of Dallas.

Of course, Laura did not know the reason for Kennedy's trip to Texas—to end the feud between Governor John Connally and Senator Ralph Yarborough. And she may have been only vaguely aware that her former neighbor, George H. W. Bush, was campaigning for the GOP Senate nomination and a chance to unseat Yarborough. What she and every other Texan did fear was that the assassination would bring shame to their state. "What wounds me most of all," Lady Bird Johnson said to a blood-spattered Jackie as Air Force One prepared to leave Dallas, "is that this should happen in my beloved state of Texas!" Jackie stared back blankly. Lady Bird regretted the remark the instant she uttered it.

But it was a sentiment shared by millions of Texans. No longer was the tragic crash that killed Mike Douglas the talk of Midland. At Lee High and everywhere else, the assassination would overshadow every other topic for months. For Laura, Mike Douglas's death must have unquestionably stood out as the single most significant event in her life. "In the end," McCleskey said, "you can't run away from something like that. It's there. It happened. There's nothing you can do to change that." Yet even Laura would later describe JFK's assassination, not the fatal crash that she caused, as "the most traumatic time in my childhood."

When she finally did return to school, Laura did not bring up Mike or the accident to anyone. Nor did her teachers or friends feel comfortable broaching the subject. "We never talked to Laura about it, not once," said a classmate. "She would have had to be the one to bring it up, and she never did."

In the end "she didn't totally withdraw from everything," McCleskey said, "but it took some time to get over it. She kept going to school. She had a good circle of friends to support her. She didn't change in any way that I could tell." But others felt it was a different Laura who returned to school that winter. "Some of the spark was gone," said a classmate. "She was more subdued, more pensive. She was still a pretty upbeat person, but it was just clear that some of the spontaneity and joy had gone out of her life."

Laura did actually drop out of a number of student activities, but chose to remain on the yearbook staff. She wanted to help write a full-page tribute to the boy whose life she had cut short. "I can still see those eyes—full of delight," Laura wrote. "The mouth—ever a smile. An armload of books on one hip, and the walk that so resembled youthful confidence." The poem went on to praise Douglas's "sense of fun, the effervescent good will, the sportsmanship, and the obedience to duty." In a touching final verse, Laura and her friends mused, "His imprint lingers in the halls, where he walked only a while ago. So I'll close my eyes. And remember. And I'll smile."

According to one teacher, the poem, accompanied by a photo of Douglas sprinting to the finish at a track meet, "made everybody cry. There is no way to describe how that accident just shattered this whole town."

But there was also mounting concern for Laura. "Everybody worried about her, wanted to make sure she'd be okay," Joe O'Neill said. There was a consensus among Laura's friends that she had been transformed by the experience. "Just look in Laura's eyes," said one. "The pain is right there. She has never gotten away from it, not entirely. And she never will. It still haunts her. People say Laura is very calm, but it has more to do with her having to suppress her emotions. She is a very controlled person—she has to be. Otherwise she'd just crumble."

In the fall of 1964, Laura entered Southern Methodist University along with her Midland friends Peggy Weiss, Polly Chappell Davis, and Lucy MacFarland Woodside. Nestled amid the stately brick mansions and well-tended parks that made up Dallas's tony University Park district, SMU was generally regarded as one of the most conservative learning institutions in the nation. Certainly it provided Laura with the kind of cosseted environment George W. Bush would later claim existed on the Yale campus in the strife-torn sixties.

Even as America sank deeper and deeper into the quagmire of Vietnam and bloody race riots erupted in city after city, Laura and her Midland buddies would spend four years at SMU insulated from the harsh realities of the outside world. Female students at the private coed college still wore skirts to class, fraternities and sororities had not fallen out of fashion, and drug use—with the exception of alcohol—was rare.

"My generation was just right on the cusp," Laura would later say. "It was a fairly conservative campus compared with how it was just a few years after that for the little brothers and sisters of my friends" entering SMU. "So we weren't wild like that. I mean, people smoked cigarettes—and I did. And they drank beer, and that was sort of the way college kids were wild when I was there."

Laura joined a sorority—Kappa Alpha Theta—and spent weekends sitting around the pool with her pals smoking, downing Cokes, and playing bridge. Regan Gammon's copy of *Meet the Beatles*, the group's debut album, was played nonstop their freshman year. "Regan liked Paul," Weiss said, "I liked John, and I think Laura liked all of them."

In keeping with her long-espoused dream to become a teacher, Laura majored in elementary education. She earned As in courses like children's literature and child growth and development, but, as in high school, that did not compromise her social life. "Laura always had a boyfriend—some good-looking guy to go out with," said one of her Midland friends. "But she would never allow herself to get serious about anyone. She kept every boy who showed signs of wanting something more at arm's length."

Less than two years after the crash that took the life of her former boyfriend, Laura returned to Midland to make her formal coming out at the Minuet Club Debutante Ball in 1965. Wearing a floor-length sleeveless satin gown and opera gloves, Laura clutched a bouquet of roses as she lined up and posed with the other beaming daughters of Midland society.

By the time she became a college senior, however, Laura was wearing the same peasant skirts, tie-dyed blouses, beads, and bell-bottoms as the rest of her generation. And no sooner did she graduate from SMU in 1968 than Laura inexplicably accused her startled father of "programming" her to become a teacher. Spurred on by the feminist argument that women had been confined to narrow roles in society, she told Harold Bruce Welch that she had studied teaching not because it was what she wanted, but because it was what her parents wanted.

"Women can do anything, Daddy," she said, "but you wanted me to do what women have always done—teach. Why can't I be a doctor? Or a lawyer."

With that, Laura's bemused father pulled out his wallet. "Then I'll send you to law school," he said without missing a beat.

"He would have loved to," Laura later recalled of the incident. "But I had to admit, when he did that, that I didn't want to be a lawyer. I wanted to be a teacher."

But before she entered the workforce, Laura told her parents that she wanted to spend the summer with her friends backpacking through Europe. The Welches thought it too dangerous, but they stumbled upon a compromise when Harold's brother Mark, a Dallas surgeon, invited Laura to accompany his family on a two-week tour of Europe. Rooming with her sixteen-year-old cousin Mary, Laura got her first taste of life abroad as she visited London, Paris, and Rome. "It was a magical experience," Laura confided to her mother. "It made all the things I'd read about in books come alive."

Once she returned to Dallas, Laura wasted no time trying to find work as a teacher in the public school system. Told that there were no teaching jobs available, she bided her time working as a clerical worker at a Dallas insurance company. She did not have to wait long. After two months a spot opened up for a third grade teacher in Dallas, and Laura jumped at the chance.

She was stunned to discover that many of her eight-year-old

pupils could not read. "Frankly, I'm not sure I was very good at teaching them," she later said. "I tried to make it fun by making the characters in children's books members of our class. We saved a web in the corner for Charlotte." Laura found she "got as much out of it as they did . . . I got more involved than ever in these very traditional stories." So much so that every time she got to the end of *Charlotte's Web,* Laura cried.

In the fall of 1969, after a year in Dallas, Laura relocated to Houston and a job teaching second grade at John F. Kennedy Elementary, a predominantly black school in the city's gritty Independence Heights neighborhood. "I think teaching in a minority school opened my eyes," she said of that time. "It made me realize how unfair life is in a lot of ways."

Laura soon proved to be one of John F. Kennedy Elementary's most popular and effective teachers. "The kids really did love her," recalled one of her second grade students, Larry Gatson. "She'd go outside and play with us. If you had problems in reading and spelling, she'd take a little more time with you."

One of the areas she was not particularly strong in was math. "I was a pretty bad math teacher," she recalled. "I'm sure they suffered for that."

Laura grew so found of Gatson and the rest of her pupils that she asked to move on with them when they graduated to the third grade. "I'm sure I learned more from them than they did from me—most importantly, I think, about the dignity of every child."

For the next two years while she taught at John F. Kennedy Elementary, Laura lived in a one-bedroom apartment at the lofty-sounding Châteaux Dijon, a turreted, four-hundred-unit residential complex built around six swimming pools in Houston's Galleria district. Trumpeted as "The Place to Live" in its newspaper ads, the Châteaux Dijon was aimed squarely at the city's affluent young singles. Coed activities of every conceivable kind abounded on the "rowdy" side of the complex, where midnight water polo matches and volleyball games, boozy barbecues, and belly-flop contests were near-nightly events. On the weekends, "things got a lot crazier," said one of Laura's neighbors.

Miss Welch, the quiet, unassuming schoolteacher with the bright smile and glasses, resided on what she called the "sedate" side of the

Châteaux Dijon, along with the other young professionals who preferred to keep to themselves. For a time, she would share an apartment at the Châteaux with her childhood pal Jan Donnelly—until
Donnelly returned to Midland and in 1972 married W.'s childhood
pal Joe O'Neill.

Laura had been living in Houston for ten months when a young
Texas Air National Guard jet pilot stationed at nearby Ellington Air
Force Base pulled up to the Châteaux Dijon in his blue Triumph
convertible and—with much fanfare—moved into the "wild" side.

Over the course of the next year, Laura Welch dated occasionally,
but without ever allowing herself to become serious about anyone.
She spent much of her time alone in her apartment, curled up with
a pack of cigarettes and a book, or sunning herself by the pool. Just
yards away, meanwhile, the jet jockey with the swagger and the smirk
partied hard and loud when he wasn't flying F-102A Delta Dagger
Interceptors out of Ellington. True to form, the National Guard
pilot often organized the noisiest, most bacchanalian events—beer
busts and midnight volleyball tournaments and drunken antics in the
pool with bikini-clad stewardesses, oil company secretaries, or Rice
University coeds.

To any of the many women who inquired about the good-
looking pilot, the building manager merely answered that he was
"the Congressman's son." Incredibly, Laura Welch would be one
of the few available young ladies at the Châteaux Dijon not to make
the acquaintance of her boisterous neighbor, George W. Bush.

He was really struck by lightning when he met her.

—*Barbara Bush*

I kind of floated and saw a lot of life.

—*George*

It was like Audrey Hepburn walking into the
Animal House.

—*Marvin Bush, on Laura's*
joining the family

4

Even before he arrived at the Châteaux Dijon, W. seemed to have made a full recovery from his breakup with Cathryn Wolfman. No sooner had she called off their engagement than W. set his sights on one of Houston's most desirable young debutantes: Christina Cassini.

The closest thing W.'s crowd had in their midst to Hollywood royalty, "Tina" Cassini was the daughter of legendary designer (and Jackie Kennedy favorite) Oleg Cassini and the stunningly beautiful film star Gene Tierney, who rose to fame in the 1944 whodunit *Laura*.

Tina's mother had been one of Hollywood's most beguiling and tragic figures, starring in films opposite the likes of Humphrey Bogart, Spencer Tracy, and Clark Gable while being romanced by Howard Hughes, Aly Khan, and John F. Kennedy, among others. After kissing an ardent fan who happened to be suffering from German measles, Tierney gave birth to a deaf and retarded child—Tina's older sister Daria—and that event triggered a series of mental breakdowns.

In 1960, Tierney wed oil tycoon W. Howard Lee (who had previously been married to another screen beauty, Hedy Lamarr) and moved to Houston. Tina had inherited her mother's spectacular looks, and whenever she visited home she was, not surprisingly, flooded with invitations.

W. found Tina "very attractive," said his friend Doug Hannah, "and since there were several other guys who felt the same way, he went after her. He's very competitive, you know." Within days they were one of Houston society's most ubiquitous young couples. The romance lasted all summer, until Tina returned to school in Europe and W. left Houston to begin his flight training in Valdosta, Georgia. "It was very therapeutic for George to have the gal," Hannah said, "that basically everyone wanted. It was just a great fling."

It would not be his last. W. did not lack for female companionship during his year learning to fly jets at Valdosta's Moody Air Force Base. Aviation groupies flocked to the officers' club, and the handsome, wealthy, well-connected, Yale-educated life-of-the-party jet fighter pilot—the only Guardsman among some seventy pilots assigned to Moody—was rarely left alone. "There was draft beer, and all the girls from town came in," recalled Ralph Anderson, who was in flight school with W. "Everybody got crazy." Said another pilot of Bush: "There were a lot of women who came to the officers' club for one thing, and like every other bachelor there he was eager to oblige."

During the last few months of flight training at Moody, however, W. was seen almost exclusively in the company of one local girl. Her name was Judy—he would later profess not to remember her last name—and every Friday he drove his blue Triumph into Valdosta to pick her up and bring her to the officers' club. "It looked like he was very serious about this girl," another pilot observed. "We kidded him about getting married. But when his tour was over, so was the thing with Judy."

There was speculation that the mysterious Judy might not have been up to the congressman's standards, particularly now that he was embarking on another run for the Senate against incumbent Democrat Ralph Yarborough. There was someone else on the horizon, however, who most certainly would have made the cut . . .

She was pretty and smart—and certainly his parents approved. In late 1969, W. was winding up his training at Moody when he was summoned by his commanding officer. That same day, Lieutenant

Bush boarded a government plane bound for Washington, D.C., and a very special mission. Once he arrived, he proceeded directly to the White House. On direct orders from the Commander-in-Chief, George W. Bush—Bombastic Bushkin, Junior, W., Tweeds, The Lip—was to take first daughter Tricia Nixon out to dinner.

The date, set up by then-president Richard Nixon, was designed to seal the political pact between the White House and Congressman Bush. Nixon was relying on Bush and former governor John Connally, who was about to bolt the Democratic Party, to bring Texas firmly into the GOP fold.

A graduate of Finch, the prestigious New York women's college that catered to the daughters of America's most socially prominent families, Tricia Nixon was wearing a pink suit and white gloves when W. picked her up at the White House in his dress uniform. They were driven by Secret Service agents to dinner at a local restaurant, where the back-slapping Texan and the genteel Miss Nixon quickly discovered they had little in common.

When he was flown back to Moody the next day, W. did not share any of the details with his buddies; he had been expressly ordered not to. "We went to dinner," he shrugged. "It wasn't a very long date."

As for W.'s role in the campaign, dating Tricia Nixon was only the beginning. Just a few months later, when he was living at the Châteaux Dijon in Houston, he would join Big George on the hustings. Clad in his National Guard flight jacket, he would often stand behind the candidate as a symbol of the Bush family's unflinching devotion to duty—and its continuing support of Nixon's policies in Vietnam.

There were other moments during the campaign, however, when he gave campaign aides cause to shake their heads in disapproval. During a charity walk in Houston, newspaper photographers snapped the button-down candidate with his son ambling behind him, shirtless and grinning in the sweltering Indian summer heat.

Campaigning for his father full-time was out of the question. In addition to weekend duties, W. had to remain on call throughout the week. But that didn't prevent the Bush campaign from fully exploiting W.'s military service. Campaign photographers were on hand to record the proud moment when the decorated World War II Navy pilot pinned his eldest son with his second lieutenant's wings.

"George Walker Bush," a National Guard Press release began, "is one member of the younger generation who doesn't get his kicks from pot or hashish or speed. Oh, he gets high, all right, but not from narcotics . . . As far as kicks are concerned, Lt. Bush gets his from the roaring afterburner of the F-102."

Indeed, W. cut a dashing figure in his bright orange scarf, flight jacket, and aviator shades. And on the ground he continued to be head cheerleader, nickname-dispenser, and all-around cutup. But once airborne, Lieutenant Bush was not one for grandstanding. Fighter jets, he later wrote, "force you to master yourself mentally, physically, and emotionally. You have to stay calm and think logically. One mistake and you could end up in a very expensive metal coffin."

There was ample risk involved in flying military jets in domestic airspace, certainly. Two of W.'s fellow pilots were killed in separate mishaps during the time he was stationed at Ellington. But there was virtually no chance that W., as a National Guardsman, would see combat. Aware that his father might encounter criticism over this issue during his make-or-break second try for the Senate, W. volunteered for Palace Alert, a special program that dispatched National Guard pilots to relieve active duty pilots in Vietnam. But W. was turned down. The program was being phased out, and he had not logged enough hours to participate anyway.

W. also adhered strictly to the rule that prohibited drinking for the twenty-four-hour period prior to going on duty. For Bush and the other weekend warriors, that meant partying began Monday and ended Thursday. W.'s off-duty hours were spent either chain-smoking Winstons and downing "red-and-whites" (iced cans of Budweiser) by the pool at the Châteaux Dijon, or tooling around Houston in his blue Triumph looking for a good time. Not *too* good a time, however—at least not during his father's campaign. "Don't want to do anything," he said whenever things began to get too rowdy, "that might embarrass Dad."

The entire Bush clan was stunned that summer of 1970 when Houston insurance magnate Lloyd Bentsen, a moderate, wrested the nomination from liberal Ralph Yarborough in the Democratic primary. The charismatic, Texan-to-the-bone Bentsen, also a decorated World War II pilot, benefited from the continuing perception that

Big George was a Yankee carpetbagger, that his Lone Star conversion was forced and artificial.

No sooner did he suffer his second defeat than George flew to Washington and lobbied with Nixon to appoint him U.S. ambassador to the United Nations. By March, he and Barbara had moved into the ambassador's official residence on the forty-second floor of Manhattan's Waldorf Towers. W.'s mother, who had cried as she always did when her Poppy lost an election, was now in her element. One of her first acts was to remove two Monets from the apartment and replace them with works by American artists like Bellows and Mary Cassatt. When he visited, W. was warned not to touch the Steuben glass *objets*—the smallest ashtray was worth hundreds, perhaps thousands of dollars—that filled the massive five-bedroom apartment.

Even though his father had managed to land the sort of high-profile appointment that would bolster his résumé, the ambassador's job was unquestionably a consolation prize. W., still devastated by his father's second major defeat, was the only Bush left behind to lick his wounds in Texas—W.'s brothers were away at school in the East and his twelve-year-old sister Doro lived in the Waldorf Towers with their parents.

It was the first time, say close friends, that W. seemed cast adrift—no longer in his father's shadow but unsure of what to do. "He was so lost and floating," his friend Doug Hannah said. "It was the first time he had kind of lost his anchor. He wasn't doing anything."

This would be the start of what W. himself would call his "nomadic period"—a time of wretched overindulgence devoted almost exclusively to drinking too much, smoking too much, and chasing women. Apartment 29-A at the Châteaux Dijon was an accurate reflection of its occupant's state of mind: soiled laundry and yellowing newspapers strewn about the room; dirty dishes piled in the sink and spilling over into the living room, empty bottles and beer cans everywhere.

"I was pretty cavalier in my early twenties," W. later admitted. "I was rootless. I had no responsibilities whatsoever." He focused on what most twenty-three-year-old males focus on. Waxing gallant, W. agreed that he "spent enormous amounts of time and energy courting women."

"You could literally have a whole social life without ever going outside the Châteaux Dijon," said John W. Link, one of W.'s neighbors. "You would date different people, and there were groups inside of groups. The guys would have contests: this week, we'll date only from this side of the street."

Still, W. had been careful to maintain his ties to that other, more rarefied world of money, power, and prestige. Unbeknownst to his rowdier friends, W. was a member in good standing of the Master's Club, a select group of bachelors who held dances at country clubs in and around Houston.

But Susan Munson, one of the women he dated in the early 1970s, was impressed by W.'s seeming disdain for formality of any kind. "He was conservative, but he hung around with people who were more liberal," she said. "Most of George's friends were the type who would sit on the floor with torn jeans and T-shirts . . . He liked to sit around and talk about serious things in a fun way. You didn't get that with most of the guys there."

W. also liked to talk about his admittedly vague plans for the future. "He knew he wanted to own a baseball team," Munson said, "and he wanted to go into politics. He wasn't sure how he was going to get to those goals."

Now that the election was over and W. felt he no longer had to "behave" for his father, the boisterous young pilot became a fixture at the Milieu nightclub, as well as several bars and lounges in Houston's garish lower Westheimer area. His modus operandi seldom varied: W. zoomed up in his blue Triumph, always with a date or a friend, made a dramatic "I'm here!" entrance, and then searched the room for familiar faces that he invariably found. There were impromptu drinking contests (W. claimed a special fondness for "The 4 B's": beer, bourbon, and B&B), dirty joke marathons, and sports trivia contests. Wherever W. went, the decibel level rose to drown out whatever was blasting from the jukebox.

Although there was no question that alcohol was always W.'s drug of choice, there would be ceaseless speculation over the years that during what he called his "so-called wild, exotic days," he also indulged in cocaine, or at the very least marijuana.

"Maybe I did, maybe I didn't," he would say decades later. "How I behaved as an irresponsible youth is irrelevant." He conceded that he "made mistakes. I've learned from my mistakes. I'm not going to talk about what I did as a child." For her part, Diane Paul, who dated W. between 1970 and 1972, said W. "never did anything like that. He was the straightest guy I knew. The most we ever did was go to a party and drink beer."

In fact, the mood-altering properties of alcohol were more than enough to change W. from, as one Milieu patron put it, "Dr. Jekyll to Mr. Hyde." When he had too much to drink, friends pointed out, W.'s natural reserves of sarcasm bubbled to the surface. Behavior that might have been dismissed only moments earlier as simply playful could suddenly turn boorish and surly. "He was not the classic mean drunk," a colleague said. "But there was a point at which he crossed the line over into nastiness, and the comments that he thought were hilarious were just asinine, and sometimes malicious. You just sort of held your breath when he walked up to a stranger in a restaurant—you never knew what he was going to do or say."

Even when he was sober, W. was prone to the sort of immature actions that made others wince. Bush was a veritable smorgasbord of tics and quirks and generally irritating behavior. He seemed to be "revved up twenty-four/seven," as one friend from those days put it—a "jumpy, can't-wait-to-get-the-party-started kind of guy." For no discernible reason, he might bump up against someone in an effort to start a mock shoving match, or pinch the other person's cheek, or stick his tongue out in the middle of what was thought to be serious conversation.

At a cocktail party in Kennebunkport, W. searched the room before spotting an elegant gray-haired woman he recognized as one of his parents' good friends. Bourbon in hand, he wobbled up to the woman and bellowed, "So, what's sex like after fifty, anyway?"

None of which boded well for the ambassador's son, whose weekend warrior duties left him with considerable time on his hands. Without telling his family, he quietly applied to the University of Texas Law School—sans string-pulling of any kind—and was promptly rejected. "I think that got under his skin a little bit," said Barbara Bush, "because I don't think he was used to not doing what he wanted to do."

Enter Poppy, who saw his son—now widely if inaccurately referred to as "Junior"—floundering. The senior Bush arranged for

W. to go to work for Stratford of Texas, a huge agricultural con-
glomerate. W. was assigned his own office, and over the next several
months his duties ranged from writing lengthy, data-filled memos
on the productivity of Stratford's nurseries and poultry processing
plants to making calls on some of Stratford's farming operations.

Every day W., who by now had moved out of the Châteaux
Dijon and into a one-bedroom luxury apartment at 2039½ South
Boulevard, showed up in a Brooks Brothers suit and worked from
nine to five. Restless and bored, he would later refer to his apprenticeship in agribusiness at Stratford as "a dull coat-and-tie job."

In 1972, he managed to wrangle a reassignment to the Alabama
National Guard in Montgomery, so he could work as a paid political
director for the Senate campaign of former U.S. Postmaster General
(and old Bush family crony) Winston "Red" Blount. Nee Bear, one
of several women W. dated in Alabama, was impressed by W.'s determination to see Blount win. "He wanted to be a hands-on guy," she
said of W., who went from parking lot to parking lot slapping stick-
ers on cars in the broiling Alabama heat. When Blount was flattened
at the polls by incumbent Democrat John Sparkman, W. chalked up
the defeat as one more in a string of disappointments.

W. was dealt another blow when family patriarch Prescott Bush
died at age seventy-five after a short bout with lung cancer. Along
with his brothers and the Senator's other grandsons, W. served as a
pallbearer at the packed funeral service in Greenwich's Episcopal
Christ Church. The grandfather he had idolized—and occasionally
feared—was buried in Putnam Cemetery, next to the small stone
marker Prescott himself had chosen to commemorate the brief life
of W.'s sister Robin.

His next major move, again without telling anyone in his family,
was to apply to Harvard Business School. At the time, Big George
was also in transition—departing his post as U.N. ambassador to
become chairman of the Republican National Committee. W.'s parents had moved into a furnished house on Washington's Cathedral
Avenue, and in December 1972 twenty-six-year-old "Junior" flew
to the nation's capital to spend Christmas with his parents.

With his fifteen-year-old brother Marvin in tow, W. took off in
one of Dad's cars to visit a friend. By the time they left the friend's
house for the long ride home, both brothers were drunk. W. got

behind the wheel and, miraculously, managed to make it to within a block of his parents' house when he smashed into a neighbor's garbage can. Without stopping and with the metal can wedged in his left front wheel well, W. drove noisily up the street and into the Bush family driveway.

Big George, who had been in the den reading when he heard the clanking of his car as it pulled up to the house, waited until an obviously inebriated Marvin came stumbling in. "Tell your brother I want to see him," Dad commanded.

W. burst into the room and confronted his father. "I hear you're looking for me," Junior shouted, shaking his fist as Big George drew himself up to his full six-foot-two-inch height. "You want to go mano a mano right here?"

By this time the entire family had rushed to the den to witness the heated exchange between father and son. Barbara was literally pulling the two men apart when nineteen-year-old Jeb, now a student at the University of Texas, decided to share with the rest of the family a secret he had been keeping. "Hey, everybody. Guess what—George has been accepted into Harvard Business School."

Everyone else in the room was flabbergasted. Mom and Dad traded unknowing glances.

"But he hasn't decided yet whether or not he'll go," Jeb continued.

Forgetting the garbage can that would have to be pried from his car the next morning, Dad turned his attention to the possibility that W. would add Harvard to his list of academic credentials. "You should think about that, son," he said.

"Oh, I'm not going," W. said dismissively. "I just wanted to let you know I could get into it." He would later say the shouting match in Dad's den was not so much an act of youthful rebellion as "the result of two stiff bourbons, nothing more . . . Real smart. I was drunk."

But those closest to him saw W.'s decision to stand up to Dad as a symptom of his mounting frustration. "You have to really understand how much his father was loved and respected by so many people," said W.'s cousin John Ellis, "to understand what it would be like to grow up as a namesake, the son of George Bush."

Tellingly, W. did follow his father's advice. Not only would he go to Harvard Business School, but he would spend the nine months before classes were scheduled to begin working at an inner-city program for disadvantaged youth. Not just any program, but the Professional United Leadership League (PULL). Big George had been honorary chairman of PULL, which paired professional athletes with kids from some of Houston's toughest neighborhoods.

Big George wondered if his son, who had never held a job for more than a few months, would buckle down this time. With good reason. "I wasn't interested in taking root," W. conceded. "I was having fun."

But W.'s first close-up look at living conditions in the ghetto would prove "tragic, heartbreaking, and uplifting, all at the same time." He played basketball with the kids (during one game a gun fell out of an eleven-year-old's pocket), listened to their problems, occasionally took them out for a hamburger, or for a drive in his 1970 white Oldsmobile Cutlass. Before he could take them for a ride, however, he would have to make room by emptying the car of its usual cargo of detritus: dirty laundry, old tennis shoes, beer cans, and styrofoam coffee cups.

W. grew especially close to Jimmy Dean, a six-year-old African-American boy who followed him everywhere. "He became like a little brother," W. would later recall of the boy. When he came to the PULL offices barefoot one day, W. took him out to the store and bought him several pairs of shoes.

One day W. decided to take several of the PULL kids on their first plane ride, and asked his sixteen-year-old brother Marvin to tag along. When his young passengers refused to stop acting up, W. put the plane in a momentary stall. Terrified, the kids did not make a sound for the rest of the trip. "For a lot of these kids, this was the first white man who really seemed to care about them," said one PULL volunteer. "They liked him. They liked him a lot."

When W. took Jimmy home one evening, he was upset to find the boy's family living in utter squalor. The woman who answered the door was "clearly stoned," he said. The room inside "was smoky, and the music blaring . . . I was incredibly sad to leave him there." Over the years, W. wondered what became of Jimmy. Sadly, he eventually found out: Jimmy made it only to his teens, when he was gunned down on the streets of Houston.

During the time he worked for PULL, W.'s own living conditions were far from ideal. His cramped apartment at 2910 Westheimer was directly above a florist who refused to use pesticides. As a result—or perhaps because of his own less-than-fastidious lifestyle—W.'s apartment was infested with roaches.

Although he was supposed to complete his tour of duty with the National Guard in May 1974, W. was permitted to leave the service early so that he could enter Harvard Business School in the fall of 1973. For the son of the man who was chairman of the Republican National Committee, it was not the ideal time to be on a college campus. Watergate dominated the news, and George Herbert Walker Bush was stuck with the unenviable task of publicly defending an embattled Richard Nixon.

But as he had done so many times before, W. quickly adjusted to his new environment. When Rudy Winston walked into the class he was teaching for the first time that year, he saw W. leaning back with his cowboy boots on the desk, flying paper airplanes around the room. In another class, Mitch Kurtz was just settling in when he heard a bizarre noise. "What the heck is that?" he thought to himself. Then he turned to see W. seated directly behind him, spitting tobacco juice into a cup. The school's heavy emphasis on class participation, teamwork, and the "Big Picture" approach to management seemed ideally suited to the antsy twenty-seven-year-old with no patience for ironing out the details. "George felt this environment," Winston said, "was something he could handle."

Once again, W. excelled as a leader despite mediocre grades. He often led discussions in class, and was one of only six students chosen by his peers to head up a team in the campus-wide business simulation competition. He was also a standout in the school's intramural basketball league—not as a player, but as what a classmate called "someone with an uncanny knack to get people to do what he wanted." Said Mitch Kurtz, "George's leadership was not based on raw brain power. He had an intangible quality about him, that there wasn't a problem that couldn't be solved . . ."

As the Nixon Administration became increasingly unhinged with each new Watergate revelation, W. remained devoutly apolitical. Yet it undoubtedly hurt to hear the chants of protesters condemning Nixon and the men like George Herbert Walker Bush who defended him. When W. wasn't on the basketball court or in the classroom, he was running for miles along the banks of the Charles River or dashing off to Boston's Hillbilly Bar to listen to Waylon Jennings and Johnny Cash playing on the jukebox. With the exception of the beers he downed there, W. also picked this time to go on a stringent diet that seemed to his friends to consist mostly of raw carrots. W.'s gaunt appearance concerned his friends and family, who knew that all of it—the compulsive running, the dieting, the trips to the Hillbilly Bar—were avenues of escape.

Big George and Barbara stood on the White House lawn on August 8, 1974, and watched a disgraced Richard Nixon leave the White House for the last time as president. Within six weeks, W.'s dad had wangled a new ambassador-level appointment from Nixon's successor, Gerald R. Ford—as head of the U.S. Liaison Office in China.

That summer, before his parents departed for Beijing, George made a farewell visit to them in Washington. At that time, he was introduced to the young man who served as his father's special assistant at the Republican National Committee, Karl Rove. At the height of Watergate, the *Washington Post* accused Denver-bred Rove of "teaching dirty tricks" to young Republicans on college campuses across the country. Rove, who was five years younger than W., let the boss's son know that he made no apologies for his take-no-prisoners approach in defense of the GOP. W. instantly recognized a kindred spirit. Later, after relocating to Texas, Karl Rove would become one his closest confidants and his principal strategist.

But for now it was all W. could do to tough out another year on an Ivy League campus overrun with placard-waving leftists who detested all that his family stood for. After graduation in 1975, W. scooped up three of his siblings—Marvin, Neil, and Doro—and flew to China for a reunion with their parents.

It quickly became clear that W. had an ulterior motive for the trip. "I'd always heard about how great Asian women were," he confided to a friend. "You know, that they really know how to make a man happy. You know?"

Much to his chagrin, W. quickly discovered that under Chairman Mao, unsupervised contact between Westerners and Chinese civilians was virtually nonexistent. "Meeting a Chinese girl—any Chinese girl—was not going to be easy," he said. "Dating one—impossible."

In Beijing, W. managed to stick to his routine of running at least three or four miles every morning near the American compound, or at least until he encountered one of the signs that read NO LOITERERS ALLOWED. Rough translation: No Chinese beyond this point, and vice versa.

With nearly all the children on hand (Jeb had remained behind with his new bride, Mexican national Columba Garnica Gallo), Big George and Barbara threw a Fourth of July barbecue for their Chinese hosts. The old Andover cheerleader kept spirits high in the sizzling summer heat as the family festooned the U.S. compound with streamers and red, white, and blue bunting. Then he pitched in with his sister and brothers to serve hamburgers and hot dogs to their Chinese guests.

Even this short trip abroad left W. longing for Texas. As soon as he got back to the United States, he jammed his belongings into the trunk of his Cutlass and headed for home.

He had already followed his father to Andover and Yale, and learned to fly military aircraft just as Poppy had. After his brief detour to Harvard, W. was once again retracing his father's steps—this time to Midland. Determined to learn the oil business from the ground up—just like Dad did—W. went to work researching oil and mineral records as a hundred-dollar-a-day freelance "land man" for several independent producers. "I was single," he later said. "My overhead was extremely low. I knew I didn't want to work for anybody for a while." He seemed unperturbed by the simple fact that he knew "next to nothing" about the oil business. "Things," he thought to himself, "will take care of themselves."

W.'s "low overhead" remark turned out to be a masterpiece of understatement. Friends of the family charged W. nominal rent for a two-room gray brick bungalow on a street that, coincidentally enough, had been christened Harvard Avenue. Once again, he made the place look as if it had just been struck by a Texas twister. He had somehow managed to break the frame of his bed ("It's not hard to imagine how," cracked a drinking buddy), and solved the problem by binding the springs together with neckties. "George," said his friend Robert McCleskey, "didn't spend a whole lot of money on creature comforts."

Everywhere one looked there was soiled clothing, half-eaten

sandwiches, old newspapers and older magazines, and unidentifiable piles of God-knew-what. By the end of his first month there, the place began to attract flies. "His apartment," said lifelong friend Charlie Younger, "was a disaster area. It looked like a toxic waste dump."

Over the next few months, W. began making a name for himself in Midland—not as a businessman or the scion of an influential family, but as the sloppiest dresser in town. When the tassels fell off his Bass Weejuns, he simply reattached them—with tape. That was if he wore shoes at all. Most of the time, whether he was attending a business conference or meeting friends at his favorite Mexican hangout, W. wore the paper-thin black Chinese slippers he brought back from Beijing.

If he had to dress up, he would wear his father's hand-me-down suits that were easily two sizes too big for him; W. would not pay to have them altered. Friends would give him clothing they intended to discard, and he ended up wearing them for the next ten years. One friend picked up a threadbare sweater at a thrift store and gave it to him as a gag gift. For the next year, W. could be seen around Midland wearing the sweater, usually with a pair of ill-fitting, slightly worn pants he managed to acquire from someone else. "George," observed Charlie Younger, "would wear anything anyone would give him."

W.'s reputation as an unrepentant slob led golfers at one Midland Country Club tournament to bestow an annual "George W. Bush Award" for the tournament's worst dresser. The prize: a pair of shabby plaid trousers.

To maintain his "low overhead," W. also became one of Midland's most notorious tightwads. He took his dirty laundry to be done by his friends' wives, all of whom were only too happy to oblige. When he went out on dates, he seldom picked up the check, and he always tried to find a way to make his buddies pay for the next round of beers. As the holidays approached, several of W.'s friends gathered up old corporate Christmas cards, and then crudely crossed out the company names and replaced them with W.'s. In the weeks leading up to Christmas, scores of business leaders throughout town received these laughably "recycled" Christmas cards from the man now regarded even by his friends as "The Biggest Cheapskate in Midland."

That did not seem to crimp his style when it came to the opposite sex, however. Despite his shabby attire, his squalid apartment, and his reluctance to pay, W. seldom wanted for female company. He was serious enough about several of these Texas belles to bring them home and introduce them to the family. "He brought some lulus to Maine in those days," Barbara Bush recalled of the young women W. invited to Kennebunkport. "They were very nice, but it would only take a day before he would decide they wouldn't fit in with the family."

As charming as he appeared to the local female population, W. was an even bigger hit with Midland's movers and shakers. Like his dad, W. belonged to the Petroleum Club, the terrazzo-sheathed monolith at the corner of Marienfeld and Wall streets where oilmen bragged about the wells that came in and drowned their sorrows over those that didn't. Unlike his dad, who had not an ounce of redneck in him, W. was utterly convincing as a tobacco-chewing (he had gone from Copenhagen snuff tobacco to Beechnut long-leaf), whiskey-drinking, cussin', yarn-spinnin', Yankee-hatin' good ole boy.

What many of them seemed to like the most—although they might not have admitted it—was W.'s penchant for adolescent behavior. While running along the high school track, he thought nothing of sneaking up behind another oilman and yanking down his shorts. At a Willie Nelson concert in Odessa, W. and Charlie Younger leapt onstage and, beers in hand, sang along with the star.

Yet W. was serious about making it in the oil business, just as his father had done. After a year's apprenticeship, young Bush decided to strike out on his own—just as his father had done a quarter-century earlier. "It smelled right and it felt right," he said. "I wanted to be my own man, my own businessman." The name of his new oil exploration company: Arbusto (pronounced Ar-*boost*-o, Spanish for "bush"). It took only a couple of dry holes for locals to slyly rename W.'s company "Ar-*bust*-o."

There seemed little chance of that happening. The Bush family name meant that every phone call from W. would be returned, and that every business proposition would be seriously considered.

Slowly, with the help of two veteran oilmen who let him invest in a few of their wells, Arbusto began making some money.

At no time, however, did W. ever stop or even temper his carousing ways. Friends like Charlie Younger and Don Evans began to notice that the Bombastic Bushkin was consuming more and more alcohol, and that the marathon partying was beginning to take its toll. Alarmingly, a week did not go by without an inebriated W. getting behind the wheel of his car and trying to find his way home.

That summer of 1976, Big George and Barbara Bush got a chance to see firsthand how their boy was faring when he visited them at Kennebunkport. The elder Bush, who left his post in China to take the reins of the Central Intelligence Agency, had been hearing stories about W.'s antics back home in Midland. Now that his son was thirty, Big George and Barbara grew increasingly concerned that W. might be developing a serious, long-term alcohol problem.

Those fears were confirmed on September 4, 1976, when W. made his usual Labor Day weekend pilgrimage to Kennebunkport with the rest of the Bush tribe. Whenever he hit town, W. hooked up immediately with his circle of drinking buddies. This time, rather than bring Marvin, he brought his seventeen-year-old sister Doro along to keep him company. They met up with Australian tennis star John Newcombe and his wife at a local dive, and after three hours spent knocking back beer after beer, headed home to the family compound at Walker's Point with W. behind the wheel.

As they made their way down Ocean Avenue, W. was having a difficult time staying on the road. The car drifted over the center line, then back in the opposite direction before sliding off the road. W. made a quick correction, but it was too late: Calvin Bridges of the Kennebunkport police department had been just about to end his shift when he saw Bush slip onto the right shoulder.

Officer Bridges turned on his lights and siren, and pulled the car over. As soon as W. handed Bridges his license, the officer realized that he had just stopped a member of the town's most illustrious family. Looking at the driver's flushed face and bleary eyes, Officer Bridges had little doubt that W. was intoxicated.

"Have you had anything to drink tonight, sir?"

"Yes, officer, I have," Bush slurred good-naturedly. "A few beers."

The policeman then asked him to take a sobriety test, and he readily complied. Not surprisingly, W. failed. Officer Bridges arrested George W. Bush on the spot for driving under the influence, placed him in the back of his patrol car, and drove him to the Kennebunkport police station.

Once at the station, a second sobriety test was administered—perhaps in the hopes that by now W.'s blood alcohol level might have slipped below the state's legal limit, saving the Bush family the embarrassment of having one of its own charged with drunk driving. But W.'s blood alcohol level still registered a substantial .12, over Maine's .10 legal limit.

George W. Bush was released on five hundred dollars bail and would appear a few days later to stand up in court and plead guilty to a misdemeanor. W.'s sentence was fairly typical for the time: a $150 fine and one-month suspension of his driving privileges in Maine. Released into his parents' custody, a chastened W. seemed uncharacteristically somber as he left the courtroom. He made no note of the other man arraigned that same morning on DUI charges—the man who twenty-four years later would recall seeing George W. Bush in court and trigger a chain of events that might have changed the course of history.

But for now W. was not worried about what it all might mean for his future. At the age of thirty, he was "going nowhere fast," as he confessed to a girlfriend. But Big George was still head of the CIA, and now there was serious speculation that he might run for the presidency in 1980. Once again, the younger Bush feared that he could prove an embarrassment to his father at a time when Big George could least afford it.

That had certainly crossed the mind of the paterfamilias, who once again shook his head as he delivered the all-too-familiar—and devastating—"I'm disappointed in you, son" speech. "You're not a kid anymore, son," Big George told him. "This is a wake-up call. You're thirty years old. It's time to start acting responsibly and cut back on your drinking."

There was no mano a mano retort this time; it was all W. could do to keep from weeping in shame and frustration. What W. did not know was that behind closed doors Big George had been coping with his wife's serious emotional problems. Over the previous six months, Barbara had been secretly battling clinical depression so severe that night after night she wept in her husband's arms. "I sometimes wonder why he didn't leave me," she later said. Barbara had even contemplated suicide during this time. "Sometimes the pain was so great I felt the urge to drive into a tree or an oncoming car," she confessed. Fortunately, when those feelings struck, she simply pulled to the side of the road and waited for them to pass.

Barbara had made steady progress, and for whatever reason the curtain of depression had nearly lifted. Now this—one more sign that her eldest son had a drinking problem. No one in the family had ever been arrested even once before, much less twice. "For Pete's sake, George. What in God's name were you thinking?" was all she could bring herself to say to W.

For the moment, however, there were more practical matters to consider. How would they be able to keep the arrest secret? What would they say when it was picked up by the press? So they formulated a contrite, no excuses response and waited for the call. But after a few weeks, it became clear that the call might never come. No local reporter had picked up on W.'s arrest, marked so clearly on the posted docket sheet. Nor had any of those in court that day uttered a word to the press.

Faced with such good fortune, Barbara and Big George told Doro and the boys not to mention their big brother's arrest to anyone. They urged their loquacious eldest son to do the same, and this time he obeyed. With a little luck, there was a good chance that no one would ever know . . .

After pleading guilty to drunk driving, W. wasted no time returning to Midland, where his driving privileges were unaffected by the court ruling in Maine. When Jimmy Carter took office in 1977, Dad's brief stint at the CIA came to an end and he and Barbara returned to Houston.

It was at this moment that W. saw the chance to redeem himself in his father's eyes. It seemed that he had been spinning his wheels in the oil business; the famously impatient Bombastic One now determined that it would take forever to get Arbusto off the ground. But an opportunity of a different sort was opening up in West Texas's nineteenth congressional district. After forty-four years in Congress, seventy-seven-year-old Democrat George Mahon was at last retiring.

W. phoned his father and proudly told him that he intended to run for Mahon's House seat. Big George approved—not, as he would later explain, because he taught his son that "you must be a politician to be successful," but because there was a family tradition of service. So long as W. could keep his year-old drunk driving arrest secret (not to mention the college pranks that had gotten him in trouble), Bush Sr. believed his son had a good chance of winning.

If for no other reason than he was George Herbert Walker Bush's son, W. would prove to be a formidable candidate. Controversial GOP strategist Karl Rove went to work for the campaign, as did old friends Don Evans and Joe O'Neill. Big George's pals in the oil business would make sure that Junior's campaign coffers were overflowing. "The opposition will not be of any concern to me," he boasted to the *Lubbock Avalanche-Journal* when asked about the crowded field in the GOP primary. "I'm accustomed to tough campaigns."

In surveying the competition, W. did make note of the fact that nearly all the candidates were married with children. So, too, were virtually all the people he had grown up with. "From a political standpoint," said one campaign worker, "it was a definite liability to be a thirty-one-year-old bachelor running for office. This was a part of the country where practically everybody was married by the time they were twenty-two, and anybody who waited too long was viewed with suspicion."

Then there was the matter of W.'s well-deserved reputation as a carousing womanizer. The churchgoing folk of Lubbock and Dimmitt and Muleshoe frowned on such behavior, particularly on the part of someone who wanted to represent them in Congress.

W. had the name, the money, the looks, the charm, the drive, and the connections. Now, his closest advisers told him, it would not hurt his chances if he had a wife.

Jan O'Neill, meanwhile, wanted nothing more than to see her good friend and former roommate Laura Welch get married and settle down. But Laura had spent the last six years focused on her profession, fashioning a new career for herself as a children's librarian. As soon as she earned a master's degree in library science from the University of Texas in 1972, she went to work at the McCrane-Kashmere Gardens Public Library in central Houston. As it happened, Laura had ulterior motives of her own for choosing the downtown location. "I didn't have the opportunity to meet that many men to date," Laura explained, "and I thought by working in a big public library in downtown Houston, I might have a different social life." Laura dated a half-dozen men over the next year, but nothing clicked.

What Laura did slowly come to realize, however, was that she missed being in an elementary school environment. In 1974, Laura moved back to Austin and took a job as the librarian at Molly Dawson elementary school on the city's primarily Hispanic south side. Laura at last had the chance to use her high school Spanish, and once again charmed her way into the hearts of the children. "Miss Welch loved reading and books so much," said one former Molly Dawson student, "that as a little kid you couldn't help but get excited, too. She was also very pretty, and a lot of the fourth and fifth graders had a crush on her."

In Austin, Laura was still on a "romantic treadmill," dating regularly but unable to make a serious connection with any one man. Increasingly, she would leave Austin on Friday afternoon and make the five-hour drive to Midland so she could spend the weekend with family and her old friends.

Joe and Jan O'Neill worried about their two single friends, and over the course of a year made a concerted, insistent attempt to bring them together. Jan repeatedly invited Laura to come to the O'Neill house for dinner and meet the young congressional candidate everybody was talking about.

Laura knew the Bush name, of course, though she did not recall the twelve-year-old boy who attended San Jacinto Junior High the same time she did. And someone did show her a picture of young George W. that had run in the local paper. But Laura's visits home were designed to get her away from the dating scene, and she did not want anything to infringe on the time she spent with Mom and Dad. Laura understood why the O'Neills were so persistent. "I think all of our friends wanted to fix us up," she said, "because we were literally the last two people left who hadn't married of all our friends."

Nor did it help that W. belonged to a high-profile political family, and that now he was running for Congress. "I was just so uninterested in politics," Laura sighed. "I thought he was someone real political, and I wasn't interested."

One unseasonably cool evening in early August, however, Laura finally relented. She showed up for a backyard barbecue at the O'Neills' home in Midland and met the young man they had been talking about for what seemed like an eternity.

W. was instantly smitten. "And why not?" asked Joe O'Neill. "Laura has always been a beautiful woman, and back then she was a definite 'ten.'"

Laura, W. later said of that first meeting, was "gorgeous, good-humored, quick to laugh, down-to-earth, and very smart. I recognized those attributes right away, in roughly that order."

Although the O'Neills had convinced themselves that opposites attract, they had begun to worry that perhaps their two friends were *too* different to ever hit it off. They needn't have doubted their matchmaking instincts. George talked nonstop, telling jokes and waxing sentimental about West Texas while Laura laughed and listened.

"By then, I'd lived a lot of life, and I was beginning to settle down," W. said of that evening. "When we met, I was enthralled. I found her to be a very thoughtful, smart, interested person—one of the great listeners. And since I'm one of the big talkers, it was a great fit."

There was another, unmistakable sign that W. was captivated by the pretty librarian. Knowing that he would have to get up at dawn the next morning to begin his daily three-mile run, W. normally left by nine. This night, however, he did not leave until midnight. "We knew then," Joe O'Neill said, "that they had made a connection. George started to pursue her right away."

"I don't know that it was love at first sight," Laura would say. "But it was close." She told Jan O'Neill that she thought W. was "really cute," and that he was "very funny" in an "outrageous way." When she got home that night, she sat on the edge of her mother's bed and told her, "The thing I like about him, is that he made me laugh."

That first night, Jenna Welch recalled, George had told Laura that he wanted to see her again. But the fact that Laura lived in Austin and George in Midland made the idea of any ongoing relationship problematic. "You know," Laura's mom said, "it was like 'Fat chance. I really like him, but how is this going to work?' "

Still, George and Laura were eager for more. The next night, the O'Neills went miniature golfing with George and Laura. The following weekend, Laura did not make the five-hour drive to her parents' house in Midland; W. went to visit her in Austin.

The match struck some of their mutual friends as odd, others as perfectly logical. "We quickly realized that they were perfect complements to one another," Regan Gammon said. "Laura loved George's energy, and George loved the way she was so calm."

"Laura does have a very calming effect on people," Jenna Welch said of her daughter. "It's just part of her nature. She's a very—I won't say controlled, but an *in* control person. I guess you have to be in control if you're a teacher and you've got to get a bunch of schoolchildren to behave."

Four days after that fateful cookout at the O'Neills', W. was back in Kennebunkport telling his family about the wonderful girl he had just met. "He fell madly in love with Laura," Barbara said, adding that that first day in Maine he was "calling back to Midland every minute." When he phoned and a man answered Laura's phone, W. caught the next available flight back to Texas.

"Regan Gammon's husband Billy was always very protective of Laura," Joe O'Neill said, "but George didn't understand that and was pretty jealous. He was always asking, 'Who is this guy Billy Gammon anyway?' "

Over the next few weeks, W. pursued the soft-spoken librarian relentlessly. They dated more or less nightly, and when she returned to work in Austin, he made several weekend trips to visit her there. Jenna Welch worried that W. was coming on too strong, too fast. Laura had brought young men home before, and when it became clear they were rushing things, it "sort of turned her off," said Jenna. "I thought George was a great catch, but I was afraid he was pushing Laura so hard he might ruin the whole thing."

Even though they were the ones who had arranged the meeting in the first place, the O'Neills had no inkling that George and Laura would still be dating weeks later. "I was not just surprised," Jan O'Neill said. "I was shocked."

But Laura had reached a point in her life—she was three months away from her thirty-first birthday—where she was eager, if not exactly desperate, to marry. "I think it was a whirlwind romance because we were in our early thirties," she later conceded. "I'm sure both of us thought, 'Gosh, we may never get married.' And we both really wanted children. Plus, I lived in Austin and he lived in Midland, so if we were going to see each other all the time, we needed to marry."

"Once you find the right person," Joe O'Neill said, "that part of the equation is done and you can get on with the other things." But Laura did worry about what it would mean to be a politician's wife. She was an intensely private, obviously shy young woman who would not mind working behind the scenes but was terrified at the thought of having to give a speech. "Don't worry, Laura," he reassured her. "If we get married, I promise you will never have to give a political speech." Then he got down on bended knee and asked her to marry him. Laura said yes. They had known each other just three weeks. "If I am anything," W. said, "it's decisive." (In contrast to his proposal to Cathy Wolfman a decade earlier, George did not immediately give Laura an engagement ring.)

The entire Bush tribe was descending on Houston for the christening of Jeb's daughter Noelle. After the church service, George brought Laura to his parents' house on Briar Drive. Although the siblings knew what was afoot, Big George and Barbara were unaware of the engagement. Laura was still standing in the hallway when Jeb, having just met her, jokingly dropped to one knee.

"Did you pop the question to her, George, old boy?" Jeb asked.

"Yes, as a matter of fact he has," Laura replied without hesitation, "and I accepted."

While the brothers applauded, their parents stood open-mouthed. "We didn't even know he wanted to get married," Barbara said, "until he showed up at the door with this beautiful creature, Laura, and announced that she was going to be his wife."

A few weeks later, George took Laura to Kennebunkport, where she met W.'s grandmother, flinty Bush family grande dame Dorothy Walker Bush. At one point, the conversation turned to athletic pursuits—a topic close to the competitive Dorothy's heart.

"And what do you do?" Dorothy Bush asked her grandson's fiancée.

"I read," Laura replied, taking another drag on her cigarette, "and I smoke."

"Mrs. Bush," Barbara later recalled, "darn near collapsed."

Once back in Midland, George took Jenna and Harold Bruce Welch to dinner and, as they expected he would, formally asked for their daughter's hand in marriage. W. had grown especially fond of Laura's affable dad—"just one of the nicest guys who ever lived."

"George and Laura's father were very much alike—very outgoing, very funny," Jenna Welch said. "I suppose that was part of the appeal for Laura." Others who knew the Welches agreed that there were strong similarities between the two couples. "George and Laura are not unlike Harold and Jenna," said Robert McCleskey, who had known them all since childhood. "Mrs. Welch was the quiet Sunday School teacher, Harold was the fun-loving type of guy who talked up a storm."

At the time, W.'s old Houston pal Doug Hannah would have agreed with that assessment. "I met her at a party," Hannah said, "and as usual George did most of the talking. In fact, he dominated the conversation so much that it was difficult to see how she—or anyone else for that matter—could get a word in edgewise."

Three days before the wedding, Big George and Barbara flew to Midland and hosted a rehearsal dinner at the Hilton. There had been no time to arrange entertainment for the evening, but when Big George heard a barbershop quartet singing at a function down the hall, he corralled them into performing for the soon-to-be newlyweds.

The nuptials were equally unpretentious—just seventy-five guests, no bridesmaids, no groomsmen, no flower girls, no ringbearers. "No fuss," W. said. "We just wanted to get married, and we wanted our closest friends and family there to celebrate with us."

It was Laura's idea that each parent be allowed to invite only two couples. "We thought we were doing them a favor," she later said, "but some of the Bush uncles got their backs up."

"They'd been to enough weddings to know that they weren't interested in a big production," a friend said. Jenna pitched in and wrote the wedding invitations by hand; there had not been enough time to have them professionally printed.

On November 5, 1977—a Saturday—Laura Welch and George W. Bush were wed in the Glass Chapel of the First United Methodist Church. The ushers were Laura's cousin Robert and W.'s brothers Jeb, Neil, and Marvin. The men, including the groom and the father of the bride, wore business suits with orchid boutonnieres. Instead of a bridal gown, Laura opted for a long-sleeved street-length dress of candlelight beige crepe de chine. She wore a single strand of white pearls, and a corsage of white gardenias at her waist.

The morning light streamed through the chapel's stained-glass windows as the Reverend Jerry Wyatt pronounced Laura and George W. man and wife at 11 A.M. It was one day after the bride's thirty-first birthday and one day before the fourteenth anniversary of the crash that killed Mike Douglas.

It had been less than three months since they met. Just how much did they really know about each other at this point? W. did tell her about his brief engagement to Cathy Wolfman, and Laura shrugged it off. "It's not like he's been married before," she told one of her Midland friends. "We're both thirty-one. We've both got a past."

But there were other, potentially explosive things that could no longer remain secret. As soon as they began talking about marriage, she knew she would have to tell him about the tragic accident in her past. What if it were to come out during the campaign that George W. Bush's soft-spoken librarian wife had actually killed someone— albeit accidentally? Certainly it could deal a crippling blow to his campaign, and perhaps even cut short his political career.

One evening, Laura told George what had happened that night of November 6, 1963—not every gruesome detail, but enough to convey the profound horror of the event. She told him the facts dispassionately, without breaking down; Laura had long ago learned to keep her emotions in check. It was the highly emotional George whose eyes welled up with tears as he heard her tell the story of how her one fleeting moment of carelessness cost the life of her former boyfriend.

George W. then told Laura that he had known all along about the accident, that their mutual friends had mentioned it to him long before they met. Besides, he, too, had made mistakes—not the least of which was the drunk driving arrest in Maine one year earlier. Even before they actually marched down the aisle, the newlyweds had come up with a basic strategy for handling these potentially embarrassing incidents. "George and Laura just agreed that they would never talk about the negative things in their pasts, period," said a friend and campaign adviser. "If someone dug up the information and confronted them with it, they would just own up to having made mistakes in their pasts, but that's it. You've got to hand it to George. He knew that Laura's accident could become a political problem, but he was that much in love with her."

Not that they shared everything with each other. At the outset Laura told George W. that she was apolitical, and even that she— like the vast majority of Texans at the time—was a registered Democrat. For the moment, however, Laura thought it the better part of valor not to mention that she had voted for antiwar candidate George McGovern for president in 1972—and against the man her father-in-law had so staunchly defended, Richard Nixon. Worst of all, in the U.S. Senate race in Texas of 1970, Laura had cast her vote not for George Herbert Walker Bush, but for Democrat Lloyd Bentsen.

The couple took off for a brief honeymoon in Mexico, then moved into their own $200,000 one-story beige brick ranch house at 1405 West Golf Course Road in Midland. The house, situated right on one of the city's most heavily traveled roads, had a shallow, pebble-paved circular drive and was shaded by mature evergreens that showered the front walkway with needles.

This would be George and Laura's home base for nearly a decade, though they spent little time there during their first year as man and wife. On their "extended honeymoon," as W. called it, the newlyweds would crisscross the Texas Panhandle from Hereford to Midland in W.'s white Oldsmobile, shaking hands and making speeches. Laura insisted that on the longer trips a young campaign worker be hired to drive them because she was still "skittish" about being behind the wheel for extended periods.

"We campaigned the whole first year of our marriage," said Laura, who fretted about the toll it would take on them as a couple. Instead, the campaign proved to be a perfect way to adjust to each other's idiosyncrasies. "We were never mad at each other," she said, "because we always had opponents. It's a great way to spend a honeymoon."

Still, they had not been married two months when he broke the promise he had made to her about never having to make a speech. Because of a scheduling snafu, W. could not make a rally in Muleshoe and pleaded with her to stand in for him. When she stood up to give her speech, she delivered the opening lines she had been rehearsing in her head. "When we got married my husband promised me I would never have to make a speech," she declared. "So much for political promises." Unfortunately, she hadn't really thought of what else to say. "I had a really good start to my speech," she recalled, "but I hadn't gotten far enough to have a very good ending. So I got up and gave a few lines at the start and then I had to mumble and sit down."

W. poked fun at Laura's awkward first attempt at public speaking. "My wife's a librarian," he said. "Her idea of making a speech is 'Shhhh!' "

In fact, Laura quickly realized that her new husband, despite his pedigree, was really feeling his way as a politician. "George did sort of leap into it," she told Texas journalist Skip Hollandsworth, "but even back then he was smart enough to know that a lot of politics was simply timing . . . If George is good at anything, it's timing."

She also recognized from the outset that her husband had an innate genius for connecting with voters—and, it often seemed, for little else. "He was just great," she remembered, "he was so terrific, he always said the right thing . . . Then he would come home, and I would think, *Well, he can't even change a lightbulb!*"

W.'s competition in the Republican congressional primary was quickly narrowed down to former Odessa Mayor Jim Reese. Despite the fact that Reese was backed by most of the GOP heavyweights, including then-presidential hopeful Ronald Reagan, George W. trounced him at the polls. The celebration at Bush headquarters that night hearkened back to W.'s days at Yale. Campaign workers drained several kegs of beer, and by 11 P.M. the police were called to quiet the raucous crowd and make sure things did not "get out of hand."

With his primary victory, W. forged ahead with even more self-assurance than usual. Not everyone in the GOP was charmed by what one ally called his "cocky side." Recalled fellow GOP activist Mel Turner: "Bush was acting like a little kid. He was an immature rich-kid brat." Another local Republican, Curtis Webster, agreed that W. was at the very least "a little immature"—the kind of guy who liked to punch people in the arm or tickle them, make faces, show off his ability to wiggle his ears, make belching noises—or worse. He also liked to sneak up behind unsuspecting people—the more dignified the victim the better—then tap them on their far shoulder so that when they turned they would find no one there. "Like you do when you're twelve," Webster said.

W.'s confidence soon evaporated as he squared off against his Democratic opponent, thirty-five-year-old Texas State Senator Kent Hance. A down-home, bred-to-the-bone Texas boy, Hance made much of his local roots: a graduate of Dimmitt High and Texas Tech in Lubbock, he went on to the University of Texas Law School. He also painted his opponent as a Yankee in Stetson and spurs, the pampered son of a rich and well-connected New England family masquerading as a True Son of the Lone Star State.

He had a point. Through his family ties, W. had managed to raise $400,000 for his campaign—a staggering amount for a congressional race in 1978—counting among his contributors the very un-Texan likes of Mrs. Douglas MacArthur (his parents' ex-neighbor at the Waldorf Towers); Baseball Commissioner Bowie Kuhn; John Loeb of the Wall Street investment firm of Loeb, Rhoades; and former Secretary of Defense Donald Rumsfeld.

W.'s Ivy League background did not go over well with the hard-bitten citizens of Odessa and Lubbock. It did not help that Dad, now being talked of as a serious presidential contender in 1980, served on the board of the Rockefeller-backed Trilateral Commission, an organization that drew fire from conservatives for advocating a "New World Order." Eventually, W. had to officially declare that he "opposed one-world government and one monetary system. And if the Trilateral Commission supports those things, I'm sure my father is a dissenting voice."

Before embarking on their campaign odyssey, Laura had asked her mother-in-law for advice on how to conduct herself as the candidate's wife. First and foremost, Barbara told Laura, "Don't ever, *ever* criticize your husband's speeches." Pushed by her husband to offer some criticism during his first run for office, Barbara had once had to sit listening for hours while Big George tried to convince her that she was wrong.

Laura took Barbara's advice to heart, and throughout the campaign only praised her husband's speechmaking efforts—until one night late in the campaign, when the couple was driving home from an appearance in Lubbock. W. knew his speech was not very good, and during the entire trip home he badgered Laura for some kind of reaction—all the while expecting her to offer some words of reassurance.

As they were pulling into their driveway, he sighed one last time, "I didn't do very well, did I?"

"No," Laura finally said of the speech, "it wasn't very good."

With that, W. drove into the wall of their garage. From that point on, Laura would claim, albeit jokingly, that she would never criticize a speech of his again.

The uphill battle got even rougher in the closing days of the campaign, when a letter went out to district voters addressed, "Dear Fellow Christians." It pointed out that an ad had run in Texas Tech's *University Daily* promising free beer at a Bush campaign rally. The letter, which was circulated at churches throughout the region, went on to state that the "Bush Bash" was designed to exchange alcohol for votes—and corrupt local youth in the process.

"It was my first confrontation with cheap-shot politics," said W., who discovered that Hance actually owned the property on which a local bar—which also happened to be a Texas Tech hangout—stood. W. decided not to use the information against Hance. "Just an instinctive move," W. said. "In retrospect, I probably should have counterattacked." Ernie Angelo, who was then mayor of Midland and one of the state's most influential Republicans, agreed that young George "should have been tougher. Texas was still an overwhelmingly Democratic state, and Republicans never won by being Mr. Nice Guy."

As it happened, Hance exercised similar restraint when he decided not to reveal what he knew about W.'s drunk driving arrest in Maine. As it turned out, he did not need to. Hance won handily, with 53 percent of the vote to Bush's 47 percent. Bush called from his headquarters to offer his congratulations, and Hance was impressed with what a "gentleman" W. was. "I never detected any bitterness." (Years later, Hance would switch parties and become one of George W. Bush's most ardent supporters.)

In truth, George and Laura were crushed by the defeat. The next morning at his postelection press conference, W. choked back tears as he talked of how unfair it was to be branded an outsider when he had for all intents and purposes grown up in the heart of West Texas. He thanked his supporters, who responded with wild applause and cheers. W. wiped away a tear as he walked out with Laura who, as always, masked her emotions behind an otherworldly *La Giaconda* smile.

The defeat was a huge blow not only to the Bushes but to their legion of friends. And once again, W. felt that he let his father down. But many Texans believed it was the best thing that could have happened to a young man who often crossed over the line between boldness and arrogance. "That experience changed him, made him more humble," said local Republican Johnnye Davis. It also taught him never to permit a political opponent to portray him as elitist. "George," said Joe O'Neill, "has gotten a lot folksier since then." Agreed George Strake, former head of the GOP in Texas, "His father had to read about Texas in a book. George W. has Texas in his gut. It's who he is, and he wants everyone to know it."

It was over. George W. went back to making a go of it in the oil fields of Midland, and for the first time Laura settled into the life of a West Texas housewife. Together, they were still trying to make good on their promise to one another to start a family.

As a businessman, W. proved to be brilliant at luring investors but incapable of actually turning a profit. "At first it never occurred to George that he could actually lose $130,000 of his own money if he dug a dry hole," said Ralph Way, who with fellow veteran oilman Fletcher "Buzz" Mills was one of W.'s first partners in the business. "You should have seen the look on his face when that happened to him for the first time. He was *shocked*."

Unfortunately, George W. dug one dry hole after another, each time being forced to call investors—many of the same Bush family friends who contributed so heavily to his campaign—with the bad news. As a result of this "humbling experience," said Midland businessman Ernie Angelo, W. "became a much more likable person. He had the reputation when he came here of being cocky and arrogant and he lived that down."

Failure—both at the polls and in business—wasn't the only thing tamping down W.'s flaming ego. Laura had been welcomed into the Bush clan as a dignified, almost regal presence. Certainly what W. would call her "calming influence" could be felt almost immediately. "Laura's the sweetest person you can imagine," said Johnnye Davis, "and some of that rubbed off on him."

Perhaps. But it would take years for Laura to truly transform her bad-boy husband. Meantime, he was as garrulous, sloppy, and penurious as he had always been. The flimsy Chinese slippers were gone. Still, the only dress shoes he owned were hand-me-down alligator loafers that were two sizes too big. "George kind of slid around in them," said one Midland friend. "Laura tried to get him to pay attention to the way he dressed, but it was always pretty tough going."

Meantime, Laura indulged her own obsession with neatness and order—at least on the home front. She relaxed by cleaning out the kitchen cabinets, or organizing her closets. The contents of her kitchen cabinets were arranged in alphabetical order, and the books in the living room and den were actually organized according to the Dewey Decimal system. ("Well," Laura shrugged, "after all, I *am* a librarian.")

Just four months after W. lost in his first bid for Congress, Big George announced his candidacy for president. While the Bush children scattered about the country to stump for Dad, W. stayed on home turf. There he could cajole the Bush's longtime financial backers into pouring even more money into the Old Man's full-to-overflowing campaign coffers.

In the end, Ronald Reagan easily captured the nomination at the GOP convention in Detroit. Finding the right running mate would not be so easy. When the idea of tapping former president Gerald Ford for the vice presidential slot was floated on the convention floor, Ford responded with demands that he be given special powers that amounted to making him a "copresident." Reagan refused. Then the candidate turned to his aides gathered in his suite on the sixty-ninth floor of the Detroit Plaza Hotel. "Who else is there?" he asked.

"There's Bush," Richard V. Allen, Reagan's national security adviser, suggested tentatively.

But during the primaries, W.'s father had charged Reagan with preaching "voodoo economics." That, coupled with Bush's pro-choice abortion stand, initially made him unacceptable to Reagan. There would be six more hours of negotiations with Ford until Reagan literally threw up his hands. "Well, what do we do now?"

"We call Bush," said Allen, and Reagan reluctantly picked up the phone. With that, W.'s father, who had barely been on Reagan's radar screen six hours earlier, became what Allen would call the "accidental vice president."

This one off-the-cuff, spur-of-the-moment decision effectively launched the Bush Dynasty—and changed the course of American history. But W., incredibly, was not that impressed. He believed that his father, and not Reagan, deserved to be heading the ticket—an opinion he shared with anyone who would listen.

All the Bushes were on hand for the swearing in of George H. W. Bush as vice president in January 1981. Just a few days later, however, W. was back in Midland, trying to talk yet another rancher into letting Arbusto drill on his land.

Not that he had given up on a political career himself; the race for Congress in 1978 had simply whetted his appetite. With the passage of time, George W. had actually come to view his defeat with some degree of equanimity. "It wasn't that people didn't like me," he reasoned. "I came in a popular second."

"Oh, George has got it bad," Laura joked with friends. "He really wants to run for something again, but he doesn't want to look like he's riding on his father's coattails." George was not shy about his intentions. "I'm getting back in the game," he would say. "I've just got to pick the right moment. It's all in the timing."

For the time being, he coached Little League, taught Sunday School at his wife's church, First Methodist, and spoke before local organizations like the United Way and the Rotary, Lions, and Kiwanis clubs. The mangled syntax for which he would become famous was already much in evidence, as he substituted the word "inebriating" for "intoxicating" ("I found the whole campaign experience inebriating") and "tenants" for "tenets" ("Those are their tenants, but I want them to accept our tenants").

Nor was he about to give up his reputation as Midland's worst-dressed citizen. When the Vice President came to town to give a speech, W. showed up in a shirt that was so wrinkled that his friend Don Evans refused to let him be seen in it. Evans literally gave W. the neatly pressed dress shirt off his back—and the color-coordinated tie that went with it.

Less than two months after the inauguration, Laura was at home doing housework when the phone rang. It was W., calling from work. "The president's been shot," he told her. "Turn on the TV." Over the next few hours, a nervous George W. waited by the phone to see if Reagan would pull through—or if, for the worst possible reason, his father was about to accede to the presidency. Ironically, the Vice President had been in Texas when Reagan was shot, and immediately flew back to Washington aboard Air Force Two. Throughout the flight, Poppy called Barbara to reassure her that everything was going to be fine.

But W. and Laura could only watch the television coverage and wonder with the rest of the nation if Ronald Reagan was still capable of running the country. When Big George did finally call Midland to say it looked as if the President would make a full recovery, W. and Laura breathed a sigh of relief.

By the spring of 1981, George W. and Laura confronted a heartbreaking problem shared by millions of couples across the nation. For three years they had been trying without success to conceive a child. "When George and I married," Laura said, "we wanted to have a lot of children—and then we didn't." Remembering her own mother's difficulties—the miscarriages that left Laura an only child—Laura blamed herself. The couple's infertility problem "has got to be my fault," she confided to friends in Midland. "Look at the size of George's family, and then look at mine. I guess it's hereditary . . ."

George and Laura consulted a number of fertility experts, but doctors finally told them that—while they could not rule out the possibility—it was highly unlikely that Laura would ever become pregnant. The news plunged her into a state of depression; Laura became so unhappy that she avoided walking down the baby aisle of the supermarket because, she said, "it was just too sad."

The Bushes were only the latest in a growing number of prosperous young Midland couples turning to adoption. Six of their closest friends—the Youngers, the Evanses, and the O'Neills—had adopted children from the Gladney home in Fort Worth. Laura's parents had also visited Gladney when she was a little girl, but ultimately decided not to adopt.

That spring of 1981, George W. and Laura grudgingly came to the conclusion that, at age thirty-five and after three years of trying, Laura was not going to become pregnant. So they, too, made the long drive to Fort Worth and the Gladney adoption home. They filled out all the requisite applications, supplied their financial statements, and had friends send in letters of recommendation.

In late May, the Gladney home called to say that the Bushes had just cleared another hurdle in their quest to adopt a child. Now all that remained was for a representative to visit the Bushes in Midland to make sure that their home was suitable for a small child.

No sooner was a date for the visit set than Laura's doctor called with the news that she was pregnant. Their first call was to Laura's parents; their second call was to the Vice President's official residence on the grounds of the seventy-seven-acre U.S. Naval Observatory in Washington. Bush then called the Gladney home with the happy news, although he was careful to keep their options open. Pending the birth of their own healthy baby, they stressed that they were simply putting their adoption plans "on hold."

Laura's pregnancy, coming at a time when the Bushes were resigned to never having children of their own, was "nothing short of a miracle," W. said. They were in for another surprise when they went for Laura's first sonogram that summer. "Here's the baby," the obstetrician said, using a pencil to outline the silhouette of the baby. Then the doctor squinted at the screen. "Oh, wait a minute. There are *two* babies, two beautiful babies." George, of course, promptly dissolved in tears. This time, the usually unflappable Laura joined him. The next morning, Laura opened her front door and was handed two dozen red roses. It came with a card: "From the father of twins."

Laura, who had seen her mother suffer through miscarriage after miscarriage, was not about to take things for granted. Nor was she willing to tempt fate by buying baby clothes or a crib for the twins, who were due to arrive shortly before Christmas. "Whenever I went to the grocery store," she later recalled, "I avoided the aisle with diapers and baby items. I just didn't want to get my hopes up."

As it turned out, she had good reason to be cautious. From the first trimester, Laura's doctors warned her that hers was a high-risk pregnancy. By her sixth month, they told Laura that she was in the preliminary stages of toxemia, a disorder that often causes blurred vision, seizures, pulmonary edema (fluid in the lungs), and kidney and liver damage. In severe cases, toxemia, also known as preeclampsia, could result in the death of the mother as well as the babies.

Worried that traveling of any kind might trigger a miscarriage, Laura declined to make the usual summer pilgrimage to Kennebunkport. "But you go ahead, George," she insisted. "I'll be fine." W. flew to Maine to see the rest of the clan, but returned the next day. He did not, he later said, want "to be away from Laura and our growing little babies."

That September Laura's physicians, fearing that she might deliver prematurely, confined their patient to bed. Nevertheless, the following month she developed full-blown toxemia. With her life and those of her unborn children in the balance, Laura was rushed to Baylor Hospital in Dallas, where Laura's uncle was a surgeon and where they believed they would receive the most sophisticated neonatal care. There were still seven weeks to go before the babies were due to arrive. Any further delay, the doctors told Laura and W., could pose a serious threat to her life.

W., terrified that he might lose his wife, urged her to follow the doctors' advice. But Laura insisted on holding off for just a while longer. "These babies," she told him, "are going to be born healthy. They will stay with me until they're big enough."

"She wanted to give our babies the best possible chance for survival," said W., who stayed at a hotel across the street from the hospital. "She was heroic. There was an unbelievable will to protect the children. I remember to this day how confident I became because of her. She's a determined woman."

W. returned home shortly before Thanksgiving, leaving Laura behind in Dallas. He was on the phone to her constantly, and when he wasn't, W. sought reassurance from friends. "That was a very emotional time for George," Regan Gammon said. "He was very worried about Laura." In fact, Gammon added, "It was probably harder on George than it was on Laura." So much so that, on more than one occasion, W. broke down in tears while describing Laura's battle to friends.

"There was a time," Laura later conceded, "we weren't sure" both babies would survive. "She held out for as long as she possibly could," W. marveled. "She was determined to have these girls."

Then, after two weeks in a hospital bed at Baylor, Laura finally agreed that it was time. Laura's doctor called George W. "You're having your babies tomorrow," he said.

"Are you sure? It's five weeks early," W. said.

"Well," the doctor replied, "unless you want your wife's kidneys to fail . . ."

W. rushed to Dallas, and was in the operating room at 10 A.M. on November 25, 1981, when their fraternal twins were delivered by cesarean section. They were named after their grandmothers— Barbara Pierce, at five pounds four ounces, and Jenna Welch at four pounds twelve ounces. Again, Dad wept for joy. "I witnessed it all. It was beautiful—the most thrilling moment of my life," he later said.

What made it especially thrilling was Laura's steely determination that, in her husband's words, "these children will come to be. It was such a resolute, powerful statement of motherhood. When the babies came and they were healthy and she was healthy, it was a fabulous moment." For George, this would be one of the defining moments in their marriage. "She loves our daughters more than anything," he said. "She would lay her life down for them, and nearly did at birth."

George W. got on the phone to his parents and, weeping, announced that they had "two beautiful girls." Then, still crying, he called Harold and Jenna Welch with the news. The girls were scarcely two hours old when a reporter called to check on the health of the Vice President's newest grandchildren. A photograph of W., wearing hospital scrubs and holding his newborn daughters, ran in the papers the following day. "They held their first press conference," George W. later cracked, "two hours after they were born."

They also experienced their first security alert. Hospital personnel had spotted a suspicious-looking character prowling Laura's floor, but the man vanished before he could be apprehended. The Vice President's son, worried that the intruder might pose a threat to his wife and daughters, phoned his friend Joe O'Neill and asked if his old Midland pal would do him a favor. "My dad had a helicopter," O'Neill said, "so we sent it to Dallas and George, Laura, and the girls were airlifted out of there."

Not surprisingly, Laura would later describe the birth of the twins as a pivotal event in their lives. "I was thirty-five when I finally had Barbara and Jenna," she said, "so we never took our children for granted. Ever."

From the very beginning, Harold and Jenna Welch would be a constant presence in their granddaughters' lives. While Jenna did not want to bother her daughter as she coped with the new arrivals, Grandpa Harold had no such compunction. He showed up every morning at 11 A.M. just as Laura was putting the babies down for a nap. "Are the girls awake?" he would ask in a booming voice, and then spend an hour doting on them. Six weeks after they were born, the girls had two more special visitors: the Vice President and his wife.

The new parents employed a nurse to help out during the first few months, but W. made a point of learning how to change diapers, give baths, and heat up the bottles for their 2 A.M. feeding. Still, they had their hands "more than full," as Dad put it. The babies cried incessantly, and to try and quiet them, Dad would pace around the house with one cradled in each arm, making faces, and singing the only song he knew that might do for a child—the Yale Fight Song ("Bulldog, Bulldog, Bow Wow Wow . . .").

"He actually got up in the middle of the night and fed the babies with me and changed their diapers," Laura later said. "One thing about having twins is you need a little bit of extra help." From the beginning, W. gloried in being a hands-on dad while Laura relished what she called the "luxury" of being a stay-at-home mom. "It's so perfect, the symmetry, with one baby for each of you to hold," she gushed. More often than not, however, it was Laura who balanced the girls on each hip while her husband was at the office trying to find a way to make Arbusto solvent.

At first, the new parents would take them on exhausting stroller rides around the neighborhood in the hope that they would nod off. After finally putting them to bed, they then moved stealthily through the house, trying not to make a sound or movement that might set them off. Often, nights were spent in the garden, where Laura pulled weeds or planted bulbs while W. filled her in over a beer on what had transpired in the oil business that day. Other times, when W. was working late or out of town, Laura would work in the garden alone. "I would still have a few hours of light left after they went to bed," she said. At one point she was kneeling in the garden, the girls were sound asleep in their room, and Laura thought to herself, "This is the life."

W.'s modus operandi as a dad was a familiar one. As soon as he returned from work, the tactile George W. would wrestle with the girls on the living room floor, tickle them, toss them in the air, make an endless variety of faces and sounds. Every night they read to the girls—children's books like *Goodnight, Moon* and *Hop on Pop*, which they did with gusto whenever he read it to them.

For Laura, the mornings were best. From the time they were infants, Mom and Dad would each retrieve one of the babies from her crib and then snuggle with them in bed. As they grew older, Laura and W. would be lying in bed with the papers spread out when suddenly the girls would bolt into the room and pile into bed with them. "Those were the happiest times," Laura said, "just having those babies and the luxury of time together."

That luxury would soon become a thing of the past as W. struggled to make his mark in the West Texas oil patch. In 1982, he renamed Arbusto "Bush Exploration," and set out to take the company public. Bush Exploration raised $4.67 million, but returned only $1.55 million of that to its investors. Going public, W. eventually conceded, was "a bad mistake."

By late 1983, as oil prices continued to nose-dive, Bush Exploration was on the verge of collapse. "George started looking seriously for someone to bail him out," said one of his closest friends. "It sure as hell didn't hurt that his father was Vice President of the United States."

Spectrum 7, a successful oil investment fund run by fellow Yalie and baseball fanatic Bill DeWitt Jr., came to W.'s rescue in early 1984. Spectrum 7 acquired Bush Exploration, and "Junior" was named chairman of the fund in exchange for an annual salary of $75,000 and more than one million shares of stock.

After eighteen months with Junior at the helm, Spectrum 7 also began to founder. Tom Dickey, a young geologist who worked for Bush, popped into W.'s office one day and found him with his cowboy boots propped up on his desk, staring out the window. Dickey—dubbed "Total Depth" because his initials happened to go with the oil drilling term—was looking for a little encouragement. But Junior had none to give. "I don't know where the hell this is all going," he said. "Dickey, you need to get out of here. You need to go where there's some *action*."

Clearly, it was W. who felt frustrated, trapped, overcome by the need for action. Laura offered a sympathetic ear. Once the girls were tucked into bed, the Vice President's son would unburden himself to Laura over a stiff drink. And then another. As these evenings wore on, he became louder and more agitated. Sometimes, Laura would have to remind him that the girls were asleep, and he would quiet down. But with each passing month, George was drinking more and more, and Laura started to confide in friends that he had a drinking problem.

George W.'s fondness for alcohol-fueled good times was well-documented. Just because he was now the happily married, church-going father of twins, the Bombastic One was not about to change his ways entirely. He was still wearing those loafers with the Scotch-taped tassels, still dawdling when it came time to pay the check, and still playing the role of good-time Charlie to the hilt.

W. never missed the three-day-long "Wildcatter" golf tournament thrown each year by the Midland Country Club ("Seventy-two hours of open bar!"). There were several events, including a costume party that W. insisted on attending. One year his friends shook their heads in amazement when George showed up wearing a Nixon mask and holding his fingers up in the victory sign—a bizarre choice given the fact that his father had risked his own political future defending the embattled ex-president. Things could get worse, of course, and did: At another Wildcatter costume party he arrived as a diaper-clad Mahatma Gandhi. "He kept doing this pretty terrible Indian accent," said one partygoer, "but I got the impression he really didn't know who Gandhi was, and why his being drunk and practically naked might be seen as offensive to some people."

Even though he was a heartbeat away from the White House, Big

George could still squirm when someone accosted him with another story about Junior's antics. When his Yale roommate Ted Livingston got married, W. had rounded up several fellow ushers to toss the groom and the fathers of the bride and groom into the pool. At a reception years later, Livingston's father shook hands with Vice President Bush. "Your son once threw me into a swimming pool," he said.

"That sounds like George," the elder Bush replied wearily.

These days, however, W. was not exactly in a celebratory mood. It seemed that, in an effort to keep Spectrum 7 afloat, the Vice President's son had personally schmoozed and cajoled and squeezed every Bush family contact in the country by 1986. Still, Spectrum 7 teetered on the verge of bankruptcy. Finally, Harken Energy, a Texas oil company that specialized in buying up small companies that were on the ropes, agreed to purchase Spectrum 7. In return, W. was paid $600,000 worth of Harken shares, and a salary of $120,000 as a consultant.

"It's obvious why they kept George Bush," Harken founder Phil Kendrick told *U.S. News & World Report*. "Just the fact that he's there gives them instant credibility."

By this time, however, W. was equally focused on his father's bid to succeed Ronald Reagan in the White House. The entire family was summoned to Washington in the spring of 1985 to meet the men and women who had been selected to run Big George's presidential campaign. W. was wary of them all. He claimed he wanted to be certain they were there "to help elect a great man as president, not to make themselves look good."

W. first took aim at Lee Atwater, the brash, flamboyant take-no-prisoners strategist handpicked to manage Dad's campaign. "How do we know we can trust you?" W. asked flatly. Atwater suggested W. move to Washington to keep an eye on him.

South Carolina–bred Atwater and the man he would call Junior quickly discovered that they were almost frighteningly alike—two outspoken, flamboyant, hard-drinking, womanizing (as W. had been before his marriage), brash-to-the-point-of-rude good-ole-boy politicos. Atwater was a practitioner of killer politics. Later in the campaign, he would concoct television spots blaming the Democratic nominee, Massachusetts Governor Michael Dukakis, for the furlough of convicted African-American rapist and murderer Willie Horton.

Not surprisingly, Atwater was not exactly the class act Barbara Bush initially had in mind to run her husband's campaign. He was a brazen self-promoter, someone who had no compunction about doing interviews in his underwear and liberally punctuating his language with words like "cocksucker" and "motherfucker." Laura shared her mother-in-law's view at first, until W. convinced them both that he was the kind of political streetfighter they needed to get the job done.

Ultimately, Barbara and W. would come to be regarded as two of the most feared figures in the Bush camp. The "Silver Fox," as George W. called his mother, became enraged when a campaign operative made a mistake, leaked information to the press, or took credit for the candidate's ideas. W., meanwhile, was the self-described "loyalty enforcer" who would launch into a tirade if there was the faintest sign that someone might be losing enthusiasm or, worse yet, doubted the "greatness" of the elder Bush.

Paradoxically, at around the same time he was giving his blessing to Atwater's cutthroat tactics—tactics Atwater would himself apologize for years later when he was dying of a brain tumor—W. was finding religion. In the summer of 1985, Laura, who had become increasingly concerned about her husband's drinking, hatched a plan with her in-laws to bring W. closer to God.

The elder Bushes' motives may have had little to do with modifying their son's behavior. In his efforts to build a winning coalition, the Vice President had failed to secure the unequivocal backing of the increasingly important Christian Right. Doug Wead, an Amway executive and Assembly of God Evangelist with close ties to Jim and Tammy Faye Bakker—among other questionable characters—would be given the task of forging a bridge between Bush and the evangelical movement. His handler: George W.

But before he could be handed this formidable job, it only seemed appropriate that W. should undergo a conversion of his own. In July, the Vice President and Mrs. Bush invited the Reverend Billy Graham to spend a weekend at Kennebunkport. George W. watched the legendary Graham deliver a sermon at St. Ann's by the Sea, then joined his parents and Graham for lunch on the patio overlooking the Atlantic. That evening, Graham sat by the fire and answered questions about God and faith and sin and redemption put to him by the Bush clan. George W. wanted to know more; the two men were locked in conversation as they strolled for hours along the beach.

That weekend, W. would later write, "Reverend Graham planted a mustard seed in my soul." George had always attended church, and had even taught Sunday School. But what the devoutly Yankee Bushes had always practiced was a kind of Christianity Lite— sanitized and rote and social and basically part of one's weekly routine. The weekend in Kennebunkport changed all that, W. would later insist. During that weekend with Graham in Maine, he would write, "my faith took on new meaning . . . I would recommit my heart to Jesus Christ."

Conveniently, W. became a vocal born-again Christian just as he was masterminding the effort to lure evangelicals into the Bush fold. Although he joined a men's Bible study group and began seriously studying the scriptures that summer of 1985, George W. gave no outward sign of having become a changed man. He continued to drink too much, to curse like a Texas roustabout, and to fly into purple-veined rages when a campaign underling made a mistake or a member of the press criticized his father.

Years later, W. would proudly agree with one journalist's description of him as the "Roman candle" in the family—"quick to spark, and that's true when it comes to defending my dad . . . I'm a fierce warrior for George Bush. And if that ruffles people's feathers, so be it." But W.'s zeal, undoubtedly heightened by an excess of alcohol, led him to behavior that, according to one fellow churchgoer, seemed "decidedly un-Christian."

In April 1986, the *Washingtonian* magazine ran a piece giving prognostications from various journalists about who might make up the tickets for the national elections in 1988. One of those asked, *Wall Street Journal* Washington Bureau Chief Al Hunt, predicted that former Reagan Housing and Urban Development Secretary Jack Kemp and Indiana senator Richard Lugar would square off against Colorado senator Gary Hart and Virginia senator (and LBJ son-in-law) Chuck Robb. Hunt was one of sixteen pundits who predicted the more youthful, charismatic Kemp would be the GOP nominee— not George Bush.

At a Mexican restaurant in Dallas, Hunt and his wife, television correspondent Judy Woodruff, were dining with their four-year-old son when a man started making his way toward them. He was clearly intoxicated—red-faced and colliding with tables and other diners as he approached the Hunt family's table. As the man came closer, Hunt finally recognized the Vice President's son, someone he barely knew and could not recall even seeing on the campaign trail.

The little boy's eyes widened as the man pointed a finger at his father and began shouting. "You no good fucking son of a bitch!" George W. screamed while other diners looked on in shock. "I will never fucking forget what you wrote!"

For the next minute or so, W. stayed at the table, continuing his diatribe against the story in the *Washingtonian*. But Hunt could not imagine what could have provoked such rage. He had not even mentioned the elder Bush in the *Washingtonian* article, much less criticized him. With that, W. weaved his way through the restaurant and out to the parking lot.

When word of W.'s drunken tirade against two of the country's most respected journalists and their four-year-old son reached Laura, she was livid. It was only the latest in a series of embarrassing public moments and wounding private ones that would make her doubt her marriage.

At restaurants and bars and in the homes of friends, George W. periodically knocked back enough beers or whiskeys to trigger the switch to Mr. Snide. This transformation occasionally happened at the Midland Country Club, which, ironically, was located on Highway 349 just past the site of Laura's fatal car crash. "He would just get a little too loud, and the jokes would get more off-color," a longtime friend observed. "Sometimes he'd do silly stuff. One time I saw him stick chopsticks up his nose. He loved to wiggle his ears, make those faces of his, that sort of thing. Just his brand of humor. You know he thought he was a riot, and you were inclined to overlook it."

Family friend Robert McCleskey thought it had less to do with the amount of alcohol George consumed than it did with his personality. "He didn't need to be drinking to get all excited about something. But when he drank . . . Let's just say he lacked tact when he drank. He'd say things without thinking first." Concurred Joe

O'Neill: "It was all pretty harmless, really. I know lots of people who drank more than George did. Sure, he'd have a few beers and get . . . exuberant. But that was all part of the West Texas culture."

Perhaps, but there were times when W.'s drunken behavior seemed anything but "harmless." There was, even his closest friends concede, a "tendency to blow" whenever W. felt someone had betrayed him. "Oh, if he was pissed off at you about something," said one Midlander, "George let you know it, all right. Especially if he had had a few."

"Once he got started," his friend Don Evans acknowledged, "he couldn't quit, didn't shut it off." If they were out together in public when W. had had too much to drink, Laura took the wheel. But Laura was not always there to be the designated driver; W. was often out of town on business or drumming up support for his father over long liquor dinners. Sometimes he drove to and from the airport in rental cars or automobiles that had been provided for him. "There were some close calls in those days," he confided to a friend about the times he drove after a few drinks. "You look back and think, how in the hell did I keep from getting killed." Or killing someone else.

To be sure, George's binges were of short duration. Because he got up every morning at 6 A.M. to run three or four miles, W. was almost always in bed by 10 P.M. if not earlier. That meant that if he was out at a restaurant or at a social function, he invariably left by 9 P.M. "We are always," Laura said, "the first to arrive and the first to leave."

Nor did W. start drinking until the sun was over the yardarm. "George never was a drinker who drank during the day," Laura said of her husband. "He never did. He didn't have a Bloody Mary at lunch—ever."

W. took particular care not to drink to excess in the company of his in-laws. "He would come over and have a drink before dinner with my husband," Jenna Welch said. "He certainly didn't drink too much around us. We never saw him out of control."

But there were times throughout the first nine years of their marriage when Laura worried that her husband *was* losing control. She desperately wanted him to quit drinking, and begged him to on many occasions. Laura did not make the request constantly, she later insisted, "but every once in a while, after some night that wasn't particularly great."

In the early years of their marriage, those "not particularly great nights" sometimes ended with W. passing out. "Laura is a very patient woman," George would say of her reluctance to criticize his drinking during this period.

But as the twins grew older, it became increasingly obvious to them that something was wrong with Daddy. Sometimes they would be awakened by the sound of their father's booming voice as he reeled about the house before collapsing on the living room couch. Although he was never violent during these booze-fueled episodes— incidents that a distraught Laura relayed to several confidantes—his bleary eyes and slurred speech confused the children and infuriated Laura. Although several acquaintances would later insist that they seldom saw W. drunk, Laura herself conceded, "He was wild when he drank too much."

As much as the couple's friends sympathized with Laura's plight, they were reluctant to interfere. One who did was Spectrum 7 President Paul Rea. With Laura's encouragement, Rea gently mentioned to George W. that perhaps his drinking was getting a little out of hand.

But W. turned a deaf ear to both his wife and his colleague. By the fall of 1985, as the children were about to enter nursery school, Laura was desperate. "George is pretty impulsive and pretty much does everything to excess," his wife conceded. "Drinking is not one of the good things to do to excess." She confronted him on an almost daily basis about his drinking, but to no avail.

According to W.'s cousin Elsie Walker, Laura "loves George's fun side, but after a while she got tired of George's edges that came from the drinking. He was a riot, but afterward, when you're older, that can wear thin. And she would never hold back whatever she felt."

Finally, in late 1985, she delivered an ultimatum to her husband: "It's either me or Jim Beam." Laura would later deny that things had reached such a crisis point in their marriage, and a few friends suggested that confrontation of this sort just wasn't her style. "I'm sure that Laura didn't like it," said her friend Nancy Weiss. "I'm sure there were plenty of discussions about it . . . Laura's not the type to say, 'You better or else,' and George is not the type to accept that kind of challenge."

But in fact, the ultimatum had become her mantra. "She said it to me maybe fifty times," one friend said. Agreed another: "Laura was dead serious. She is a strong woman. I mean, she put up with his drinking for *ten years* without whining. But she was obviously upset over how George's drinking was affecting their daughters then and what it was going to do to Jenna and Barbara in the future. She told me she was going to take the girls and leave him if he kept it up."

One evening in June 1986, an inebriated George W. became so loud that he inadvertently woke up his daughters. Usually Laura would wait until the next morning to confront him about his drinking. But this time she waited until the girls were asleep to sit her husband down in the kitchen and, Laura would tell one of her closest friends, "really let him have it." W. sat silently as his wife told him yet again that the decision was his: either their marriage or the bottle.

"This," Laura told George one final time, "has got to stop!"

George studied her face for a moment, his mouth twisted in that all-too-familiar smirk. Then he rose slowly, ambled over to the kitchen counter—and poured himself another bourbon.

George was on the road to nowhere at age forty.

—*John Ellis, George's cousin*

He was ready to be rescued.

—*Laura*

Laura's quiet, but she accomplishes a great deal with that quietness.

—*Barbara Bush*

She played a huge role in every aspect of his life. Before he quit drinking, she put her foot down. She's a gentle person, but the reality is she's got a strong side that's important to George.

—*Marvin Bush*

She's serene. He's very . . . rambunctious.

—*Katharine Armstrong Idsal,*
friend

He makes life more exciting for me.

—*Laura*

1

2

3

4

Two future presidents (*opposite*): Dad was still a junior at Yale when "Georgie"
was born in 1946. Four years later, the family moved to Texas,
where Georgie quickly became comfortable on horseback. Barbara (*above left*)
made sure Georgie wore his cowboy boots when grandparents Dorothy
and Senator Prescott Bush paid a visit to Midland in 1950.

5

After the death of his little sister Robin, Georgie made it his mission to cheer up his grief-stricken parents. In 1954, Georgie posed with Jeb— forty-six years before the historic presidential elections in which both brothers would play decisive roles.

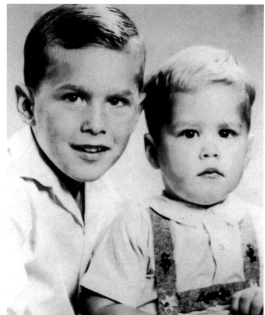

6

At age twelve, Georgie proudly accompanied his dad, then CEO of
Zapata-Offshore, to the christening of yet another Zapata oil rig.

8

As Head Cheerleader at Andover,
George W. shouted slogans and
wisecracks through a giant
megaphone, took a call while his
fellow cheerleaders crammed into
a phone booth, and reenacted
one of his famous naps in the
school library.

9

10

George W. was one of the most popular undergraduates at Yale in 1968, but he was eager to "get back to Texas and away from the snobs." His well-deserved nickname at Yale: "The Lip."

11

12

George W. spent the Vietnam War flying F-102A Delta Dagger Interceptor jet fighters in the Texas Air National Guard.

13

George W., a thirty-one-year-old bachelor when he started the race, talked to West Texas oil workers in 1977 while seeking his party's nomination for Congress.

14

Two-year-old Laura took her tricycle for a
spin, then smiled for the camera in 1948.
At age ten, she posed with Mom and the
mailbox in front of their new home.

15

16

17

18

At sixteen, Laura sported a Patty Duke hairdo for a school photo and for a portrait taken with her parents, Jenna and Harold Welch. Later that year—and less than two months after the November 1963 car crash that changed her life forever—Laura sat on her living room floor opening Christmas presents.

19

20

21

Laura and her friend Candy Poage packed up for their sophomore year
at Dallas's Southern Methodist University in September 1965.
Three years later, Laura was among SMU's smiling graduates.

22

The happy couple on the dance floor. Three weeks after they met,
George asked Laura to marry him.

23

Moments after tying the knot in Midland on November 5, 1977,
the bride and groom posed outside the church with the Bush clan (*from left*):
brother Marvin, sister Doro, brother Neil, Jeb and his wife Columba,
Barbara Bush, George H.W. Bush, and matriarch Dorothy Walker Bush.

Newlyweds George and Laura campaigned from the flatbed of a pickup truck in the sweltering summer of 1978; he made sure she was a major part of his campaign literature.

George Bush for Congress

ON NOVEMBER 7,
VOTE FOR WEST TEXAS.
VOTE FOR
George Bush for Congress

Dear Voters,
Laura and I would like to take this opportunity to thank you for the many kindnesses you've shown us during my campaign for the Congress.
You've listened to me, and you've told me what you think. And hundreds of you have actively worked in my campaign.
I am very grateful to all of you.
During the past twelve months I have told you how much I want to represent you in the Congress. I mean that. I know I can do a good job.
Again, our thanks.

George W. Bush

26

Smiles during a Bush family Christmas at Kennebunkport concealed George and Laura's difficulties in conceiving a child. Standing (*from left*): sister Doro, Mom and Dad, Jeb's wife Columba, and Laura and George. Seated: Marvin (holding Jeb's daughter Noelle), Jeb (holding his son George P.), and Neil.

27

"He's brought a lot of excitement to my life," Laura said of her husband, here with her during one of their frequent visits to Maine.

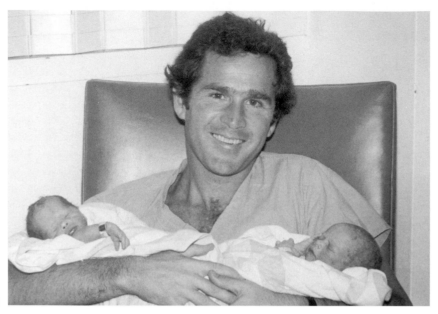

28

After a life-threatening pregnancy, the twins—Barbara and Jenna—
arived via cesarean section on November 25, 1981.
"She was heroic," George said of Laura's battle with toxemia.

29

Laura held Barbara, and George dandled Jenna on his knee,
while Vice President Bush spoke at a Texas rally during the
1984 Reagan-Bush reelection campaign.

30

31

Temperamentally, Barbara (*top,* on Laura's lap at age four) more closely resembles
her mother while Jenna favors Dad. When they posed in Kennebunkport
four years later, the girls shifted sides—but still remained
closest to the parent they were most like.

George W. was his dad's self-described "Loyalty Enforcer" in the White House. The senior Bush's bitter defeat at the hands of Bill Clinton in 1992 left Laura wondering why her husband would want to "put himself through that sort of pain" by running for office.

33

34

Barbara and Jenna shared their mother's early reservations about Dad seeking office. After he decided to run for Texas governor in 1994, W. got an affectionate squeeze from his twelve-year-olds. Later during the campaign, they challenged Dad to a water pistol competition at the Texas State Fair in Dallas.

35

After George was sworn in for a second term as Texas governor on
January 19, 1999, he and Laura rode in the inaugural parade.

36

Jenna and Barbara applauded as their mother gave the kickoff address at the
2000 Republican National Convention in Philadelphia. Each had already completed
a year in college: Jenna at the University of Texas and Barbara at Yale.

After securing the GOP nomination for president, George and Laura
were engulfed by balloons as they waved to convention delegates.

38

39

40

The candidate and his wife
shared a private moment on
the tarmac after arriving for
a campaign appearance in
Dayton, Ohio.

41

George and Laura airborne. When they weren't on the road together,
W. often raced home to Texas to spend weekends with his wife.

42

"Now, Mrs. Bush . . ." Clowning around before a TV interview in the
governor's mansion, George puts a bemused Laura in the hot seat.

43

Laura helps untangle the GOP presidential candidate from streamers
during a rally at Missouri State University in Joplin.

44

At the governor's mansion in Austin, George and Laura go over plans
for their 4,000-square-foot ranch house in Crawford, Texas.
Laura was adamant that the house "fit into the landscape."

45

Campaigning in Florida just two days before the 2000 presidential election, George clearly enjoys what his wife is telling him on the flight from Miami to Tampa.

46

The Bushes celebrated W.'s apparent victory on election night, but the smiles quickly vanished when the results in Florida were challenged. George would be declared the winner—thirty-five days later.

Only seconds after being sworn in, an intensely emotional moment between the forty-third president and his first lady. Daughter Jenna beams at right.

Oops. At one of the nine inaugural balls, President Bush grins as Jenna quickly adjusts the wayward bodice of her gown.

49

Usually the more stoic of the two, Laura wipes away a tear during the February 19, 2001, dedication ceremony for a memorial to the victims of the Oklahoma City bombing. The 1995 bombing killed 169 people.

50

At the Austin Community Court, nineteen-year-old Jenna pleaded no contest to charges of alcohol possession. Much to their parents' chagrin, the Bush twins made headlines after minor scrapes with the law.

George and Laura unwind at the Western White House—their 1,583-acre
spread in Crawford. "There are very few places," George said of his ranch,
"where a president can get kind of lost."

The President could not mask his shock—even for a classroom full of schoolchildren—when White House Chief of Staff Andy Card told him that a second plane had hit the World Trade Center. "America," Card whispered, "is under attack."

52

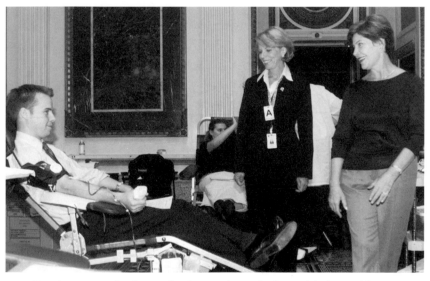

53

Less than twenty-four hours after the terrorist attacks, Laura visited a special room set aside at the White House for those who wished to donate blood.

54

Concern etched on their faces, Laura and George comforted a family member of one of the victims of the Pentagon attack during a visit to the Washington Hospital Center on September 13.

55

An emotional George Bush spoke at the annual National Fallen Firefighters tribute in Maryland three weeks after 9/11.

56

A week after Operation Enduring Freedom drove the Taliban from Afghanistan,
George and Laura were cheered by soldiers at Fort Campbell, Kentucky.
A few hours later, the First Lady and the Commander-in-Chief ate
Thanksgiving dinner with the troops.

57

"It gets lonely around here," Laura said of the post-9/11 cancellation of
White House tours during Christmas 2001. Still, Boston schoolchildren
were invited to the East Room to hear the President read
Clement Moore's *A Visit from St. Nicholas.*

Returning to Washington after spending the Easter 2002 holidays
at their ranch, Laura and her mother, Jenna Welch, watch as
the President tries to rein in Barney the Scottish terrier.

59

Just hours after a routine colonoscopy, the President takes a brisk four-mile walk
at Camp David with Laura, brother Marvin (*second from left*),
Chief of Staff Andy Card, and Card's wife Kathleene.

60

Spot the springer spaniel watched as George and Laura went
their separate ways on the South Lawn of the White House.
The war on terrorism, said one friend, has "energized them both."

5

They were about to turn forty, so George and Laura decided to celebrate with friends facing the same milestone. On the weekend of Don Evans's birthday, the Evanses—Susie and Don—joined the Bushes and Joe and Jan O'Neill at Colorado Springs' Broadmoor Hotel. With its three championship golf courses and palatial seven-hundred-room hotel, the three-thousand-acre resort nestled at the foot of the Rocky Mountains had been luring kings, prime ministers, presidents, and movie stars since before the turn of the century. It had also long been a cherished vacation destination for the Bush family.

The three couples made plans to visit one of Colorado's most popular tourist attractions, the chapel at the U.S. Air Force Academy, on Sunday morning. But first, they partied. As the evening wore on, W. became louder and more profane and—though he was convinced he had never been so funny—indefensibly obnoxious. Laura, more exasperated than ever with her husband's loutish behavior when he was under the influence, excused herself and went to bed. George remained in the bar for hours, stumbling down the corridor to their hotel room not long after midnight.

Incredibly, W. managed to pull himself together enough to go on his customary run early the next morning. But when he returned to his room, Bush could summon the energy to do little else. Nor were his friends, all suffering from the same head-pounding, stomach-churning hangover, in any condition to follow through on their plans to visit the Air Force Academy Chapel.

"The next morning," Joe O'Neill allowed, "nobody felt great. It was one of those things where it was fun at the time, but the next day you say to yourself, 'What were we thinking?' "

It was then, after some considerable time spent on his hands and knees in the bathroom, that W. made the abrupt decision to stop cold turkey. "I'm quitting drinking," he told Laura, who had heard it all before. "I'm not sure she believed me, at first," he allowed, "but I can be pretty stubborn about myself." Besides, this time there was a difference: "This time," George W. said, "I meant it."

Why then? "I'm not sophisticated enough to find out if I had a clinical problem," W. would later say. "And I can't say there was something significant that happened to make me change my life." His stated reason for quitting: "The best explanation is to say that alcohol was beginning to compete for my affections—compete for my affections with my wife and my family. It was beginning to crowd out my energy and I decided to quit."

Even more than the pain he was causing his wife and children, W. seemed obsessed with the notion that alcohol was somehow robbing him of energy. "I'm a high-energy person," he said, "and alcohol competes with your energy. It really does, so I quit."

But there were others close to the Bushes who felt that this explanation was designed to conceal the fact that George W. quit to save his marriage. "His marriage was falling apart," one friend insisted, "and he cared about his girls. That's what turned him around."

At first, Laura was skeptical. She had heard similar promises before. But over the coming months, she was impressed with his ability to remain firmly on the wagon. Although he did not appear to have the strength of will to moderate his alcohol intake, Laura insisted that her husband was "very, very disciplined—he's an incredibly disciplined person, really.

"He just said, 'I'm going to quit,' and he did," Laura went on. "That was it. We joked about it later, saying he got the bar bill and that's why." When friends asked how she got him to change, Laura refused to take credit. "I said I thought he ought to quit drinking," she allowed. "Of course, I told him that. But the person who stopped drinking was George."

For his part, George H. W. Bush, who had worried for years about his son's overindulgence in alcohol, now seemed in denial concerning the true extent of his son's drinking problem. "He was never an alcoholic," Big George said. "He just knows that he can't hold his liquor."

W. was under no illusions about the kind of person he became when he was under the influence. "I would tend to talk too much when drinking," he conceded. "If you're feisty anyway, you don't need any reason to be more feisty." Alcohol, he continued, "magnified aspects of my personality that probably don't need to be larger than they already are . . . I wasn't so funny when I drank. Just ask my wife."

Laura notwithstanding, it was in part because of his deep, worshipful love of his father that George W. finally made the life-altering decision to quit. "I'm afraid I might do something to embarrass my father," he confided to Joe O'Neill. "I just don't want to do anything that could get my dad in trouble."

What most impressed those who knew George was his ability to quit drinking without professional counseling or treatment of any kind. "That was something," Jenna Welch said, "he apparently never even considered."

"He didn't make any big announcements about it or anything like that," said the Bushes' longtime friend Robert McCleskey. "There was no fanfare, no drama. You just sort of gradually noticed that he wasn't holding a beer in his hand anymore. He never made a big deal about it, never even brought it up. When you asked him about it, he said he wasn't drinking anymore and changed the subject."

There was, in W.'s mind, no turning back. "I quit for the rest of my life," Bush said, "and if you catch me drinking, it's not going to be a good sign for your old buddy George." Now W. could share his last remaining addiction with his wife. Both he and Laura were and continued to be unrepentant chain-smokers.

Laura was, in fact, more of a free spirit than she might have seemed on the surface. As part of her own fortieth birthday celebration that year, she ventured out with friends Margie McColl, Regan

Gammon, Jane Ann Fontenot, and Peggy Weiss on a week-long rafting trip through the Grand Canyon. When they were done with the rafting segment of their adventure, the group hiked up from the canyon floor—a grueling ten-mile trek. As they climbed up the steep, narrow trail "it was hot," Weiss remembered, "very hot. Over one hundred degrees. At one point, we were just sort of dizzy, just putting one foot in front of the other. The rest of us complained, but not Laura—never once."

With his $120,000 annual consultant's fee and a net worth of more than one million dollars, W. was free to throw himself into the effort to get his father elected president. In April 1987, George, Laura, and their daughters pulled up stakes, moved to Washington, and settled in a town house on Massachusetts Avenue.

For Laura, the move was wrenching. She had already settled into her life as a housewife and mom—the "traditional women's roles" that she claimed left her "completely satisfied." W.'s wife had joined the PTO, volunteered at the school library, even joined a car pool with other moms in the neighborhood. Laura "set the schedule" for the twins, as Jenna Welch put it, and Dad was occasionally called in "to crack the whip" as chief disciplinarian. Now that George had his drinking under control, Laura said, life seemed "awfully close to perfect."

Yet the move to Washington was what Junior wanted, and Laura was not about to stand in his way. From this point on, Lee Atwater's budding political protégé stayed close to the center of power, working out of the Bush campaign's shabby headquarters at 733 15th Street NW. Although he was the candidate's son, W. was paid five thousand dollars a month plus expenses as a senior adviser. With the door to his office always wide open, George W. leaned back in his chair, put his eel-skin boots up on the desk, and spit wads of chewing tobacco into a styrofoam cup.

As both self-described loyalty enforcer and gatekeeper, George W. vetted all journalists who wished for access to Dad. "Why you?" he would demand. "Give me one reason why I should let you talk with George Bush." It was a way to fend off practitioners of what he called "that goddamned psychobabble crap"—the writers who wanted to delve too deeply into his father's psyche, who sought to explain what it was that "made him tick."

W. quickly impressed his fellow campaign workers with his total commitment to the candidate, his boundless energy, and his easy charm. With the ubiquitous styrofoam cup that served as a spittoon in one hand, he stuck out the other and introduced himself with a down-home twang. He routinely poked fun at his role in the campaign, referring to himself as "Maureen" in a sly reference to President Reagan's somewhat bossy eldest daughter.

Yet he was also the stern disciplinarian who monitored everyone working on the campaign. W. would not hesitate to take a worker aside to tell him he was not pulling his weight. "I'm blessed," Andy Card said of W. then, "that I never got taken to the woodshed."

Once in the spring of 1987, Junior was about to board a plane when he spotted a Bush campaign aide yelling at an airline clerk. Later, as he passed the man seated in first class, Junior confronted him. "Where are you sitting?" the man sputtered. "You should be up here. I'll talk to them for you . . ."

"No, I don't waste taxpayers' money," Junior replied. "I don't waste campaign money. I ride coach." The aide was dismissed not long after.

According to Doug Wead, Junior delighted in "putting people who thought they were big shots in their place." His usual gambit: "Harassing them with wisecracks and booming it out so everyone would hear it."

As his father's gatekeeper, Junior would make a few friends among members of the press. But most would find him abrupt, abrasive, and presumptuous. If an interview or piece was critical of his father or simply not sufficiently flattering, he would not hesitate to confront the offender and, in the words of one observer, "let the expletives fly."

In the summer of 1987, rumors began to circulate that Big George was having an affair with one of his longtime aides. Initially, the campaign decided to ignore the unfounded gossip. But as the drumbeat grew louder, Laura told Junior that it was time "somebody said *something*." Otherwise, she said, people would see the candidate's no comment stance as a tacit admission of guilt.

Before he could take his wife's advice, however, W. bluntly asked his father at a meeting of his top advisers if there was any truth to the rumors. "I knew it was all bullshit, but before I went out there,"

W. said to one friend, "I wanted everybody to hear it from my dad's lips." Junior's cleverly worded denial, which the campaign leaked to *Newsweek,* said: "The answer to the Big A question is N-O." With that, the rumors subsided virtually overnight.

For Junior, the adultery question was easier to handle than the persistent suggestion that his father was weak, limp, an effete preppy elitist—a wimp. When *Newsweek* ran a damaging cover story by staffer Margaret Warner entitled "Fighting the Wimp Factor," Junior exploded. He then blasted Warner over the phone. "This is disgraceful!" he said. "You ought to quit if that's the kind of journalistic integrity you have."

"I was furious," W. conceded—something he would never stop being when it came to the *Newsweek* cover that branded his father a wimp. More than a dozen years later, he said that whenever he thinks about the story, "my blood pressure still goes up."

Another time, Junior watched from the sidelines as one network reporter was questioning the senior Bush's selection of Indiana Senator Dan Quayle as his running mate. As soon as the reporter signed off, Junior ran toward him and then showered him with blistering epithets. The broadcaster just stood in stunned silence as W. vented. When he wasn't scolding journalists, Junior often made known his feelings by simply treating them with contempt. He might respond to a question with "No comment, asshole," or simply employ the patented smirk.

In late 1987, W. was very nearly handed a "Big A" situation of his own to deal with. One of the more attractive women on the campaign staff had been flirting with him for months, and things had heated up to the point that there was actually an office pool on whether she would succeed in seducing him.

When they were on the road together, Bush asked religious right expert Doug Wead to stay with him until late at night in his hotel room. "He wanted everyone to know," Wead said, "that nothing was happening."

Finally, with the door to his office open as usual, W. told the woman off. "I don't want you going around telling people there's something between us, because there isn't," he shouted loud enough to be heard down the hall. "I am a married man, for God's sake."

Shaken and fighting back tears, the woman fled Junior's office.

Moments later, one of the Vice President's top campaign operatives burst into Junior's office. "She's hurt," he told W. "You really hurt her."

"Good, good," Junior answered. "I'm a married man. I'm glad she got the signal."

Laura had known about the woman all along; W. told her before anyone else could. But she claimed she was never worried that he would take the ardent volunteer up on her offer. "Our marriage is based on trust," she told a friend. "I know George is too smart to get caught up in something like that."

That became agonizingly clear to a congressman and a senator who were flying one evening with George W. on a private plane. As the scotch flowed, the two legislators began talking about how hard it was to hide their girlfriends from their wives and the press. Then they began sharing some of the more graphic details of these sexual liaisons. All the while, George W. laughed uproariously and drank ginger ale as the stories got bawdier and bawdier.

Finally, the senator and the congressman turned to W. and waited for him to regale them with stories of his extramarital affairs. "I'm a lucky man," Bush said, "to have Laura."

There was an awkward pause, then the senator lifted up his scotch and soda. "Let's toast Laura!" he said, and with that George and the other men clinked glass in honor of the wife Junior had remained faithful to.

In fact, as dedicated as he was to his dad, Junior was not willing to go on the road if it meant being away from his own family more than two days at a time. Unlike other campaign workers who would be expected to willingly spend weeks, even months away from their families, W. insisted that every two days he be flown home to Washington. If he was in Los Angeles, he would fly home to spend an evening with Laura and the girls, then return to California the next morning.

During these eighteen months based in Washington, Laura, George W., and the twins grew especially close to "Gampy" and "Ganny." The younger Bushes spent every weekend at the Vice President's stately official residence at the U.S. Naval Observatory. They had the same thing for lunch every week—hamburgers—then learned the finer points of tossing horseshoes from the master, Big

George. Into the afternoon, the Bush men would talk about the direction the campaign should take while their wives traded war stories about raising children.

W. and Dad also found time to engage in what they called "aerobic golf"—a version of the game where they dashed from green to golf cart to green in a race to polish off eighteen holes in under two hours. Barbara had been an avid golfer for years, but aerobic golf was not for her. "It's strictly a father-son thing," she explained. More accurately, it was a peculiar approach to the game that satisfied a father's need to crowd as much as possible into his schedule and a son's almost compulsive need to run. Laura, meantime, adhered to the adage that golf in any form was just another way to "spoil a nice walk."

It was during this time that Laura grew particularly close to Barbara, who shared her all-consuming interest in books. Georgie's mom was already planning what she would do if her husband won the presidency. She would use her position, Barbara told her delighted daughter-in-law, as a platform to battle illiteracy in America. In Laura Bush, Bar found an eager protégée.

Laura also came to realize just how much alike W. and his mother were. "His personality comes from Barbara," she concluded. "They both love to needle and they both love to talk."

Conversely, Barbara grew to appreciate what she saw as Laura's "dignified demeanor masking a will of steel." She was also pleased that Laura, like Jeb's wife Columba, made such an effort to become a part of the extended Bush family. "Laura is a very special person," Barbara observed, "and I always felt that being an only child . . . she was amused by us."

There was also plenty of time for the six-year-old twins to spend with their Gampy and Ganny. Often when W. and Laura were out of town campaigning, Barbara and Jenna spent the night at the Vice President's residence. One evening, when Big George was preparing for his second televised debate with Michael Dukakis, little Barbara complained that she could not get to sleep without her stuffed dog Spikey. For over an hour, the Vice President of the United States scoured the mansion before finally locating Spikey and tucking him into bed alongside his granddaughter.

During the last week of the campaign, George W., Laura, and the girls joined the candidate on a final campaign swing through South Bend, Indiana. Since it was Halloween, the twins were allowed to make the trip in costume—Barbara as a vampire and Jenna as a pack of Juicy Fruit gum. Aboard Air Force Two, the girls decided to play a little prank on Gampy, stuffing wads of paper into the plane's toilets. Taking matters into her own hands—literally—Grandma foiled the plot by reaching into the toilets and pulling the paper out herself.

W. was so devoted to the Bushes and what he saw as their legacy that campaign issues were of little interest to him. Loyalty was the only thing that mattered, so much so that during the 1988 campaign there was not a single instance where he advocated one policy over another. "The upshot is," observed journalist Nicholas D. Kristof, that W. "proved immensely talented at steering his ship to avoid shoals and rough seas . . . but sometimes seemed less concerned with precisely where the ship of state was headed."

Junior made no apologies when it came to his blind allegiance to Big George and the family name. "My motivation was," he explained, "he's been a great dad."

Indeed, no sooner had his father won the presidency and started the transition process, than Junior began plotting his return to private life in Texas. "Once his father won," said his Yale buddy Roland W. Betts, "he was very unhappy. He did not want to be there. He was looking for 'what am I going to do next?' "

When he posed the question to his aide Doug Wead, they both decided it might be a good idea to determine what generally became of presidents' children. Wead's researchers took the assignment seriously, and several weeks later handed over a forty-four-page study that was far from encouraging.

According to the report, many presidential children died young, were chronically ill, or at the very least became alcoholics. Many never graduated from college, or had difficulty keeping a job. A total of sixteen had actually managed to make it to Congress, but none were elected governor. John Quincy Adams's son George Washington Adams, burdened by the knowledge that both his father and his grandfather had achieved the ultimate political prize, was believed to have killed himself at the age of twenty-eight.

Like his other close friends, Betts was well aware that Junior— despite the grim news contained in Wead's report on presidential

children—still harbored political aspirations of his own. But ironically, by working so ferociously to put his dad in the Oval Office, the
younger Bush now faced the grim reality that he might never
emerge as his own man. "You need to do something," Betts told his
friend, "to step out of your father's shadow."

He did not have to look far. While he was still immersed in his
father's campaign, Junior had received a call from his old oil partner,
Spectrum 7's Bill DeWitt. One of the things that had brought the
two Yalies together was a shared passion for baseball, and now
DeWitt had a proposition involving the sport they both loved.

The Texas Rangers were up for sale, DeWitt told Junior, and the
owner just happened to be old Bush family pal Ed Chiles. Another
West Texas oil tycoon, it was Chiles who flew W.'s sister Robin and
her parents to New York on his private plane after the little girl was
diagnosed with leukemia.

DeWitt's dad had owned the Cincinnati Reds and the St. Louis
Browns, and now DeWitt saw his own chance—with a little help
from the Bush family ties—to own at least a piece of a major
league team. It was a dream shared by Junior, whose great-uncle
George Herbert Walker had been one of the three owners of the
New York Mets.

First, he ran the idea by Laura. Beyond attending high school
baseball games back in Midland, she was no great fan of the game
when she met her future husband. But W.'s unbridled enthusiasm
for the national pastime soon proved contagious, and before long she
was sitting next to him on the couch watching the games on television, barefoot and munching popcorn as he provided a running
commentary. To Laura, buying the Rangers seemed a perfect opportunity for George to make a not inconsiderable amount of money
doing the thing he most loved. Her simple advice to George: "Go
for it."

Over the next few months leading up to his father's inauguration,
George worked the phones drumming up support from potential
investors. But he still wielded power in Washington as chairman of
the incoming administration's "Scrub Team" (later renamed the
"Silent Committee")—a top-secret task force that made sure that
only the most scrupulously loyal Bush backers were offered jobs in
the new administration.

Her husband had worked so hard to get his father elected that Laura was happy to see him share in the joy of the inauguration. On the eve of the big event, Junior decided to get up at dawn and walk the route of his father's inaugural parade. The streets were eerily empty, and as he walked alone down Pennsylvania Avenue, W. was suddenly overcome with emotion.

The next day, he watched proudly as his father was sworn in as the forty-first President of the United States. After his parents and other dignitaries cleared the podium, Junior leapt up and seized it for a moment, waving his fists in the air in a triumphant "Rocky" gesture. Laura then joined in, waving and mouthing words to friends she recognized in the crowd. Later, at one of the many inaugural balls, Laura and George W. stood solemnly on the stage while the new President praised them for all they had done to help make the moment possible.

George W. made no secret of his distaste for Washington. While Laura merely spoke of her own desire to return to their "beloved state of Texas," her husband decried an "inside-the-Beltway mentality" that he said was "completely out of touch with the rest of the country . . . I've just had enough." Besides, he stressed, "I'm proud to have done what I could for my dad, but I've got to get back to living my own life."

In January 1989, the Bushes settled into their spacious new ranch house with pool on Northwood Road in the leafy Preston Hollow section of North Dallas. Barbara and Jenna were at first enrolled in the local public school, but would soon transfer to the exclusive Hockaday School. The family also joined Highland Park United Methodist Church, where every Sunday they worshiped with some of the nation's richest and most influential Protestants.

The "mustard seed" planted by Billy Graham four years earlier had taken root—so firmly, in fact, that W. embraced his Christianity with an evangelical fervor. On a visit to the White House, W. and Barbara began arguing about "who goes to heaven."

George proclaimed that the Bible left no room for misinterpretation—only Christians have a place in heaven. "Mom, look, all I can tell you is what the New Testament says," W. insisted.

"Surely, God will accept others," Barbara said.

"No, Mom. Here's what the New Testament says," he pressed as he leafed through the Bible in search of the appropriate passage.

"Okay," Barbara replied, picking up the telephone. "Get me Billy Graham," she told the operator.

"Mother, what are you doing?"

Two minutes later, the Reverend Graham was on the line. Barbara posed the question, and Graham conceded that he agreed with W. "I agree with George," he said. "The New Testament has been my guide. But I want to caution you both. Don't play God. Who are you two to be God?"

When he wasn't debating scripture, W. was invariably holed up in his home office with the gilt-framed western paintings on the walls, working the phones in search of potential Rangers investors. He went after the deal, W. would later concede, "like a pit bull on the pant leg of opportunity." Bush once again approached several well-heeled Yale buddies, as well as East Coast–based relatives and friends. But this time it would not be so easy. Baseball Commissioner Peter Ueberroth determined that the Rangers' new owners should have strong Texas ties, so that meant W. would have to work that much harder to raise dollars on his home turf.

Eventually, he would put together a consortium of seventy investors that would pay eighty-six million dollars for the franchise. The biggest piece of the pie—18 percent—would go to W.'s friend Rollie Betts and Betts's partner Tom Bernstein. Their Silver Screen investment company had earned millions backing feature films ranging from *Gandhi* and *The Little Mermaid* to *Pretty Woman*. Betts and Bernstein had agreed to pay seven million dollars for the privilege of owning at least part of a baseball team. George W.'s contribution of $606,000 would be the smallest amount of any major investor, earning him a 1.8 percent stake in the team.

It was agreed that Bush, along with another partner, Edward "Rusty" Rose, would run the team together. Rose, who shunned the spotlight, would serve as chairman of the board while the outgoing George would handle the public as managing general partner. For this, W. was to be paid an annual salary of $200,000. In addition, since W. had essentially put the deal together, he stood to make a 10 percent bonus once the partners' initial investment was repaid.

The team's new owners left the day-to-day operations to General

Manager Tom Grieve, but George W. quickly became the new face of the Texas Rangers. Like any political candidate, he got to know the team's foot soldiers first; within months he was on a first-name basis with the ticket takers, the hot-dog vendors, the cleaning crew, the security guards, and the ushers.

Eschewing seats in the air-conditioned owner's box, he sat next to the dugout at virtually every game. With his trademark cowboy boots perched on the railing and the red bill of his Rangers cap pulled down to shield his eyes from the blazing sun, W. spit out sunflower seeds and signed almost as many autographs as the Rangers' star player, the legendary pitcher Nolan Ryan. He also logged plenty of television time, although what the cameras captured was not always flattering. There was nationwide coverage of Ryan's three hundredth victory, but when the cameras zeroed in on George W., they caught him picking his nose.

Still, W. gloried in his newfound status as a bona fide Texas celebrity. His place was front-and-center at the old Arlington, Texas, stadium because, he explained in typically graphic George W. fashion, it was important for "folks to see me sitting in the same seat they sit in, eating the same popcorn, peeing in the same urinal."

The Texas Rangers quickly became a family affair. By his own estimate, over the next five years George W. and Laura went to nearly three hundred home games together, often with their young daughters in tow. At some point in nearly every game Laura and George chewed bubble gum, blowing bubbles that burst and stuck to their noses and cheeks. It was "part of the baseball experience," they would tell bemused guests.

"If you're going to a baseball game," George W. later said, "you'd better go with someone you like, because you have ample time to talk. I went with someone I loved."

During those games, Laura recalled, they talked not only about baseball, but about politics, their faith, their daughters ("Our daughters grew up there"), their friends, even their pets. When Millie, First Lady Barbara Bush's famous springer spaniel, gave birth in 1989, the female puppy that went to George and Laura was named Spot Fletcher in honor of Rangers shortstop Scott Fletcher.

Jenna and Barbara spent countless evenings at the beginning of each season huddling with their parents beneath a blanket that protected them from the April chill. Later, they would go off to summer camp just as their parents had. Three weeks during each summer were also set aside for the girls to spend time with pushover Gampy and no-nonsense Ganny in Kennebunkport—"basic training," Laura liked to call it.

As idyllic as his life as a team owner seemed, it quickly became evident to W. that the old Arlington ballpark—urinals and all—had fallen into a horrible state of disrepair. A new stadium was needed if the team was going to flourish. Over the next three years, W. lobbied hard for a new venue that would combine the architectural feel of a traditional American ballpark with all the modern accoutrements, from luxury sky boxes to facilities for the disabled. For her part, Laura lobbied for more women's facilities. "Men never have to wait in line to go to the rest room," she said, "so why should we?"

After more than a year of heated public debate, in 1991 the voters of Arlington approved $135 million in bond issues to build a new home for W.'s team. When it finally opened in the spring of 1994, the new stadium, with its walls of native granite and red brick and its Texas Longhorns in the facade, was an immediate hit.

In the meantime, W. took his act on the road, adding to his star power with Texans. At one event after another, he carted out the same opening line. "I'm sorry the most famous Bush couldn't be here tonight," he would deadpan, "but Mom was busy."

George W. had stepped boldly into center stage, but his wife still stood tentatively in the wings. With her well-connected and extremely wealthy friend Nancy Brinker to guide her, Laura began navigating the often treacherous waters of Dallas high society. Brinker, whose husband Norman owned a controlling interest in the Chili's restaurant chain, made sure that her protégée joined all the right charity fund-raising committees and that her name was never left off the guest lists for Big D's most glamorous events.

Of course, simply being the President's daughter-in-law gave Laura an instant cachet. Nor did it hurt that George W. was fast becoming one of the best-known figures in the state as the salt-of-the-earth savior of the Texas Rangers. "These women can be pretty catty," one Dallas socialite observed. "But even the nastiest ones liked Laura because she was just so unassuming and so *classy*. It's not what everyone expected after watching her husband spit and scratch himself on television."

Gala fund-raisers and formal dinner parties were, in fact, anathema to Laura. "I'd much rather have a backyard cookout or, even better, go out for Tex-Mex," she said. But W.'s wife also realized that he still harbored political aspirations of some sort, and that she could help him by building bridges to Dallas's elite. "Laura may not be naturally gregarious," one of her Preston Hollow neighbors said, "but she knew the importance of networking. She learned from the masters."

Laura was most impressed with her husband's ability to stay off the bottle, even when she indulged in a glass of wine or two. As a result, she told friends, George was noticeably less frantic, more focused, and more comfortable in his own skin. "George was very disciplined in a lot of ways—except for drinking," she said. "And when he was able to stop, I think that gave him a lot of confidence and made him feel better about himself and easier about himself."

With his star rising in his home state, George W. Bush was approached by Republican Party leaders in 1989 and asked if he would consider challenging popular Democrat Ann Richards in her first try for governor. Junior was tempted by the opportunity to take on the feisty Richards. It was she, after all, who brought down the house during the 1988 Democratic Convention when she declared that then–Vice President Bush ("Poor George") had been "born with a silver foot in his mouth." (She later topped this remark by proclaiming W.'s dad was "born on third base and thought he hit a triple.")

"If I run, I'll be most electable," young George said. "Absolutely, no question in my mind. In a big media state like Texas, name identification is important. I've got it."

But W. was also enough of a realist to know that being the President's son was not enough to get elected. He had yet to prove himself. "My biggest liability in Texas is the question, 'What's the boy ever done? So he's got a famous father and ran a small oil company. He could be riding on Daddy's name if he ran for office.'"

Of course, W. was not about to deny that having a dad in the White House had its privileges. "Being the President's son puts you in the limelight," he admitted. "While in the limelight, you might as well sell tickets." He quickly added, however, that by Texas standards he was far from rich. "You've heard of all hat and no cattle?" he routinely cracked. "Well, I'm all name and no money."

To be sure, all that was changing—and rapidly. "Now I can say I've done something," he said of his tenure at the helm of the Rangers. "When all those people in Austin say 'He ain't never done anything,' well, this is it." Besides, he hastened to add, "there are a lot of parallels between baseball and politics . . ."

Laura, meanwhile, had adjusted to the role of presidential in-law with relative ease. Now she felt comfortable enough around the trappings of power to look forward to their periodic weekend stays at the White House. Usually George and Laura slept in the Queen's Bedroom just across from his parents, and the girls shared a room down the hall. More than once, Junior and his wife stayed in the Lincoln Bedroom. "Everyone who sleeps there says the same thing, and it's true," she told her pals in Midland. "You can feel Lincoln's presence in the room."

Just as Jackie Onassis had worked diligently to keep her two children from being "inhaled" by the Kennedy clan, Laura balked at the notion of giving herself over entirely to the Bushes. "They liked her and she liked them," said one longtime friend of the family. "But Laura was still very much her own person. She went along, but politics wasn't in her blood the way it was in George's."

Indeed, Laura tensed at the very notion of hitting the campaign trail again. "In case you hadn't guessed," she liked to say, "I'm not as gregarious as my husband." Besides, she was having a difficult enough time establishing a beachhead in Dallas society. "Laura still had to overcome that mousy librarian image," said one society matron. "Everybody was getting to know George, but she was still a mystery. At first people mistook her serene demeanor for timidity. Laura is a shy person, but not a fearful one. She can shine when she gets the chance."

Laura urged W. to sit out the 1990 governor's race—not because she was terrified of the prospect, but because she was convinced it was too soon and he would go down in defeat. In the middle of a speech to a group of Dallas attorneys, W. dropped a bombshell. "I've decided at this time," he declared, "that I would not run for gover-

nor of Texas in 1990. For now, I want to focus on my job as managing general partner of the Texas Rangers and more importantly as a good father and good husband."

That did not mean, however, that he had entirely absented himself from the world of politics. That spring, his youngest brother, Neil, was being pilloried for his role in the billion-dollar demise of Denver's giant Silverado Savings & Loan. W. sprang to the defense of Neil, who sat on Silverado's board. "There's not a devious bone in his body," Junior said of his brother, whom he described as having "the biggest heart in the family." Ultimately, Neil was fined fifty thousand dollars for his part in the Silverado collapse.

Soon it was W. who found himself in the crosshairs of federal regulators. In 1990, Harken Energy, the oil company in which George W. still had a significant interest, beat out giant Amoco to land its first offshore drilling deal in Bahrain. W. knew that it would be immediately perceived as an Arab nation wanting to deal with the son of the American president, and he shared those concerns with Laura.

"I'm afraid it's going to embarrass Dad," he told her. "They're gonna say that the only way Harken is getting a deal like this is because they want something from the White House."

Laura never upstaged or competed with her husband and, unlike Barbara Bush, did not offer scathing opinions for public consumption. (It was during the vice presidential debates of 1984, for example, that Barbara famously described Democratic vice presidential candidate Geraldine Ferraro with the words "rhymes with witch.") But behind the scenes, George W. often sought her advice. When he didn't, she often gave it to him anyway.

This time, Laura told George point-blank that if he felt the Bahrain deal would embarrass the President, then he "ought to get up in front of the board and tell them not to go through with it."

W. did just that, pleading with the Harken board not to proceed. But it did, and—as Bush predicted in an interview with the *Dallas Morning News*—there would be plenty of "bad political fallout."

Laura's husband would again be accused of shady business dealings after he sold most of his Harken stock in the summer of 1990 for $848,560—more than twice what he paid for it. When Iraq invaded Kuwait just six weeks later, triggering the Persian Gulf War,

it was feared that the Harken deal in Bahrain would be canceled. Harken stock plummeted, only to take another hit when the company announced unprecedented losses in its quarterly report.

W. explained that he had borrowed the $606,000 to pay for his small piece of the Texas Rangers, and now he had to raise the cash to pay back those loans. But the timing seemed suspicious, since George W. was a member of a company committee specifically assigned the task of finding ways to placate creditors. As much as any Harken executive, he was keenly aware of the company's deteriorating condition. In addition, W. waited eight months to tell the SEC that he had sold his stock; he explained that he had filed the notice, but that it was "lost" by the SEC. The commission, in turn, could find no evidence that any such documents had been received in the first place, much less misplaced.

Laura once again weighed in, advising Junior to fight back. He had, after all, gone ahead with the sale only after being given a green light by his attorneys. "I'm not," he said to a reporter for *USA Today,* "a punk kid." Nothing about the sale of his Harken stock, he insisted, was legally, morally, or ethically wrong. "No, I don't feel American troops in Saudi Arabia are preserving George Jr.'s drilling prospects," W. said, his words dripping with sarcasm. "I think that's a little farfetched."

The SEC investigation into W.'s stock sale would drag on for years before being abandoned for lack of evidence. In his October 1993 letter to W.'s lawyer, the SEC's Bruce A. Hiler stated that the investigation had "been terminated as to the conduct of Mr. Bush and, at this time, no enforcement is contemplated with respect to him." Hiler went on to say, however, that "it must in no way be construed as indicating that the party has been exonerated or that no action may ultimately result."

Meantime, the President continued to lean heavily on his eldest son as loyalty enforcer and, when the occasion called for it, high executioner. W. "had a good sense of what wasn't going right," said Wyoming Senator Alan K. Simpson, a longtime Bush family friend. "And when things weren't going right, George W. would suddenly be on the front porch."

When it came to Dad, no slight went unnoticed—or was entirely forgiven. The first summer of his father's presidency, as press boats

bobbed off Walker's Point waiting to catch a glimpse of the First Family, W. and the twins went out with Gampy on the Bush speedboat—the same speedboat featured on the infamous "wimp" cover of *Newsweek*.

This time, knowing full well that television cameras were trained on them, W. bet his dad that he wouldn't dive into the frigid Atlantic. Then he handed the stakes—the eleven dollars he had in his pocket—over to Jenna and Barbara for safekeeping. The President dove off the side of the boat, then climbed back on board to collect his winnings from his granddaughters. When images of the presidential dive were broadcast on the evening news, Laura patted her husband on the back. With this one seemingly spontaneous act, the President now appeared to the public to be anything but effete. "Muy macho," W. said with a sly wink.

When the President became disenchanted with his ambitious White House Chief of Staff John Sununu, George W. was called in, said one White House staffer, to "wield the ax." More accurately, Junior sat down in Sununu's office and told him point-blank that the President would be better served if he quit. Faced with an offer he couldn't refuse from the First Son, Sununu resigned several days later.

For all his access to the corridors of power, Junior showed virtually no interest in formulating policy. His correspondence with Dad over the course of the elder Bush's presidency never mentioned the issues being confronted either domestically or abroad. Instead, they dealt with paying back favors—an autographed picture here, a White House invitation there—to those who had proven sufficient "loyalty" to the Bushes. "George, the Texas Rangers man," the President would invariably scrawl, "did indeed pass along your letter."

But even this meticulously tended old-boy network could not keep the Old Man from facing a grim political reality. With 1992 shaping up as a three-way race, Bush had slipped behind Democrat Bill Clinton and independent Ross Perot in the polls. The feisty, fast-talking billionaire with the Texas twang had surprised everyone in the Bush campaign—everyone but George W., who had warned his father that Perot's grassroots campaign was gaining momentum.

That May of 1992, George and Laura were among the guests at a

White House luncheon for Queen Elizabeth II. The First Lady told Her Majesty that she had seated George W. as far away from her as possible and instructed him not to speak.

"Why is that, Mr. Bush?" the Queen asked W. "Are you the black sheep of the family?"

"Yes, Your Majesty." He nodded. "I suppose that's true."

"Well, I guess all families have one," the Queen replied.

"Oh, does your family have a black sheep?" George W. shot back. "And if so, who is it?"

Her Majesty laughed and turned to Barbara. "I don't know why you think your son is so dangerous," she said.

"Because he says what he feels," the First Lady answered. She also warned the Queen that he had threatened to wear cowboy boots to the state dinner planned for that evening. "And they either have Texas flags on them or 'God bless America.'"

"Which pair do you plan to wear tonight, Mr. Bush?" Queen Elizabeth asked.

"Neither," he said. "Tonight's pair will say 'God save the Queen.'"

Laura, seated out of earshot at another table, glanced over nervously to see George and the Queen engaged in conversation. When Her Majesty tossed back her head and laughed, the girl from Midland breathed an audible sigh of relief.

That night, George and Laura moved through the receiving line at the state dinner. When he got to the Queen, she looked down smiling and, without missing a beat, W. lifted up his pant leg to reveal his boots emblazoned with the Stars and Stripes.

However amusing the Queen may have found him, George W.'s biggest fan was still Mom. He still needled her shamelessly. Warned that Barbara was grieving over the death of her beloved dog C. Fred, W. burst through the door and shouted, "Hey, Mom, where are you, *doggone* it?"

Not long after Junior showed off his boots to the Queen, Laura and George decided it was time to host their own first black-tie affair. W. had been appointed to the board of Paul Quinn College, an African-American college on Dallas's south side. To raise money for the financially ailing institution, Laura put together a glittering fund-raiser at Symphony Hall featuring the actor Danny Glover and Dionne Warwick.

When the IRS threatened legal action against Paul Quinn College not long after, W., afraid of another scandal that might cost his dad the election, resigned. But the fund-raiser itself had been a huge success, raising both Bushes' social profile and bolstering Laura's confidence.

As the 1992 Bush reelection campaign stumbled onward, W. grew ever more resentful of the press. On the floor of the GOP convention in Houston, he sparred verbally with CBS anchor Dan Rather, who ended their brief exchange with, "Tell your mother hello for me." As one TV interview got under way, an enraged First Son ripped off his microphone and stormed away. From that point on, the offending station was frozen out of all access to the Bushes—a fate that befell any media outlet George W. felt had been "unfair" toward his father.

If anything, W.'s mantra—that his father and for that matter the entire Bush family was being savaged by a hostile liberal press—reinforced Laura's feeling that she could not find happiness as a politician's wife. She had seen her husband so frustrated by his inability to get the message across that he sometimes broke down in tears. Her most vivid memory of the 1992 reelection campaign would be "waking up every morning and feeling anxious when George went out to get the newspaper. I'd think, 'What's it going to be today?'" She added, "It really hurts to see someone you love attacked. It gets to you after a while."

So much so, in fact, that while her husband had more or less given up cigarettes for chaw by 1992, Laura was back to smoking a pack a day. Although she would later claim that she had also given up smoking in 1992, in truth Laura would, in times of stress, bum cigarettes off friends and sometimes even from reporters so long as no photographers were around to snap a shot of her with a cigarette in her mouth.

By the end of the campaign, there was more than enough reason for Laura to light up. Fully aware that Ross Perot would split the vote and hand the presidency to Bill Clinton, George and Laura joined the rest of the Bush family aboard Air Force One on election eve. As the presidential plane flew back to Washington, the Oak Ridge Boys led the passengers in a mournful rendition of "Amazing Grace" that reduced both the President and Junior to tears. Barbara and Laura, both far less inclined than their spouses to give in to emotion, joined them.

Two weeks after Poppy lost his reelection bid to Clinton, Dorothy Walker Bush—"the most competitive living human," according to Barbara—died after suffering a stroke at age ninety-one. George W. and Laura and the girls were among the one hundred mourners attending the private funeral at Greenwich's Christ Episcopal Church. Along with the rest of the family, they later drove to Putnam Cemetery and hung their heads as Dorothy Walker Bush's ashes were interred next to her husband the Senator and her long-deceased granddaughter, W.'s little sister Robin.

Back on home turf in Dallas, W. dealt with stress the best way he knew how without turning to alcohol—he ran. He ran every morning through the streets of Preston Hollow, stopping to chat with neighbors about the Rangers and his mom and dad and the political climate in Texas.

At his Rangers office, nothing had changed. There was an autographed photo of Nolan Ryan on the wall, along with pictures of Laura and the girls and Barbara in a Rangers jacket. But the rest was strictly dorm-room clutter: bats, gloves, balls, and caps; a folded Texas flag; a personalized license plate, a half-eaten bag of popcorn, an empty can of Diet Coke.

Nor had he altered any of his personal habits. As soon as W. walked into his office, he flung his eighty-nine-dollar Hagger sportcoat on the floor, loosened his tie, flopped behind his desk, and began making phone calls. With one hand in the bag of popcorn and the other gripping the receiver, he phoned one old buddy after another, pausing only to shout orders to his secretary through his perpetually open office door.

At home, W. was no less frantic. In his home office just to the right of the front door, he managed to channel-surf, chat on the phone, and help Jenna and Barbara with their homework—all at the same time. Then he would dash outside and play fetch with Spot, the family's springer spaniel.

It quickly became evident to Laura that her husband was no longer satisfied with simply being the managing partner of an American League baseball team. "I wouldn't say that patience," she sighed, "is one of George's greatest qualities."

At this juncture, the same GOP leaders who had approached him in 1990 to run against Ann Richards were again pressing him to run against the popular Democratic incumbent in 1994. With her trademark upswept hairdo and Texas cowgirl accent, Richards had managed to hold on to the national prominence she gained by uttering the famous "silver foot in his mouth" line at the 1988 Democratic Convention.

There were unmistakable similarities between the grandma-turned-governor and the President's son. Both had overcome a serious drinking problem, though by different means: W. went cold turkey, while Richards checked herself into rehab after an intervention by her friends. Both were charismatic in that seductive down-home, aw-shucks way that their fellow Texans found all but irresistible. Both possessed keen political instincts, a sarcastic streak, and the desire—the *need*—to win.

Ideologically, they were on opposite ends of the spectrum. Richards was a populist, a liberal, and a darling of the entertainment industry who counted among her supporters Barbra Streisand, Sharon Stone, Steven Spielberg, Robert Redford, and Willie Nelson. George W., conversely, was the consummate conservative—not only the son of a Republican president but a high-profile business leader with roots planted deep in the oil fields of West Texas.

Trouble was, George did not want to be governor—or at least not as much as he wanted to be commissioner of baseball. When long-time Bush family ally Fay Vincent was deposed as commissioner in the autumn of 1992, W. told Laura that the job would constitute nothing less than the fulfillment of a lifelong dream.

"Laura wasn't sure about George running for governor," one of their Midland friends said. "So when he said he wanted to be base-ball commissioner, she really pushed for it."

She did not have to push very hard, since W. made it patently obvious to anyone who would listen that he craved the top job in baseball. W. called Fay Vincent and told him that he wanted Vincent's old job, but that party bigwigs were pressuring him to run for governor. Vincent urged Junior to challenge Richards. "I'm going to have to make up my mind one of these days," W. sighed. "I think I'd rather be commissioner than governor."

Over the next several months, W. bided his time in hope of

becoming baseball commissioner. But a firm job offer, dangled in front of Bush by acting commissioner Bud Selig, never came through.

Meanwhile George W. decided to wait and see how fellow Republican Kay Bailey Hutchison did in a special election to fill the Senate seat being vacated by Lloyd Bentsen, Bill Clinton's newly appointed treasury secretary. George and Laura were at Hutchison headquarters in Dallas's Anatole Hotel the night of May 1, 1993, and cheered with the rest of Hutchison's backers when she won. As W. walked up to the podium to introduce Texas's newest U.S. senator, the crowd began chanting "Governor Bush! Governor Bush!"

Laura studied her husband's face carefully that night. She told friends the next morning that she had "a sinking feeling" right then that her husband was "hooked." But Laura did not share his enthusiasm. "Is running for governor something *you* want to do?" Laura asked George, "or is it something you're doing because people are pushing you to do it?"

W. would complain to friends that his wife was "throwing cold water" on his plans to run. "She wanted to make sure I wasn't running," he recalled, "because I felt I had something to prove." He acknowledged that her fears were not entirely without merit. Laura had worried that family pride was at stake, that her husband was being sent into battle to avenge his own father's honor. If this was merely part of a Bush family vendetta against Ann Richards, then Laura did not want George to be a part of it.

She had ample reason to believe that was the case: When W. asked his mother what she thought about his running against Richards, Barbara replied, "Go get her!" But she also added, "I don't think you have a chance in hell of winning."

Barbara wasn't the only Bush family friend who thought Ann Richards was unbeatable. Nearly all of those closest to George W. told him to wait four years until she was out of office to challenge someone less popular. He would not only ignore their advice but use their comments to poke fun at himself—and reinforce his image as the underdog. "Even my own mother," he would say, much to Barbara's chagrin, "doesn't think I can win!"

Mom's initial lack of confidence in W. contrasted sharply with her faith in his younger brother Jeb. After a stint as Florida State commerce secretary, he was now running against incumbent Democrat Lawton Chiles for governor. The aged and ailing Chiles had slipped badly in the polls; among those governors seeking reelection, he was considered one of the most vulnerable.

Convinced that a backlash was building in Texas not only against Richards but against President Bill Clinton, George forged ahead. By midsummer, Laura gave her blessing to her husband's plans—so long as she would not be required to campaign extensively. "She was the very last one," W. said, "to get on that train."

W.'s first move (after buying four new suits at Dallas's Culwell and Son) was to eliminate the need for a primary by quietly visiting with his potential GOP rivals and convincing them only he could win. Then, having carefully laid the groundwork for his campaign, W. announced his candidacy for governor before a crowd of three hundred cheering supporters in Houston. A beaming Laura stood beside him, but Mom and Dad were nowhere to be seen. Although they lived just a dozen blocks away, the senior Bushes were noticeably absent.

Big George and Barbara were in total agreement with this strategy, both in Texas and in Florida. If either son was to win, it was important he not appear to be trading on his father's name. "My job," said the former president, "is to stay out of the way . . . I've had my chance, it's their turn now."

"As hard as it was on George and Jebby," Laura said of the 1992 defeat, "in a lot of ways it was the first time in their lives they were liberated from the shadow of their dad. It was literally the first time they felt like they could say whatever they thought, without it reflecting on their father, without having to think: 'How will this sound?' "

Certainly both sons were making it clear that—in theory at least—Dad was no longer a significant part of the political equation. "I'm not running because I'm George Bush's son," W. would tell reporters. "I'm running because I'm Barbara and Jenna's dad." In Florida, Jeb echoed the sentiment: "I'm not running because I'm George Bush's son. I'm running because I'm George, Noelle, and Jebby's dad."

Over the next year Richards, who had built her career on baiting the Bushes as born-to-the-purple lightweights, went on the attack. Pelting her opponent with insults, she referred to W. alternately as

"Shrub" and "Junior." During one interview she went so far as to dismiss the Republican candidate as "some jerk." In others, she derided his lack of experience: "You can't be shaving one morning and look at yourself in the mirror and say 'I'm so pretty I'll run for governor.'" Richards also repeatedly bemoaned the fact that it was hard to run against somebody "who doesn't have a clue" and told audiences they should feel sorry for George Herbert Walker Bush's son George W. because "the poor boy is missing his Herbert."

When it was revealed in the press that W. had once told his mother he believed only Christians could get into heaven, Richards's strategists put out the word in the Jewish community. "It was, of course, picked up and politicized," W. later recalled. "You know, 'Bush to Jews: Go to Hell.'"

The candidate's retort was muted and to the point. "I believe God decides who goes to heaven," W. said, "not George W. Bush."

"It was very ugly," Bush said of Richards's highly personal attacks. "It hurt my feelings." Away from the press, W. was not hurt so much as livid.

Laura urged him to stay calm. "They're just trying to get to you, Bushie," she said, invoking one of her favorite pet names. "Don't let them. Don't take the bait."

It was advice he was also getting from the experts, like his chief strategist and longtime friend Karl Rove. At the modest vacation house the Bushes bought on Rainbo Lake in East Texas, Rove and other advisers drilled W. on ways to maintain his composure, fashioning the kind of above-the-fray comments that would only make Richards look petty and vindictive.

"It's not easy," Laura told her friends. "George would just love to let her have it." But with Laura and the others reminding him several times a day not to play Richards's game, W. resisted the temptation to launch a stinging counterattack.

Laura was happy to offer advice and encouragement, so long as she could remain out of the limelight. She would much prefer to confine her speech-making to her women's book club, like the critique she delivered on Laura Esquivel's *Like Water for Chocolate*.

That was fine with George, who characterized his spouse to one Texas reporter as the anti–Hillary Clinton. "She's not always trying to butt in," he said of Laura, "and, you know, compete. There's nothing worse in the political arena than spouses competing." Family friend Joe O'Neill agreed: "There's no burning ambition here. She's not pushing George from the back. But she truly changed him."

So W. took his wife's advice and kept laughing along with Richards, telling audiences and reporters that she was "a very funny lady" but that her politics were basically out of step with what was a conservative Texas electorate. As far as Richards was concerned, W. said he was determined to "kill her with kindness."

He would take the same uncharacteristically cool approach to the press, which hammered away at the persistent rumors of past indiscretions that allegedly included cocaine use. Bush defused the issue with the kind of casual, off-the-cuff remarks that journalists and voters would find refreshingly candid—if notably disingenuous. Did he use cocaine? "Maybe I did, maybe I didn't," he replied to the *Houston Chronicle.* "What's the relevance?" Once again, he conceded that he had been "wild" in his youth, particularly at college and during the oft-mentioned "nomadic period" between Yale and Harvard Business School. "Look, I'm not proud of what I did when I was twenty-one," he said. "None of the baby boomers can be proud of what we did then. But I've learned my lessons." That was the difference, he would later say, between himself and Bill Clinton—"I grew up."

Both sides had refrained from bringing up the issue of substance abuse. Richards not only shared W.'s history of alcohol dependence, but she had also been the subject of speculation concerning past drug use. By the same token, there was little concern that the Democrats would raise the issue of Bush's past drunk-driving conviction, assuming they were even aware of it. The arrest in Kennebunkport remained a carefully guarded secret, known only to family members and key members of Bush's inner circle like Rove (whom W. insisted on calling "Turd Blossom," or sometimes simply "Turd") and W.'s handpicked press secretary, former TV newswoman Karen Hughes. W. did not take long to christen Hughes, whose major general dad was the last governor of the Panama Canal Zone, "The High Prophet," a cunning play on her height (six feet) and her maiden name, Parfitt.

At about this time, the arresting officer in W.'s 1976 drunk-driving case, Calvin Bridges, was working a detail for the former president and first lady in Kennebunkport. When Bridges identified himself, W.'s dad thanked him for arresting his son seventeen years earlier. It was, the senior Bush said, "the best thing that could have happened" to young George. As a token of his appreciation, he gave Bridges a presidential tie clip.

W. would spend the next year barnstorming the state aboard his campaign plane, *Accountability One*. With his young aide Israel ("Izzy") Hernandez on hand to make sure he had ample supplies of Altoids (a postsmoking addiction he shared with Laura; W. gobbled down at least two dozen a day) and his favorite peanut butter and jelly and egg salad sandwiches, Laura's husband would visit virtually all of the state's 254 counties, hammering away at his basic campaign themes: cracking down on juvenile crime, paring down welfare rolls, handing over control of education to local school districts, cutting back on the frivolous litigation that he claimed was poisoning the state's business climate. Bush's rallying cry, squarely aimed at the swelling federal bureaucracy was: "Let Texans run Texas!"

That included Texas's large Mexican-American population, which W. courted with a special zeal. His heavy American accent aside, Bush would often deliver part of his speech in serviceable Spanish. *"Hola, amigos!"* he would sometimes begin. *"Me llamo Jorge Bush y quiero ser su gobernador."*

No matter the number of stops or the distance traveled, W. insisted on one thing: At the end of every day on the hustings, he returned to Dallas to sleep in his own bed. Laura and their girls, he liked to remind voters as he shook their hands, were at home waiting for him.

Not that the twins, now almost thirteen years old, were overly impressed. While they possessed two distinctly different personalities—Jenna was the fun-loving blond, and quiet, studious brunette Barbara took after their mom—they were in agreement on one thing: Everything their parents did mortified them.

"His feelings were sort of hurt," Laura would later recall, "because Barbara and Jenna did not really want to travel with him." They did go along grudgingly on a trip that brought them to the North Texas town of Quanah. "You know," he told his daughters, "I was here thirty years ago when Gampy campaigned for the Senate." Both girls stifled yawns. "They couldn't have cared less," Laura remembered.

Then an elderly man approached W. and said, "I remember when you were here the last time." Laura looked over at her husband. "It was very touching for him," she said. "It made him want to weep."

None of this registered with the girls, who insisted on staying home in Dallas for the remainder of the campaign. But W. was determined to remain a part of his daughters' lives. After another grueling day stumping the state, he nevertheless offered to pick up his daughters at a party that was scheduled to end at 11 P.M.

They would allow him to pick them up at the party, with one proviso. "Dad," they said in unison, "whatever you do—don't come inside!" So the Republican candidate for governor parked at the curb and waited as other parents cheerfully marched inside to pick up their children. At 11:30—two and a half hours past his own bedtime—the girls finally walked out to the car and got in.

If his adolescent daughters sometimes tried his patience, George W. still took solace in the fact that Laura was always there for him. "She is a very wise person," he said, "and when she talks, I pay close attention to what she has to say." However, her contribution would remain largely unseen. Still somewhat stiff and uneasy in front of audiences, the candidate's wife did little campaigning. In the end she did manage to travel to 30 of the 254 Texas counties, but only to speak to sympathetic groups of Republican women. Even then, she "panicked" if she did not have a rehearsed text in her hand. "The idea of ad-libbing," she said, "scared me to death."

Given her innate shyness, W. was not surprised. Laura, he observed, "wasn't really comfortable doing a lot of campaigning, which was fine with me."

As Richards's verbal attacks on George W. escalated, Laura also grew more and more concerned that some enterprising politico would dig up the story of how she once ran a stop sign and killed her former boyfriend. Laura's accident had been widely covered in the Midland press at the time, and the Richards camp was well aware of what transpired that horrible night in November 1963. But if Laura was known to the Texas electorate at all, it was as a wholesome-looking librarian-turned-stay-at-home mom. Worried that any attacks on Laura could only backfire, Richards explicitly instructed members of her campaign not to bring up Laura's fatal accident. Moreover, she hoped that the press would not dig it up on its own. "We'd be blamed," said one Democratic strategist, "whether we had anything to do with it or not."

Fortunately for both sides, the press virtually ignored the most significant event in Laura's past. It was a thirty-one-year-old event, said one Austin reporter, that had "nothing to do with the political landscape in 1994."

There was another, more personal reason why Laura felt it was important to stick close to home. Her father Harold had been diagnosed with Alzheimer's, and his condition was deteriorating rapidly. "Laura was under a lot of stress," a friend said. "But of course she'd never let you see it."

There were a few lighter moments during the campaign. In an effort to impress Texas's large population of hunters, W. went out on a dove-hunting expedition and accidentally shot a protected species of songbird known as the kildee. Bush promptly confessed, paid a $130 fine, and then held a press conference. "Thank goodness it wasn't deer season," he said. "I could have shot a cow."

At the state fair in Dallas that October, Jenna paused to play a midway game and won a stuffed bird. With television cameras everywhere, she handed the toy to her dad with a flourish. "Oh, look, Dad," she said, "a kildee!"

On election day, George and Laura went to the polls early in the morning for the traditional photo op. When he reached in his back pocket for his identification, the noticeably exhausted candidate realized he had left his wallet at home. "That's okay, Mr. Bush," said one election monitor as she led him to a voting booth, "I think we have a pretty good idea who you are."

Later that day, George, Laura, and the girls boarded *Accountability One* for the flight to Austin. There they would await the election results at the Capitol Marriott. It was never even close. By 10 P.M., Ann Richards threw in the towel, calling George W. at the hotel to concede. No sooner did he hang up the phone than the phone rang again—it was his father checking in from Houston for the twelfth time to see how the race was going. The numbers would show that W., initially given a slim chance of unseating the immensely popular

Ann Richards, had trounced her 54 percent to 45 percent. With a radiant Laura and their giggling daughters beside him, George W. told the cheering supporters who thronged the Marriott's Capitol Ballroom that he was particularly grateful to two Houstonians—one of whom "wears pearls."

That evening, Ganny and Gampy were torn between the prodigal son who triumphed in an upset victory and the dutiful son whose own statehouse bid was going down in defeat. Immediately after watching his brother's victory speech on television, Jeb phoned Florida governor Lawton Chiles to congratulate him on his reelection victory. "The joy is in Texas," the former president explained, "but our hearts are in Florida."

It was then that the reality of what had transpired suddenly hit Laura. The shy librarian who shunned the spotlight was now first lady of Texas. "I knew she was uncertain about moving to Austin," George recalled. "She was a little fearful, maybe, about whether any of this life would be to her liking."

"For as long as I've known her," said her friend Regan Gammon, "this is someone who has steadfastly refused to pursue the limelight." More to the point, Laura told her husband, "I'm not sure I can handle this. And the girls—they have a right to lead a normal life."

"Laura," he replied, "if you want to sit in the governor's mansion during my term in office, that's fine with me. You and the girls didn't ask to be put in this position, and I promise I'm not going to make any of you do anything."

Even before he took office, W. would be forced to deal with a minicrisis involving one of his daughters and the press. A TV crew was on hand to record the Bushes decorating their tree that Christmas when the phone rang. "Oh, that must be your new boyfriend," Dad blurted out.

"Da-ad!" Jenna objected, stamping her foot. The awkward moment, captured on tape, would air that night across the state. From then on, Jenna and Barbara were strictly off-limits to reporters and photographers. Besides, Laura guessed that the girls would be "totally humiliated" by a photo shoot. "And I know this sounds strange," she added, noting that she was concerned about their safety, "but I'm just not ready to have everyone know what they look like."

Of course, George and Laura would not escape the special fate of all parents of teenagers. To celebrate the inauguration, the twins threatened to dye their hair flaming red. Mom and Dad said no. When they asked to attend a public high school instead of a perhaps more secure private school, Laura passed the buck to the governor, who reluctantly agreed.

On Tuesday, January 17, 1995, the Bush clan gathered in Austin to witness the inauguration of George W. Bush as Texas's forty-sixth governor—and only the second Republican to hold the office since Reconstruction. An hour before the swearing-in, a reporter asked Barbara Bush what her emotions were as she prepared to watch her eldest son take office. "Don't ask me," she said. "I'll cry."

Barbara didn't, but in keeping with the tradition among Bush family males, the former president did. Sitting on the platform next to their granddaughters Barbara and Jenna, Gampy wiped away a tear and Ganny clapped as W. stepped up to the podium. Laura, smiling and confident, held Sam Houston's Bible as her husband placed his hand on it and recited the oath of office.

National Guard cannons boomed a nineteen-gun salute, and smoke wafted over the platform. The new governor, suddenly looking like the cocky Head Cheerleader he had been at Andover, pointed and winked at friends he spotted in the crowd. "It was definitely," said one, "a 'Can you believe this?' moment."

That day, the Bushes moved into the 140-year-old Greek Revival governor's mansion just across from the capitol building and only a short walk from Austin's Town Lake. With its massive Ionic columns and porte cochere, the mansion had once been home to Republic of Texas President Sam Houston. A huge painting of the *Battle of the Alamo* by Robert Onderdonk—lost for a time but found in an antiques store by a little boy who dashed off to tell his mother—graced the front hallway. The main stairway had a long banister that the children of Governor James Hogg used to slide down—until he solved the problem by having nails hammered into it.

In his search for just the right painting to hang on the wall of his newly expanded second-floor office, W. settled on *Sam Houston as Marius Among the Ruins of Carthage*—Washington Cooper's grandiose depiction of a toga-clad imperial Houston. "Houston regretted that he ever posed for the portrait," Bush said. "I hung it there as a reminder that you're never too important to make a total ass of yourself."

Once again W., who had placed his interest in the Texas Rangers in a blind trust, filled his office with baseball memorabilia—most notably his collection of 250 baseballs autographed by such legendary players as Ted Williams, Mickey Mantle, and Willie Mays. The balls filled two tall display cases; a bust of Benjamin Franklin looked down from atop one of them.

Laura took an eclectic approach to the living quarters. On the walls hung two abstracts by New York artist John Clem Clarke, husband of her SMU roommate Jane Clarke. Laura's bookshelves were lined with painted ceramic bean pots from Mexico. Because of the twins, the mansion was "like Grand Central Station," said Laura's friend Adair Margo, an El Paso art dealer. "It was filled with their school friends, with jeans, and baseball hats on backward."

Both self-confessed creatures of habit, Laura and George continued their daily routine in the governor's mansion: Up at 6 A.M., W. padded down to the kitchen in his robe and slippers, fed the pets, then brought coffee and the papers back to Laura. Spot and the family cats Willie and Cowboy, both rescued from an animal shelter, often sprang into bed with them. (The Bushes later coaxed a six-toed stray cat down from a tree in the backyard of the mansion. They named him Ernie after Ernest Hemingway, who had a special fondness for six-toed felines. Ernie would eventually be joined by a black cat, India.)

Governor Bush would walk out the back door of the mansion and across to his capitol office at 8 A.M., then hold meetings virtually nonstop for the next three hours and forty minutes. The meetings were mercifully short, seldom lasting more than twenty minutes. An aide would then knock on the door to signal the appointment was up and the Governor would spring to his feet. At most, a meeting would be allowed to run an extra five minutes.

At 11:40, George headed off to the University of Texas for a run—between three and five miles at seven and a half minutes a mile—then back to the mansion for lunch with Laura at 1 P.M. Returning to the office, W. occasionally played computer solitaire or video golf until three. Then the meetings resumed until 5 P.M.

When the family got together to lounge around in the evening, they often gravitated toward Laura's favorite room, the green-walled library near the front door. On one wall hung the only portrait Davy Crockett ever posed for, and hidden in a cabinet was a television set. It was here that their teenage daughters curled up to watch *Beverly Hills 90210* and *Melrose Place*—two shows their mother hated. "Those aren't my values," Laura sniffed.

The Bushes often entertained guests for dinner, but no one would keep Bush up past his bedtime. At 9 P.M. sharp, W. would announce "Okay, you're outta here," and escort his guests to the door before heading straight to bed. There both he and Laura would read themselves to sleep—though the Governor usually chose books for their soporific effect. The pattern would vary little over the course of their marriage.

Before long, Laura decided she would cope with her newfound celebrity on her own terms. "Well, if I'm going to be a public figure," she said, shrugging, "I might as well do what I've always liked doing—which means acting like a librarian and getting people interested in reading." Laura's own passion for literature had not dimmed over the years. She read dozens of novels in the course of a year and for fun audited courses on Greek mythology and William Faulkner. She also periodically revisited her favorite work—the "Grand Inquisitor" section of Fyodor Dostoyevski's *The Brothers Karamazov.*

Laura's first act as Texas's First Lady came during inaugural week, when she hosted a reading by several Texas authors. Filled with dread at the thought of having to give her first speech as First Lady, she was awakened by nightmares—"anxiety dreams," she called them—the night before.

She needn't have worried. Laura delivered her remarks flawlessly, and the writers—most of whom had opposed Bush in the election, were instantly won over by his charmingly down-to-earth wife. "I just have to say how impressed I am y'all would invite a raging liberal like me," said novelist Sarah Bird. "It gives me a lot of hope for this administration."

Laura's love of books, however, was not exactly shared by her husband—something she readily conceded. "George," she cracked, "thought a bibliography was the story of the guys who wrote the Bible."

Joe O'Neill agreed that his friend was "not what I'd call a lover of reading . . . He's just always on the go. Boom, boom, boom. And he has been since Day One. Nervous energy. I just don't see how he ever got through Yale. I mean, you have to read. I don't see him settling down and reading, but he does read a lot. He's not like Laura, who reads *a lot*."

Less than two weeks after they moved into the governor's mansion, George W. and Laura returned to the White House for the annual black-tie dinner in honor of the nation's governors. It marked the first time they had been inside the executive mansion since his dad was replaced by Bill Clinton two years earlier. Laura still sent Christmas cards to some of the White House staffers she had gotten to know during the Bush administration. But as usual, she only smiled inscrutably when a *Washington Post* reporter asked her and her husband how it felt to be back. George, whose emotions were never far from the surface, cocked his head, his eyes suddenly filling with tears. "Nostalgic," he said, gripping Laura's hand. "It makes me feel nostalgic."

Emotions would run high once again that spring, when Laura's father succumbed to Alzheimer's on April 29, 1995, at age eighty-two. "It got so he couldn't walk," Jenna Welch said of her husband. "He'd think he could—he'd get up and then he'd fall. Right at the last, when he was bedridden, I was trying to help him one time and he looked up at me and said 'I don't want to be a burden to you anymore.' Three days later he was gone."

Laura could take solace in the fact that her dad had lived to see his quiet, eager-to-please little girl become First Lady of Texas. The family gathered in Midland for the funeral at First United Methodist Church—the church where Laura had attended Sunday School, where she sang in the children's choir, and where she was married. "Laura was very close to her dad," one Midlander said of the emotional service. "So were the twins. Harold was a doting grandfather. There were tears behind the dark glasses, but it was George who looked the most torn up. He was really hurting for Laura."

"He was a gentle, decent man," W. said of his father-in-law. "He didn't have a mean bone in his body." Bush fondly recalled how Harold Welch liked to hang out at Johnny's Barbecue watching football games. "I don't know if there was wagering going on or not," W. said, "but let me just say that the boys seemed to take an avid interest in the outcomes of the games." Laura had no trouble recognizing the similarities between her father and her husband. "Both my dad and George tried to make people feel good."

Laura returned to Austin and dove into her chosen cause—literacy. Predictably, there were those who pointed out that literacy had first been her mother-in-law's cause as First Lady. "I didn't want to step on Bar's issue," she said, "but it had also been my issue long before I became a Bush. And I think Bar loved what I was doing."

Over the next five years, Laura would become a driving force for literacy in her home state. In her small, sparsely furnished office tucked into the underground annex at the state capitol, Laura and a lone staff member put together a list of some of Texas's most celebrated authors. Then the First Lady phoned each one, as well as some non–Texans, personally inviting them to be part of the first-ever Texas Book Festival.

Featuring panel discussions, readings, and signings—as well as storytellers, food, and music for the children—the three-day festival attracted such literary stars as Larry McMurtry, Robert James Waller, John Graves, and Frank McCourt. By the time she left Austin, Laura's brainchild would raise more than one million dollars for the state's libraries.

"My mother-in-law took an interest," Laura would say, "and you know what happens when Barbara Bush gets involved in something." Teaming up with the Barbara Bush Foundation for Family Literacy, Laura's own First Lady's Family Literacy Initiative for Texas would dole out another million dollars in grants to a wide variety of literacy programs. Laura would also work with RIF (Reading Is Fundamental) and launched the Experience Corps, a program that enlisted retired seniors to teach reading to disadvantaged children.

Before long, Laura was championing an array of causes. She traveled the state advocating Rainbow Rooms to provide a safe haven for neglected and abused children, and urged churches, schools, and businesses to provide support to child abuse caseworkers through her Adopt-a-Caseworker program. Even before her husband took office, Laura was active in promoting breast cancer awareness. Her close friend and social mentor Nancy Brinker had established the

Susan G. Komen Breast Cancer Foundation in memory of her sister, and Laura was one of the foundation's most vocal supporters.

Texans were also discovering a warm, tactile side to their new First Lady. Not surprisingly, she instantly connected with the small children she visited in schools and day-care centers. "There is a definite warmth about her," Nancy Weiss said, "a natural desire to hug children and reassure them. She's maybe a little restrained around adults, but not around kids. Right away she gets down so she can talk to them at their eye level, or she scoops them up in her arms. Laura's just a very nice, very kind and caring lady, and kids get that right away. They're drawn to her."

There was already speculation that Laura might wind up being as popular as her mother-in-law. "Oh, please," Laura demurred. "Bar is very funny, very acerbic, very entertaining to listen to. I'm, well, none of those things." Perhaps, but no one was more impressed with the job she was doing than W. himself. "To me," he said, "it has been remarkable—and I emphasize the word 'remarkable'—to watch what has happened to her."

While Laura was winning the hearts of Texans, her husband was changing minds in Austin. He quickly set a tone of compromise for his first term in office, eschewing strict partisanship to win over the conservative Democrats who controlled the state legislature. Under Texas's quirky constitution, the governor wielded little real power beyond a bully pulpit. Oddly, it was Texas's flamboyant Lieutenant Governor Bob Bullock, the state's most influential Democrat, who to a large extent determined what would and would not get accomplished.

Yet another Texas politico with a drinking problem, Bullock was larger than life in the Lyndon Johnson mold—loud, scatological, given to administering pop quizzes on Texas history and firing off guns indoors. In George W. he found a kindred spirit—a bred-to-the-bone, twanging, squinting, knee-slapping Texas pol. "Bully," as W. would call him, quickly became one of the Governor's most ardent fans. With Bullock's help, Bush saw his agenda take shape as bills were passed to slash the welfare rolls, return local control to the schools, enact tort reform, and stiffen the penalties for juvenile crime.

In the summer of 1996, George and Laura were on hand in San Diego when Republicans met to nominate GOP warhorse Bob Dole as the party's candidate for president. W. had been named cochair of the convention, one highlight of which was to be a tribute to Dad. Although dozens of television, radio, and print interviews had been set up to maximize the Governor's exposure, it was Laura who gave an address in prime time.

"Reading is to the mind what food is to the body," she proclaimed over the din of the convention floor. "In Texas, nothing will take higher priority." From the sidelines, W. watched with a genuine look of wonder on his face. What did he think of her performance? "Awesome," he answered.

"I always think of myself as basically reserved and shy," Laura mused. She managed to conquer her fear of public speaking when she began to look out at her audiences and make a mental image of the children she used to read to when she was a single working woman. "I wouldn't have thought of this before I started giving speeches, but reading over the top of a book like I did millions of times as a children's librarian is great practice."

Back in the Lone Star State, Laura pushed her own agenda relentlessly. Ultimately, House Bill 1640—known among Texas lawmakers simply as Laura Bush's bill—would earmark more than $215 million for reading programs aimed at both children and adults. Vowing to "break the cycle of illiteracy," Laura argued that children would never be able to read by the third grade—her goal—unless the adults around them read, too. "Children have never been good at listening to their elders," she quoted the writer James Baldwin as saying, "but they have never failed to imitate them."

The job she had once dreaded, it now became apparent, was fast becoming her passion. When a reporter asked if Laura had lost herself in the endless blur of committee hearings, ribbon-cuttings, luncheons, and fund-raisers, she looked genuinely puzzled. "I haven't lost myself," she objected. "I've *found* myself."

As dedicated as she was to her causes, Laura was not about to sacrifice her children in the process. "Even if I'm traveling all over the state," she said, "I get home by four, which is right before the children get out of school. And George works hard to be at home to have dinner with them."

Of course, at fifteen, the girls were not so keen to spend every evening with Mom and Dad. "They're typical teenagers," Laura said. "They don't even want to admit they have parents." They certainly did not spare either parent when it came to critiquing their fashion sense. *"Day-ud,"* one would say as he headed out the door to make another public appearance. "You're not going to wear that windbreaker, are you? It's so *dorky."* For Mom, the refrain was similar: "Mama, you're not going to wear *that,* are you?"

They had a point. "I've never really been that interested in clothes," Laura conceded. "Before I had the job as the First Lady of Texas, I wore jeans, pants, and T-shirts. I had very few clothes. So I got a new wardrobe—suits, jackets, skirts, and pants sets." For these, Laura relied on Dallas designer Michael Faircloth—although she made it clear that she intended to keep things simple. No cardigans, no scarves, nothing she viewed as "frivolous and unnecessary." She wanted her hemlines to fall at precisely the right spot just below the knee, and if there was the tiniest variation from this length—even by a fraction of an inch—she gently but firmly insisted that the problem be corrected.

Her taste in cosmetics was equally uncomplicated—Cover Girl makeup purchased at the local drugstore, red or pink nail polish and lipstick. "I have a lot of contrast with dark hair, blue eyes, and fair skin," she explained. "And I think people with a lot of contrast look better with less, so that's what I like." Actually, Laura insisted that the single most important element of her beauty regimen had nothing at all to do with cosmetics. "I drink water all day," she said. "It is absolutely the best thing you can do for your skin." Both daughters simply rolled their eyes.

Mama's hairstyle was another source of concern. For years now, Laura had her hair cut short, and she visited her hairdresser only once every six weeks to keep it that way. The girls complained that their mother's hairdo was so stiff it "moves as a unit," and begged her to do something about it. Sighed Laura: "Teenage girls love to make a mother humble."

Laura took solace from her tight circle of girlfriends, most of whom were dealing with teenagers of their own. To celebrate her fiftieth birthday in 1996, she got together with her friends Regan Gammon, Marge Petty, Peggy Weiss, and Jane Ann Fontenot and headed off for another girls-only white-water rafting trip—this time in Utah. Nancy Weiss, another longtime friend, was among the group that went with Laura on a vacation trip to Mexico in 1997. "She's the most even-tempered, centered person I've ever known," Weiss would say of her pal. "We're both sort of laid-back people. It doesn't take a whole lot to entertain us. We could lie by the pool, read, or go the movies together and really enjoy it."

Determined not to miss out on anything, Texas's fun-loving First Lady accepted an invitation from author Lee Byrd for a day of hiking and talking at a ranch outside Austin. Laura brought blueberry cobbler for dessert, and everyone set out on a hike through the tall grass to a nearby creek. It was a typically hot summer day, the water looked inviting, and before long Laura and the others jumped into the water fully clothed. Laura laughed as she floated along with Byrd and the others. "My girls make fun of my 'hair helmet,'" she said, pointing to her head. "You know, always perfect, never mussed. Wonder what they'd think of this." Laura also noted that in this state everyone would be able to see her roots. "Can y'all see the gray hairs? Earned every one of 'em."

"Everyone was wet," Byrd recalled. "We just had *fun.*" Everyone had been warned to bring an extra set of clothes, so they changed for lunch. While they ate Laura's blueberry cobbler, "all our bras and undies hung on a clothesline. We all got a big hoot out of that."

By all accounts, Laura was resolute in her desire to lead as normal a life as possible. She could no longer attend an aerobics class as she did when she was the wife of the Texas Rangers owner, but she still strolled out the front door of the governor's mansion alone and took long walks along the banks of Austin's Town Lake with her friends. And there were still excursions to her favorite family-owned Mexican restaurants for salt-rimmed margaritas on the rocks and her favorite dish, enchiladas. "You'd walk into the most unlikely dives," Margo said, "and see her picture under glass by the cash register."

Laura found that, despite the fact that she was perhaps the state's most recognizable female face, she could still take the girls to the dentist, drop in at the hardware store to buy gardening supplies, or catch a movie with an old friend. At a Wal-Mart near the Texas town of Athens, for example, Laura was standing in the checkout line with Barbara and Jenna when another shopper turned to her and asked, "Don't I know you?"

"I'm Laura Bush."

"Sorry," the woman replied. "That doesn't ring a bell." Once outside, the twins doubled over laughing.

On another occasion, the actor and playwright Jaston Williams walked into the post office one morning and saw Laura standing in line. Williams, who had performed at the governor's mansion the previous evening, asked her what she was doing there. "I'm mailing a letter," she replied matter-of-factly.

As chatelaine of the governor's mansion in Austin, Laura thrived on informality. During her entire five years as First Lady of Texas, Laura did not host a single black-tie event at the governor's mansion. Instead, she opted for tailgate parties and Tex-Mex barbecues, sometimes inviting the likes of country star Lyle Lovett to perform. When the Bushes threw a joint "33⅓ Reunion" for Midland's Lee and Midland high schools, the reception was held in a tent on the lawn. There was an unexpected rainfall, but Laura remained unfazed. She slipped off her shoes and, with her similarly barefoot guests, danced to Van Morrison (her favorite) and other golden oldies on the wet grass until 1 A.M. "We had a blast sloshing through the mud and water," said Laura's friend Cindy Klatt. "Laura was right there with us going through the puddles." And the First Lady of Texas didn't leave the party "until she had danced with everyone who wanted to dance with her."

"Laura much prefers riding around in my old white Ford pickup truck than a Suburban," said her friend Bill Bostelmann. "My friends tell me, 'I can't believe you get Laura Bush in that truck!' But this is a girl from Midland."

The common touch was continuing to work wonders for George W., as well. He sometimes supplemented his ever-present cowboy boots with a white Stetson, and his encounters with Texas lawmakers—even members of the opposition party—often left them swooning. "He's our Clinton," party leaders were saying of W.'s hands-on style and undeniable charisma. "People in Texas," Bush soon became fond of saying, "*love* their governor."

To get his message across, W. employed the same techniques for disarming people that he had been perfecting since his Andover cheerleader days. He did not shake hands so much as grab them. His eyes never wandered about the room, but focused intently on the person he was talking to. He nodded as if to agree with the points he was making, and literally shook as he laughed heartily at his own bawdy jokes. Even when a conversation might be at its most serious, W. might suddenly pretend to bump heads with a state senator, or pinch his cheeks—or even playfully put him in a hammerlock. At one point, spotting a group of lobbyists outside the capitol, he rolled down the window of his car and shouted the famous Tom Cruise line from the film *Jerry Maguire:* "Show me the money!" Obligingly, the men whipped out their billfolds.

Then there were the nicknames. Attorney General John Cornyn became "General Corndog." State Senator Teel Bivens was "Biv," and Senator David Sibley, who weighed in at 250 pounds, simply "Big."

Even when he wasn't getting his way, W. often managed to seize the moment. Over breakfast in 1997, bombastic Lieutenant Governor Bob Bullock would tell the Governor that he was going to throw his weight behind a piece of legislation Bush opposed. "I'm sorry, Governor," Bullock said, "but I'm going to have to fuck you on this one."

W. got up, grabbed the Lieutenant Governor, and planted a kiss on his lips. "If you're going to fuck me," said the born-again Governor, "you're going to have to kiss me first." Bullock, the lifelong Democrat, would later endorse Bush for reelection.

Indeed, despite his newfound piety and his clarion calls for personal responsibility and restoring dignity to public office, Bush occasionally peppered his language with raw Anglo-Saxonisms. On the subject of his critics, for example: "Does anyone ever say 'Fuck you'? I don't care if they do."

Often his profane remarks were reserved for unsuspecting colleagues. "Biggest lobbyist in town," he whispered about one as soon as the unsuspecting victim was out of earshot. "Gonna try to fuck me on the tax bill." Moments later, he warmly greeted a key legislator. No sooner did the man walk away than W. muttered, "That guy is trying to kiss my butt now. But he's not on our side, and I know it."

George carefully monitored what he said around Laura and the girls, though an occasional slip would bring a swift reprimand from his wife. It was, in fact, often left to Laura to keep the Governor from getting carried away. "People who dismiss Laura Bush as a mousy librarian are missing her key role," said *Houston Chronicle* columnist Julie Mason. "She's the iron rod at her husband's back. She keeps him from going too far off the deep end when he gets all caught up in his cock-of-the-walk behavior."

Things would take a deadly serious turn in January 1998, when he was faced with the decision of whether or not to spare the life of convicted double murderer Karla Faye Tucker. Tucker, who had admitted to experiencing orgasms with every swing of the pickax she used to kill her victims, was scheduled to become only the second woman executed in Texas since 1863.

Executions were nothing unusual in Texas; Bush would preside over 152 of them during his tenure as Governor. What set Tucker apart was she claimed to have undergone a spiritual awakening, to have found Christ during her thirteen years in prison. She was now a different person, she claimed, one who could only make up for the evil she'd done if she were allowed to live. The case swiftly drew international attention. An emissary for Pope John Paul II sent a letter to W. pleading with him to spare Tucker. Bianca Jagger, acting on behalf of Amnesty International, flew to Austin to try and persuade W. to commute Tucker's sentence to life. Hundreds of other protesters came to Texas, some camping outside the governor's mansion.

As the countdown toward Tucker's scheduled execution continued, CNN's Larry King interviewed the condemned woman from the Mountain View Unit of the Texas prison system. W. had refused to meet with King, just as he had refused to meet with Bianca Jagger and all the others, but the Governor did watch King's televised interview. "It affected me more," he later said, "than I wanted to admit."

W. was also getting pressure from his own supporters among the Christian Right. They saw Tucker as the perfect example of someone who had found salvation through Jesus Christ, and joined the chorus of voices demanding that she be given a reprieve.

Two days before Tucker's scheduled execution, Barbara confronted her dad at the dinner table. "Why are you letting them go ahead with this?" she asked. "I don't think it's right. And besides, I'm against the death penalty."

Dad may have been impressed that his daughters were paying attention to the issue. Until now they had shown, in W.'s words, "almost no interest whatsoever in politics." He told his girls that they had a right to voice their opinions, and that he wanted to hear them. Then he patiently explained his philosophy that capital punishment was a deterrent "if administered swiftly and justly"—and that regardless of what he thought he had a responsibility to uphold the law.

When a journalist asked Laura if she disagreed with her husband on the death penalty, she snapped, "If I differ with my husband, I'm not going to tell *you* about it!" In fact, she and her husband were in agreement on the death penalty, although she declined to weigh in with an opinion on the fate of Tucker. "I wouldn't want to be in your shoes," she told W., "but I have total faith you'll do the right thing." As she watched her husband toss and turn night after night, Laura did grow more concerned about W.'s well-being. "I don't think I've ever seen George so anxious," she told one friend. "This one is really getting to him. I know he's upset—he's having a really tough time falling asleep."

On February 3, 1998, all avenues of appeal had been exhausted, and the U.S. Supreme Court refused to intervene. In one of the hardest and most widely publicized decisions he'd have to make as governor, George W. stepped before the television cameras and announced his final decision. "Like many touched by this case," he said, "I have sought guidance through prayer. I have concluded judgments about the heart and soul of an individual on death row are left to a higher authority." By way of reminding viewers that Tucker's had been a heinous crime, he concluded, "May God bless Karla Faye Tucker, and may God bless her victims and their families."

Then George returned to his office, where he paced the floor as the hour of execution approached. On a night so charged with emotion, Laura stayed home at the mansion with their daughters. Outside the gates, a group of protesters held a candlelight vigil. At 6:35 P.M., W. received word that the lethal dose had been administered. Ten minutes later, Karla Faye Tucker was dead.

W. sighed and telephoned Laura to tell it that it was over—and that he was coming straight home. "The truth is," he later wrote, "I wanted to hear her voice."

That night, Laura reassured her husband that he had done the right thing—that it "took guts" to stand up to all the critics. Politically, he felt he could afford to anger the Christian Right but not the vast majority of Texans who supported the death penalty. When Tucker hinted on *Larry King Live* that the Governor was surrendering to election-year pressure from pro-death penalty factions, W. shook his head.

W. later claimed to have felt some sympathy for Karla Faye Tucker; the night of the execution, he said he felt as if he was being "crushed by a huge piece of concrete." But a year later, Bush would shock one journalist by mocking Tucker. At one point Karla Faye had been asked by Larry King what she would say to Governor Bush if she had the opportunity. When writer Tucker Carlson later asked Bush how Karla Faye had responded to King's question, W. mimicked her reply. "Please don't kill me," he whimpered.

"It seemed odd and cruel," recalled Carlson, "even for someone as militantly anticrime as Bush." (Angry that Tucker Carlson had supposedly printed remarks that were off the record, Bush's handlers coined their own nickname for him: "Mothertucker.")

Nevertheless, W.'s popularity was growing exponentially—both inside and outside the state. For Karen Hughes, the possibility that her boss might be a serious candidate for president first became evident in the fall of 1997, when she held a press conference to deal with the rumors of his candidacy and a Danish television crew showed up. "That's when I knew," she later said, "that it was really starting." By the summer of 1998, polls were showing that W. was not only the favorite for the Republican presidential nomination in 2000, but that he would beat Vice President Al Gore in the general election.

W.'s father warned him not to take the polls too seriously. The only way he would ever win the party's presidential nomination, Poppy told his boy, was to win reelection as governor—"and win *big.*"

Not that W. was admitting to anyone that he had even discussed the subject with his father. When a reporter good-naturedly asked Governor Bush about his dad, Junior snapped, "What about him? This is my life. I was the loyal son, but I'm the guy now!"

Yet W., who had lusted after the job of baseball commissioner, was not even sure he wanted to be president. One of the obstacles to a presidential run was removed in September 1998, when George received an expected windfall. The Texas Rangers were sold, and George and Laura pocketed $14.9 million from his initial investment of $606,000. "It's more money," W. said, "than we will ever need." To those who criticized W.'s more than twenty-fold return on his investment, he responded, "I saw a business opportunity and I seized it. I worked hard to put it together . . . This was not a gimme."

With his family amply provided for, George considered what a run for the presidency would mean. "I'm not sure I want to spend the rest of my life living in the bubble," he would say, referring to the existence led by anyone seeking national office. "I've never been a person who has had every chapter of my life planned out. A year before I ran for governor, I wouldn't have thought I was going to do it. I did not run for governor to be President of the United States."

Laura had her doubts, as well. By the summer of 1998, W. was beginning to broach the subject with his family. "What would you say if I told you I might run for president?" he asked her.

Laura shook her head. "Are you sure, Bushie? You know what it's like . . . Don't forget '92." Stepping up from First Lady of Texas to First Lady of the nation was something Laura had not even considered, much less aimed for. "It's sort of a stretch for me," she said with a shrug, "because I could just as soon, you know, hang around and work in the yard."

Of paramount concern were the girls, who would be headed for college in the fall of 1999. As children they had spent some time in the "bubble" when Gampy was president. They knew it meant a complete loss of privacy, and no chance for anything resembling a normal life. What's more, they would be pursued by the tabloid press or perhaps even cruelly mocked the way Chelsea Clinton had been on *Saturday Night Live*. (Laura claimed she wouldn't mind being spoofed on *Saturday Night Live*, "as long as John Goodman doesn't play me" the way he did Monica Lewinsky whistle-blower Linda Tripp.)

Both Jenna and Barbara tearfully begged their father not to run for president. He would later say that his daughters "cried and cried" whenever he brought up the idea. "One of my great hesitancies about making this race," he said, "is I really don't want their lives to be affected by me, and I know it's going to be . . . I know what it's like to be the son of a president. But I don't know what it's like to be the son of a president at eighteen years old. I'm worried about that point."

By late 1998, W. was concentrating on beating his Democratic rival in the race for governor, Texas land commissioner Gary Mauro. Laura pushed him to use the catchphrase "compassionate conservatism," believing it made her husband more sympathetic and softened the public perception of hard-hearted fat-cat Republicans. The phrase also came with its own built-in retort for critics. "What part don't you like," W. would ask, "the compassion or the conservatism?"

During the reelection campaign, W. rehearsed other lines that might prove useful if he took his act on the road in 2000. "Laura is a great First Lady. Now," he would say with a nod to his enormously popular mother, "the same thing is happening to me that happened to my dad. My wife is more popular than I am.

"You know, they announced recently that my mother's inaugural gown is the only thing from the Bush Administration the Smithsonian is including in its exhibit. The next week," W. cracked, referring to his father's decision to skydive on his seventy-fifth birthday, "the old man jumped out of an airplane.

"My father's been having an identity crisis," the routine went on, "My mother was getting her hair done, and the hairdresser said 'I can't believe I'm doing the hair of the mother of the Governor.'" Another variation on this theme: "I was getting my hair cut the other day, and the barber said, 'I can't believe I'm cutting the hair of Barbara Bush's son.'" Or, "'I can't believe I'm cutting the hair of Laura Bush's husband.'"

He could even joke about his father and the lingering perception that the senior Bush was more Connecticut Yankee than Texan. "Someone said of my dad that he got to Texas a little too late in life, he was already well bred. That wasn't the case with me!"

W. was also not above using his daughters to get a laugh. "No one warned me!" he said of what it was like to be the parent of twin teenage girls. "There are not enough D.P.S. officers in Austin to protect my fellow Texans from these new drivers."

One-liners aside, Dad did worry about his daughters being out on the road. Laura, perhaps because of her own past experience as a teenage driver, did not want to seem overly cautious or "smothering," as she put it. When Mom and Dad bought the girls their first car—Barbara and Jenna would have to share—Laura stood in the driveway and snapped photos, posing them in and out of the car.

"I think I probably worry all the time about my kids," said her friend Katharine Armstrong Idsal. "Laura is much more serene. She's completely entertained by her daughters." To keep them from feeling isolated, Laura urged the girls to invite their friends to the mansion. As a result, the mansion's lot was, said Idsal, always "filled with a million cars—and they're all the girls' friends."

As his first lady grew in stature, W. searched for some public way to pay tribute to her. When she casually mentioned that she would like to do something for her alma mater, W. secretly sprang to action. That Christmas of 1998, W. watched with pride as Laura unwrapped a porcelain replica of the Fondren Library Center at Southern Methodist University. The Governor had given $250,000 to SMU to build a tree-lined brick walkway outside the library in her honor. Laura's in-laws as well as several of their friends contributed to have benches placed along the walkway.

"This is a gift that reflects its namesake," W. said at the dedication of the "Laura Bush Promenade" in the spring of 1999. "This is a serene and peaceful place, just like Laura . . . This promenade reflects a visionary, a decent soul, one who loves books . . . And it reflects my love for Laura." W., his voice choked with emotion and his eyes brimming with tears, came to a sudden halt in the text. As he tried to regain his composure, Laura walked to the podium, embraced her husband, and quietly led him back to his seat.

She holds his feet to the fire. My impression is that privately she tells him exactly what she thinks.

—*Mike Barker, West Texas*
writer and Bush friend

I'll tell you: She's no shrinking violet. If I do something she thinks needs to be toned down, she'll tell me.

—*George*

Rein it in, Bubba.

—*Laura to George*

She is his safety net for life.

—*Bush adviser Mark*
McKinnon

He's a late bloomer, let's face it.

—*Joe O'Neill*

People are going to find out that I've been loyal to my wife.

—*George*

In politics, you always have an opponent. It shouldn't be your spouse.

—*Laura*

6

———◆———

Yesterday was Speculation Day!" W. shouted to the throng of reporters gathered outside the governor's mansion. "Today is Reality Day!" The reality for George W. Bush on November 4, 1998, was that he was about to be reelected by a landslide—the first Texas governor in history ever to be reelected to a consecutive four-year term.

Laura stepped out the front door of the mansion, sidled up to her husband, then clung to him as he went on to talk about his philosophy of compassionate conservatism. How did he feel? one reporter asked. "I feel great," he said with a chuckle. Then, gazing at Laura, he added, "We know how to run an incumbent's campaign."

"That's right, Bushie," she answered softly as she grasped his hand. "We sure do."

By the time the final returns came in, they showed that Governor Bush had trounced his Democratic rival Gary Mauro by a phenomenal 2–1 margin. It was the Big Win Big George said his son needed if he was to mount a viable campaign for president.

For the Bush family, W.'s victory in Texas was only half the reason for celebrating. At the Austin Convention Center ballroom, a blizzard of balloons was released from the ceiling as George and Laura took to the stage. "Tonight is a historic night," he said as Laura stood at his side, occasionally waving to familiar faces in the crowd. "And I want to say something to the newly elected governor of Florida: Good going, brother!" As he always did, W. also thanked his parents, who this time around had thrown themselves into Jeb's campaign against Florida's Democratic Lieutenant Governor Buddy MacKay.

Laura knew at this moment that their fate was sealed. Over the following weeks, she watched and worried as Karen Hughes, Karl Rove, and other key advisers began implementing the strategy that they were convinced would secure the GOP presidential nomination—and ultimately defeat the man they were convinced would be the Democratic nominee, Vice President Al Gore.

Laura made no mention of reluctance publicly, other than to say that the Bushes would "have a life" whether he sought the presidency or not. But behind closed doors, she repeatedly asked her husband if this was what he really wanted. "His dream was to own a baseball team," she said, "or maybe to become baseball commissioner. But run for president? Never." On this point, she got no argument from George. "It was never on my radar screen," he conceded. "If I choose to run and lose, so be it. I'll finish my term as governor and be a happy guy."

Several of their old friends shared Laura's reluctance to see her husband run for president. "We all understood it when he went after Ann Richards in the governor's race," Doug Hannah said. "That was a real blood feud, a real vendetta. But after what happened to his dad—I was shocked that George would subject himself and his family to that. It was just mind-boggling."

Memories of the mudslinging that went on during the 1992 campaign were still fresh in Laura's mind. And she was still "petrified," as one Midland friend put it, that she would have to relive the fatal crash that killed Mike Douglas. Either way, Laura decided that she could no longer shield her daughters from the knowledge that their mother had once killed someone, albeit accidentally.

Jenna and Barbara had known only that their mother had once been involved in an auto accident in which a friend had died. Now Laura felt it was necessary to share the details of what transpired that night in November 1963. "It's probably going to come out during the campaign," she explained, "so you should know exactly what happened . . ." When Laura finished reliving the nightmare, both girls put their arms around her. "It really hit them," said one of Jenna's friends, "just how terrible it had been for their mom—how this was something she had always carried around with her. It also said a lot about the kind of person their mother was—not withdrawn at all, but quiet, thoughtful."

As much as she dreaded the prospect of having to answer questions about the crash, Laura worried even more that W.'s bad boy past might prove embarrassing to the family. "Laura hated it when people made fun of him, or tried to make him look like some ignorant redneck or irresponsible frat boy. It upset her, although she would never show it the way George would."

Nor was she ready to have her children learn all there was to know about their father's past. Jenna and Barbara had been kept in the dark about Daddy's drunk-driving arrest. George and Laura were both afraid that his earlier behavior set a bad example for the girls. "I don't want them looking at me," he explained, "and saying, 'See, Daddy got away with it.'"

The family debate raged on over whether or not they could endure life in what George and Laura called "the bubble" of public scrutiny. The twins were still adamant, even desperate, in their opposition to Dad's candidacy.

Until now, the press had left the girls alone, and they had been able to enjoy something approximating the lives of normal Texas teenagers. Following in Dad's footsteps, brunette Barbara excelled at cross-country as well as softball and soccer at Austin High. She was also Homecoming Queen, made the National Honor Society, and was regarded by her classmates as something of a style-setter. Classmates voted Barbara, who favored vintage clothes, "most likely to appear on the cover of *Vogue*." Jenna, an outgoing blond with a fondness for tank tops and jeans, was active in student government and wrote for the school newspaper. Fellow students predicted she would be "most likely to trip on prom night." Fortunately, the accident-prone Jenna did not.

Both girls were graduating that June, and would be heading for college in the fall—Barbara to Yale ("which thrills her father," Laura said), Jenna to the University of Texas at Austin ("which thrills her mother.")

As they contemplated trying to go on dates with Secret Service agents hovering on the sidelines—not to mention the horror of having their every foible trumpeted by the unforgiving press— both Bush daughters began to panic. More than once, Jenna and Barbara angrily demanded to know why their father was "doing this to us."

Not surprisingly, W.'s stock explanations—that it was in the national interest that he run, that there was no one else to assume the mantle, that personal sacrifices often had to be made for the greater good, that the Bushes had a tradition of public service—fell on deaf ears. "It was really rough on both George and Laura for a time," said a friend of the family. "Anyone who has kids that age knows what it's like under normal circumstances. There was a lot of arguing, a lot of crying, a few scenes at the dinner table where one of them would leave in tears."

Jenna proved to be the sassier of the two. "You know, Dad," she said more than once, "you're not half as cool as people think." This was the reason that family members called Jenna "Barbara's revenge" on her wiseacre son. For the time being, Laura was willing to laugh off her daughters' rebellious streak. "They kind of give each other permission to misbehave," she sighed.

Laura shared in her daughters' anxiety. But she took solace in the fact that, after the initial round of cruel *Saturday Night Live* skits poking fun at Chelsea, the media essentially left Bill and Hillary Clinton's only child alone for the remaining seven and a half years of the Clinton presidency. "Chelsea Clinton has been able to have a pretty normal life," Laura reassured her daughters. "The media has pretty much left her alone. I don't see why they wouldn't do the same for you." As for their role in the campaign: "You won't have one," Laura said. "You don't have to talk to the press. You don't have to do anything you don't want to do."

In the end, it was left to W. to promise his daughters that he would "do what it takes" to ensure their privacy during the campaign and beyond. "We'll just make it clear to everybody that my girls are off-limits to the press. Period. Anyone who has a problem with that will have to answer to me."

Laura had already taken steps to protect her daughters. When *Newsweek* got hold of Barbara's impressive SAT score, Mama phoned the magazine to ask that the score not be published. "Please,

I would like it to remain private," she said. "Barbara would be so embarrassed."

In their zeal to protect their daughters' privacy, both George and Laura never lost sight of the fact that the twins were leaving home. "Especially now as we look ahead to the empty nest," a suddenly vulnerable-sounding Laura told a group of Republican women in Louisiana, "we remember those times when they were babies. It goes so fast. So this is a sort of bittersweet time for us as well."

Soon, both Bush girls were telling their friends they were confident they could continue to avoid the media spotlight, even if Daddy became president. "It's not like we're going to live at the White House," they told high school pal Angela Salas, "so coverage won't be like it was for Chelsea. We'll have our normal lives."

There was one last nagging doubt Laura harbored—one that she shared with one of her closest friends. "Laura was afraid about what might happen if he won," said a confidante of nearly thirty years. "She had faith in George, but she also remembered what it was like when he drank too much—and keep in mind that he drank too much for the first ten years of their marriage. Laura was concerned that the stress of being president might start him to drinking again."

"It's going to be an incredible change to our family," W. said of his candidacy. "Laura wanted to make sure it was something I had my heart set on. She understands exactly what we're fixing to get into." Later, whenever it was mentioned that Laura had been last to board the bandwagon, she protested, "Last? I was the *first.*"

"Twenty-five years ago, who'd have thought that he'd run for president?" asked Joe O'Neill, echoing the sentiments of their friends back in Texas. "It took Laura, some dry holes, and some talks with himself to get settled down."

Even as they made their first tentative steps toward the White House, Laura and George agreed that they would need a place all their own—a refuge from the stress of campaigning and, if he won, the presidency. After considering several properties throughout Texas, they plunked down $1.3 million for 1,583 acres in the dusty, one-stoplight town of Crawford (population 700), some twenty-five miles west of Waco and a two-hour drive from Austin. The former pig farm had belonged to the Engelbrecht family, descendants of German immigrants who settled in Texas in the mid-nineteenth century. With the new owners' permission, Kenneth Engelbrecht would still run Brangus cattle on the Bush ranch.

At first glance, the spread on Prairie Chapel Road seemed anything but inviting with its parched terrain ("Flat as a cow chip," said one local wit) and sizzling temperatures. But on closer inspection, the property also boasted a river, fields of wildflowers, sprawling oaks, hundreds of pecan trees, and what one Bush adviser called its own scaled-down version of "the Grand Canyon"—a gorge that is "absolutely spectacular."

George and Laura had no intention of actually working the land themselves. "I'm what you call a windshield rancher," he explained. "I get in my pickup and drive all over the place, ranching through the windshield." Often he stopped along one of the dirt roads that wound through his property and hopped out to inspect the livestock. "I love to go walking out there, seeing the cows," he said. "Occasionally, they talk to me—being the good listener that I am."

Cows were, for the most part, the only creatures George and Laura could see for miles. "It's a very, very lonely landscape," conceded David Heymann, the architect they hired to build a home on the property. "The sky feels very large. You walk around there, and you really feel alone."

That was the idea. Ostensibly, all George asked for was "a king-size bed and a good shower." He also said he wanted the house to be the kind of informal place where he could invite people over for "beans and hamburgers."

But over the course of several months, they painstakingly reviewed every construction detail. Every weekend, the Bushes would join Heymann at the house site, where the architect would hammer stakes into the ground and the Bushes would stand inside the staked-out area visualizing what the view would be like from different angles.

"Laura has a very, very clear emotional knowledge about her world," Heymann said, "and the way she wants it to be, and she uses that to make decisions. She wants you to feel about the house that while it is not demanding of you, it is clearly intelligent."

"One thing we wanted was to make sure the house fit into the landscape," Laura explained. Toward that end, it was low and long and narrow—essentially one room wide—and constructed of limestone native to the area. To get from one room to the other, the Bushes had to walk outside to the covered porch that ran the length of the structure. A modest four thousand square feet, it included a living room, three bedrooms, and two studies. Virtually all the rooms had floor-to-ceiling windows; when they opened the drapes in the master bedroom, the early-rising Bushes could drink in the sunrise. To the north and south, there were views of the distant hills. A ten-acre man-made pond stocked with five thousand bass shimmered to the east, and to the west a large grove of oaks protected the house from the afternoon sun. Only steps from the main residence, just before the detached garage, was a two-bedroom guest house. Although the architect felt it clashed with the overall design of the house, there was also a swimming pool—"The Whining Pool," Bush called it, because his daughters kept whining ("There's nothing to do out here!") until he relented and put it in.

Out of deference to Laura's octogenarian mom and the senior Bushes, there were no steps or thresholds in the house. "We also wanted to grow old ourselves here," Laura said.

W. had angered environmentalists by, among other things, advocating drilling for oil in wilderness areas. But his Crawford ranch house was decidedly eco-friendly. A silent underground geothermal system provided both heat and air-conditioning, and household waste water as well as rainwater were collected and reused for irrigation.

With her husband understandably preoccupied, it was left to Laura to keep a tight rein on expenses. Despite their wealth, the Bushes impressed Heymann as "frugal people." In choosing doorknobs, plumbing fixtures, cabinets, and the like, Laura eschewed the most expensive choices. "That's too grand," she would say. "I don't want people coming in here and going, 'Ohmigod, they've spent every last penny.'"

Laura's lingering doubts about her husband's presidential candidacy aside, the W. juggernaut rolled on. By the spring of 1999, the anointing of George W. Bush as the Republican candidate was made to seem all but inevitable. *Newsweek*'s cover proclaimed W. the "Rising Son," while *U.S. News & World Report* called him "The Man to Beat." Both *Time* and *Fortune* magazines opted for a simple "President Bush?" on their respective covers.

The first real test would come that summer at the straw poll in

Ames, Iowa. In mid-June 1999, Bush departed Austin on an MD-80 christened *Great Expectations*. As the plane taxied down the runway, W. got on the intercom. "Please stow your expectations securely in the overhead bin," he said. "They could fall and hurt someone."

It had been only four months since the impeachment trial of President Clinton. The Senate had voted 55–45 to acquit President Clinton on the perjury charges and tied 50–50 on the obstruction of justice charges—both falling far short of the two-thirds needed to convict. Yet Rove and other Bush strategists were convinced that Clinton's wanton behavior in the Oval Office would almost certainly taint Al Gore's campaign.

From the outset, W. claimed the moral high ground while acknowledging his own questionable past. "I've made mistakes," he told supporters in Iowa, "but I'm going to bring honor, integrity, and dignity to the office."

It was a strategy endorsed by Big George who, despite his claims to the contrary, was virtually in constant touch with his son the candidate via phone, fax, and e-mail. Big George weighed in on virtually every aspect of the campaign. When he was not advising his son directly, the elder Bush spent countless hours on the phone rounding up support—monetary and otherwise—for W. Her husband was, Barbara Bush said, "obsessed" with their eldest son's candidacy.

Among other things, Big George urged his son not to overlook Laura's appeal to voters. If W. was portraying himself as the antidote to Bill Clinton, then Laura the soft-spoken school librarian was typecast as the anti-Hillary. Barbara Bush believed her daughter-in-law would be different from Hillary because "she would not get into foreign affairs or controversial subjects." Then, Bar added wryly, "I think she would rather make a positive impact on the country. And I'm not criticizing Mrs. Clinton. But it's like oil and water. We're talking about two different subjects. They're two different people. I think Laura thinks of others."

To stress that she had no political agenda of her own, Laura told ABC's Barbara Walters that she did not give her husband "a lot of advice" other than to "sit up straight . . . Not really. I mean not that I can think of. We talk about issues, of course. Um. I don't give him a lot of advice. I really don't think George wants a lot of advice from me."

"That's not true," W. objected.

But before he could go on, Laura quipped, "I don't want a lot of advice from him."

Laura made it clear to anyone who asked that she would not be proposing health care legislation or setting up her own run for the Senate. "Hey, Laura," W. joked during an interview, "about that Medicare plan—will you work out those prescription costs?"

"Oh, yeah," she replied with a wink.

Laura again pointed to her mother-in-law as her role model. "Maybe she wasn't so out-front in policy meetings," Laura said of Barbara Bush, "but she's very strong." Indeed Laura, like Bar, would continue to influence her husband's thinking on a wide range of issues from education and, yes, health care to crime and the Middle East. But instead of a paneled conference room, these intimate discussions would invariably take place in bed, over coffee and the morning papers.

Ultimately, Laura always deferred to her husband on the issues: "I'm not the candidate," she liked to remind those who pressed her for opinions. But on one topic—abortion—Laura felt strongly enough to try and talk W. out of his rigid right-to-life stance. Although she would not state her own pro-choice view publicly until well after the election was decided, behind the scenes Laura counseled George not to knuckle under to antiabortion groups that wanted him to campaign on the issue. She also told him flatly that she did not think *Roe v. Wade,* the 1973 Supreme Court decision legalizing abortion, should be overturned. It was an opinion long shared by George W.'s own mother.

Officially, W. continued to oppose abortion except in cases of rape, incest, or when the mother's life was endangered. But he rarely campaigned on the issue. When he did mention the subject, Bush argued that the number of abortions in America could be reduced by teaching personal responsibility and abstinence. "He still thinks abortion is wrong," a staffer said, "but he also has a great deal of respect for Laura's opinion. She convinced him to tread lightly on that particular subject during the campaign, definitely."

The candidate also respected his wife's political instincts, and her fine-tuned sense of what would—and would not—appeal to voters. Particularly women voters. At various times, W. ran his statements by

Laura to see if they were too harsh. When his parents were visiting the ranch that Easter, he wondered aloud if the wording of a policy statement was too strong. Rather than ask his father's opinion, W. told his staff, "Read it to Laura. See what she thinks." And Laura was not shy about telling her husband who she liked—and who she didn't. "I'm not George's adviser," she insisted. "I'm his wife. I don't advise him about policy, but we do talk issues—and personalities."

One personality she clearly disapproved of was the same man W. wanted to succeed in office. Several times, Laura told her friends that she found Bill Clinton "disgusting," that his behavior was "disgraceful," and that she felt "truly sorry for poor Chelsea. It's just terribly sad." In a not-so-subtle reference to the incumbent president's peccadilloes, Laura told a crowd in Ames that "Americans want somebody who they do trust, someone who they feel won't embarrass them but instead will make them proud." Her husband, unlike the then-current occupant of the Oval Office, was "a man of strong conviction and strong faith who keeps his word and loves his family . . . Governor Bush has represented Texas with dignity and honor. I'd like to see him do the same thing for our nation in its highest office."

To show where his priorities stood, W. passed up a preprimary debate in New Hampshire to attend a black-tie dinner honoring Laura as an SMU "distinguished alumna." Why? asked a reporter. "Because I love my wife," he answered incredulously.

The race had scarcely begun, and already Laura was proving a valuable asset on the campaign trail. Yet she was not the only woman George would come to depend upon. Condoleezza Rice, Stanford University provost and a former member of the elder Bush's national security team, was charged with keeping him abreast on all foreign policy matters. Throughout their marathon briefings, W. eschewed the minutia that Al Gore found so fascinating and zeroed in on the Big Picture. In meeting after meeting, he interrupted Rice and the other experts on foreign and domestic policy with the kinds of blunt questions that cut to the heart of the matter. "What exactly," he would typically ask, "is in the best interest of the U.S.?"

Still, he was scarcely prepared for an encounter with a Boston television reporter that left him groping for the not-always-easy-to-pronounce names of four world leaders. When asked to name the

Pakistani leader who had just grabbed power in a military coup, W. stammered, "General. I can't name the general. General." (Two years later Pakistan's president, General Pervez Musharraf, would be a key ally in America's war on terrorism.)

The pop quiz, which just happened to occur on Laura's fifty-second birthday as W. geared up for the New Hampshire primary contest, proved to be one of the campaign's more embarrassing moments. It underscored what many perceived to be Bush's lack of knowledge when it came to foreign policy. Hours later, W. was back in Austin celebrating with Laura and her friends. "Don't worry, Bushie," Laura comforted him. "Nobody's going to blame you for not knowing how to pronounce the name of the President of Pakistan."

Laura spent much of the following day, their twenty-second wedding anniversary, with her mother. George, not surprisingly, spent hours behind closed doors boning up on foreign affairs with Condi Rice. Less than two weeks later, they confronted a tragedy close to home as a bonfire students were building collapsed at Texas A&M, killing twelve and injuring dozens more. On November 25, George and Laura joined Poppy and Barbara at a candlelight vigil in honor of the victims.

Turning his attention back to the campaign, W. realized that the fallout from the failed pop quiz, which aired repeatedly in the coming weeks, had not dissipated. Over the years he had been to Mexico several times, and to Scotland and to China and Argentina and Gambia and the Middle East—yet there was a mounting perception that W. had never left the country.

Condi Rice was to continue to play a key role as the candidate's foreign-affairs tutor. Over the next several months, she grew increasingly close to both George and Laura as she spent more and more time in Austin and at the ranch. Laura felt Crawford, in particular, was the perfect setting for these sessions. The ranch had "the best walks ever," Laura explained. "Steep walks into canyons by the creeks. Condi Rice explained the Balkans to George walking up one of those canyons. We congratulated her for never stopping to catch her breath or even breathing hard." The Bushes named that particular trail "Balkan Hill."

Yet as close as Rice was to the governor and his wife, from a strictly political standpoint the most important woman in W.'s life was the "High Prophet" Karen Hughes. Easily W.'s most trusted and influential adviser, Hughes would become virtually indispensable to the candidate. Theirs, according to W.'s pal Andy Card, would be a "mystical bond."

Laura knew why. "She and my husband have the same great instinct," Laura would later say, "the same gut. A lot of it has to do with his mother. Now I'm really putting him on the couch—he'll hate this." Laura traced it all back to Robin's death, when Georgie took it upon himself to comfort his grief-stricken mom. As a result, he developed what Laura called a "completely subconscious sensitivity" to strong, outspoken women. Because of Barbara, Laura said, W. "likes women. He feels comfortable with them."

Hughes was the person he turned to when sportswriter and author Mickey Herskowitz stopped working on the George Bush autobiography that was planned for release in 1999. The High Prophet holed up in her Austin home and wrote *A Charge to Keep* (the title is based on a hymn by Charles Wesley) in time to make the original publication schedule. George and Laura, meanwhile, spent Thanksgiving with daughter Barbara in Rome, where she was spending a junior semester abroad. It was W.'s first trip to Italy—a country that impressed him as being "full of beautiful art and mopeds." Determined to seize the opportunity to look more presidential, W. went on to Cairo to have dinner with President Hosni Mubarak, then hooked up with a group of Republican governors touring Israel.

However shrewd Hughes and the rest of W.'s advisers may have been, they were not always able to save the candidate from himself. No sooner had he won the Iowa straw poll than W. began making the kind of equivocating comments regarding his past drug use that he had so assiduously avoided in the past. First he claimed he could pass the background check that asks all White House appointees whether they have used drugs in the past seven years. The next day, W. claimed he could even have passed the fifteen-year background check that was in place back when his father was inaugurated in 1989—meaning that he had not used drugs for twenty-five years.

But the damage was done. The headline on the front page of the *Dallas Morning News* blared "Bush Says He Hasn't Used Drugs in

Last Seven Years," and the press was suddenly demanding to know exactly when W. *had* used illegal drugs—assuming, of course, that he had.

Laura joined with her mother-in-law in urging W. to hang tough. "Just tell them you've said all you're going to say on the subject," Laura told her husband, echoing the sentiments of Hughes and other top advisers.

But George couldn't resist offering up his own his rationale for not going into too much detail. "I choose not to inventory my sins," he said, "because I don't want anybody to be able to say, 'Well, the governor of Texas did it, why shouldn't I?' Whether it's my daughter or somebody else's child. That's why I have been somewhat mysterious about my past." Not surprisingly, such remarks only made matters worse. "His nondenial was not as bad as Clinton's infamous 'I never broke the laws of my country,' " observed *Time* magazine's Nancy Gibbs, "but it was sung in the same key."

It was left to another important woman in W.'s life to put the issue to rest. "His father and I never asked him [about past drug use]," Barbara Bush told ABC. "We had no need to. He's always been a fabulous son . . . I'm very glad he's taken the stand he has, because the time has come to say, 'Enough!' "

There were other delicate moments for both George and Laura. As she feared, a few newspapers reported the basic facts surrounding the fatal auto crash Laura had caused in 1963. But to her profound relief, no one pursued the story in any detail. She was also surprised that W.'s drunk-driving arrest had somehow remained off the radar screen.

The rumors about his "wild past" persisted, however—from the time he supposedly danced naked on a bar during his college days to the completely contrived story that had him crashing a military jet while flying under the influence of alcohol. "I tell her the rumors, of course," said W., who claimed that she got a "good laugh" out of most of them. "Except the womanizing stuff," he said. "Everyone knows, or should know, that I have been faithful to my wife for the past twenty-one years. I have never committed adultery—not once, not ever, not since the day I put my hand on the Bible and said 'till death do us part.' "

"We laugh about all those crazy stories," she said dismissively.

"You have to—they're so silly." What she found less amusing was the growing perception that her husband was, well, dim.

After suffering an unexpected defeat at the hands of Arizona Senator John McCain in the New Hampshire primary, George called his advisers to his room at the Manchester Days Inn. "What the hell happened?" he shouted at them.

"He was pretty darn angry," recalled one. "We were pretty convinced that heads were going to roll." Then Laura, whose duties in New Hampshire had included participating with her husband in a pancake-flipping contest, stepped in to calm her husband down with a few soothing, reassuring words. "Now, Bushie . . ." she invariably began.

"Don't worry, I'm not blaming any of you," a cooled-down W. told his staff, acknowledging that he simply had not campaigned as hard in the state as he should have. "Nobody is going to be fired."

It would not be the first time Laura came to the rescue of her husband's overworked staff. "Laura can be plenty tough, and she can chew him out," said W.'s longtime friend Robert McCleskey. "I saw them once when he was giving orders to all these people and rattling off commands, and she just looked at him and said, 'Bushie, you're not president yet!' "

Mike Proctor, another close friend of both W. and Laura since early childhood, agreed that "Laura has had a profound impact on keeping his mouth shut. In many ways Laura is not unlike George's mother. She has a quiet strength, but when Laura gets a burr in her saddle you can see the fire in her eye."

Brother Jeb echoed the rest of the family's appreciation of Laura's grit, not to mention the stabilizing role she played in W.'s life. "She," Jeb said, "is his check and balance."

At the same time it was Laura who, after cooling down tempers, told George to launch a strong counterattack against McCain. "You've got to get out there, Bushie," she said, "and let people see that you're the better man for the job." Said Bush media adviser Mark McKinnon: "Laura was the one after New Hampshire who told her husband he had to fight back."

Accordingly, Team Bush regrouped for the next primary battle in South Carolina. However outwardly pacific her demeanor, Laura was feeling the stress. During the weeks leading up to New Hampshire she had been eagerly devouring the works of Truman Capote, but her nerves were so frazzled in the wake of the McCain victory that she had to abandon the book she was reading—Capote's gruesome true-crime epic *In Cold Blood*—and turn her attention to bolstering her husband's spirits. "It's so foreboding," she said of the book, "and I was reading it during the most anxiety-provoking time and I had to quit."

In addition to changing her reading material, Laura turned to an old stress-reducing habit. Whenever she was satisfied there were no members of the press around, Laura bummed a cigarette off the nearest smoker and appeared to savor every drag.

For George, the next ten days proved to be one of the most grueling phases of the campaign. Exhausted and coming down with a cold, George called his old friend Charlie Younger and admitted to feeling "terrible, wiped out. I've never been this tired before in my life. But you just do it—it's out of your control . . ."

W.'s determination paid off. After derailing McCain's campaign with an overwhelming victory in South Carolina, W. steamrolled over the competition in the remaining primary contests. By mid-March, he had more than half the number of votes he would need to win the nomination at the Republican National Convention in Philadelphia.

Through it all, Laura cringed every time her husband mangled a sentence or gave birth to yet another awe-inspiring non sequitur. Whenever he was forced to veer from his "I'm a uniter, not a divider" mantra, there was, in the words of one top adviser, "sometimes no way of telling what he might say."

On the question of education, one of his principal campaign issues, W. stated, "Rarely is the question asked: Is our children learning." As for teachers: "We want them to know how to teach the science of reading. In order to make sure there's not this kind of federal cuff link." At a school celebrating Perseverance Month, he remarked, "This is Preservation Month. I appreciate preservation. It's what you do when you run for president. You gotta preserve."

When it came to his own daughters' education, he observed that "Laura and I really don't realize how bright our children is sometimes until we get an objective analysis."

Bread and butter issues were no less taxing for the Governor. W.

told working moms, "I know how hard it is for you to put food on your family." To expand opportunity, Bush insisted that "we ought to make the pie higher." On capitalism: "I understand small business growth. I was one." The main problem with Social Security: "There's not going to be enough people in the system to take advantage of people like me."

Quotas would not "Balkanize" society, they would "vulcanize" it. Tariffs and barriers became "bariffs and terriers." Kosovars became "Kosovians" and Greeks "Grecians." At one point W. declared, "If you're sick and tired of the politics of cynicism and polls and principles, come and join this campaign." As for his own résumé: "The most important job is not to be governor, or first lady, in my case." W.'s voice choked with emotion as he thanked his campaign workers. "I'm very gracious and humbled," he said. W.'s most famous malaprop: transforming "subliminal" into "subliminable."

There were other awkward moments that had nothing to do with his grasp of English and everything to do with his lack of interest in pop culture (with the obvious exception of sports). At various times during the campaign, he had to be told who Leonardo DiCaprio and NBC's Stone Philips were, what the word "vegan" meant, and that *Friends* was a TV sitcom. When a *Glamour* magazine writer asked him what he thought of *Sex and the City,* W. was about to fly into a purple-veined rage when an aide informed him it was a hit HBO series, and not an impertinent question about his own personal habits.

"You know, I don't really mind people picking on me," he replied when asked if he had the intellectual heft for the job. "I know what I can do. I've never held myself out to be any great genius, but I'm plenty smart. And I've got good common sense and good instincts. And that's what people want in their leader."

For the most part, W. handled the gaffs with characteristic self-deprecating humor. Indeed, he seemed unusually relaxed—so much so that at times he sometimes kicked back and waxed nostalgic about past addictions. As his campaign plane headed for the Kentucky Derby the first week in May, Bush mused about his smoking days. "The coolest thing of all," he said, "was to light up a butt." Then he rambled on about his tobacco-chewing days, and how he eventually reached the point where he no longer spit out the tobacco juice but swallowed it for that extra nicotine rush.

Once he arrived at Churchill Downs, W. was greeted with shouts of "Go get 'em, W.," and "Good luck, George." He judiciously declined to sip a mint julep—or to place a bet. "You should have seen me twenty years ago," W. said. "I'd be betting and drinking all at the same time."

The attacks on George's intellect—or the perceived lack thereof—did nothing to dampen his sense of fun. W. continued his relentless clowning, tweaking reporters, bestowing nicknames (he often fell back on the generic "Dude!"), mugging for the cameras, making light of his linguistic shortcomings. Periodically, he shocked the reporters covering his campaign with what appeared to be inappropriate behavior. During a memorial service for the victims of a mass shooting in Fort Worth, for example, he repeatedly turned from his pew at the front of the church to make faces at reporters sitting toward the rear.

What may have seemed like bizarre behavior was only logical to Laura, who wore sunglasses throughout the memorial service and surreptitiously dabbed behind the dark lenses with a Kleenex. "Humor," she said, shrugging, "is just the way he copes with things." The incident in Fort Worth was simply the legacy of his childhood, when in a time of soul-crushing sorrow—the death of his sister Robin—it was left to Georgie to lift his mother's spirits.

In the end, most of the journalists covering Bush were disarmed by his ability to poke fun at himself. "It really hurts to know," he quipped, "that my dad's idea of the perfect son is Al Gore." When the *New York Times*'s Frank Bruni told W. he had to "seize the window" of opportunity for an impromptu interview, the candidate said, "Seize the window? You're talking like me!"

Yet there were plenty of moments when W.'s behavior was over the top, and when Laura was around she did not hesitate to point it out to him. "George can really get wound up, and she puts up with him—to a point," their longtime friend and accountant Robert McCleskey said. "But when he goes on a rant, she's the one who'll rein him in. Laura can bring him back to earth real quick."

"George is a lot like his mother," Charlie Younger observed. "He says what's on his mind. That means that sometimes he'll blurt something out and it's a real zinger. Laura has always tried to keep that habit of his in check."

One of George's favorite targets, in fact, was Laura. "From the very beginning, George would go to some lengths to try and get under Laura's skin," Younger said. "He would push her to the limit, and she would take it only so long and then—well, he knew when to back off. Then it was her turn to bait him. It was a real give-and-take relationship."

Aboard the Bush campaign plane, the candidate's wife cut short his antics more than once with an affectionate, "Now, *Bushieee,*" or "Bushie, you *know* that isn't true!" Other times a more exasperated Laura cut him short with a crisply delivered "Rein it in, Bubba."

Her chief role, as it had been from the beginning of their relationship, was getting her husband to "bring it down a notch," said one adviser. "She's very good at relaxing him," added former Bush media adviser Stuart Stevens. Before the taping of a television interview, for instance, "if she was around, he would go from being pulled from one thing to another to being in a zone where he was relaxing, laughing at all their private jokes." Unlike Bill Clinton, whose mood soured when Hillary entered the room, W. became visibly more serene with Laura around. "A lot of times when the candidate's wife is around, it adds tension to a situation," Stevens said. "But this was just the opposite."

Not that Laura was without her mischievous, playful side. She took an avid interest in the love lives of her younger, single staff members, and was not above playing matchmaker. Those who viewed Laura as the quintessential sheltered, shy librarian were also surprised to learn that back in Texas she numbered several openly gay males among her friends. "Laura is one of those people who really opens up once she trusts you," one said. "She's got a wicked, very dry sense of humor, and she's a lot more sophisticated about things than she lets on."

Despite her best efforts to keep W. "reined in," there was little she could do to keep him from being skewered in the press. "Laura knows that George can mangle the language sometimes. But of course it always hurts to see someone you love made fun of," said a friend who had known Laura since her days at SMU. "George is an intelligent man. He went to Yale *and* Harvard, for gosh sakes. For all their kidding around, I think Laura has always felt that he's smarter than she is. Always. So she's understandably frustrated when he's made out to be some kind of idiot."

No one knew better than W. that, as he put it, "perception is everything in politics." One way to offset any nagging doubts about his abilities was to surround himself with heavyweights from George H. W. Bush's administration. As the convention approached in July, W. again followed his father's advice and tapped former Defense Secretary Dick Cheney to screen potential running mates.

Colin Powell was everybody's first choice, but Powell let it be known that he would rather be secretary of state. Former Missouri Senator John Danforth and New York Governor George Pataki were largely unknown to the vast majority of Americans. And W. was wary of John McCain, who for all his undeniable star power could not be counted on as anything remotely resembling a team player. "Everybody felt that McCain had to at least be considered," an aide said, "but there was no way he was going to be picked. Laura made it pretty clear that she thought he had his own agenda—she just didn't trust McCain to do what was best for George Bush, and Laura's opinion mattered a great deal to her husband."

Both Bushes agreed that there should be one paramount consideration in the selection process. "The most important thing," W. told his advisers, "is that I pick someone who likes me."

George and Laura flew to Crawford for one final long weekend at the ranch before the convention in Philadelphia. There they took reporters on a tour of their dream house—the next Western White House, should he win. W. half-jokingly explained that they hoped to see the house finished "by election day." A few visitors were lucky enough to be taken on an extended tour of the spread. When they came to Rainey Creek, one asked if the water was drinkable.

"Sure," W. responded, as the man cupped the water in his hand and brought it to his lips. "Except for the cowshit." He later apologized. "Couldn't resist," he said, smiling.

While the new house was under construction, the Bushes stayed in what they called "the Governor's House," an older dwelling on the property that was situated just over a small ridge. There, where a singing "Billy Bass" plaque hung on the living room wall and Spot the springer spaniel curled up on the floor, W. and Dick Cheney mulled over Bush's dwindling options for choosing a running mate.

Sitting across the kitchen table from each other, the two men chugged Diet Cokes and gobbled sandwiches as they debated the pros and cons of the few remaining candidates. At dusk, W. cooked up hamburgers and steaks on the grill while Laura and Condi Rice made the salad. Although Cheney's serious heart condition prevented him from joining W. on his morning runs in the sweltering heat, the former defense secretary rode shotgun in the Bush pickup while W. indulged in a little "windshield ranching."

It would be left to Laura to come up with an obvious solution. She had been privately sharing her thoughts on all of the possibilities—offering up her own assessment of how each might mesh with W.'s personality. Finally, she blurted out, "So why not pick Dick?" Cheney had been unfailingly loyal to two generations of Bushes, she pointed out. And his years of experience—Cheney was only thirty-four when he was appointed Gerald Ford's chief of staff and served for a decade as Wyoming's sole representative in the House—could only lend substance to the ticket. Though she did not use the term, Cheney would provide Republicans with that indefinable something all the pundits had been talking about: "gravitas." And besides, the two men obviously got along with each other.

At about the same time, Poppy came up with the same idea—pick Cheney. Karl Rove, seeing that such a move might make W. look like a surrogate for his father, resisted the idea. But Laura and Karen Hughes argued that it was precisely what the ticket needed.

At W.'s coronation in Philadelphia, the delegates seemed to agree with Laura and Poppy, welcoming the candidate's unexpected choice of Cheney as his running mate. But they were also impressed by the candidate's wife, who arrived at the convention with her daughters in tow.

It remained to be seen what, if any, role the girls would play in the campaign. "I'm concerned about these girls, I really am," W. said. "I want them to be happy. To the extent possible, I want them to be shielded from all the news and all the noise of politics."

Laura would not be so lucky. Karen Hughes had convinced her to give the kickoff address at the convention, a prime-time event that would for all intents and purposes serve as her national political debut. Again, she hearkened back to the day he promised her she would never have to give a political speech. "But I said I was going to jog with him every day," she admitted this time. "I failed my part of the prenuptial agreement, too. We're even now."

W. knew all too well what he was asking of her. "If [back in 1977] I'd have said, 'Honey, you'll be the kickoff speaker at the Republican convention in the year 2000,' she would have said, 'You've totally lost your mind, and I'm not marrying you.' "

As he and Laura made a final swing through the Midwest in the days leading up to the convention, W. was eager for "America to get to know her." Her strongest appeal, he suggested, was her "down-to-earth quality . . . She cuts right through, through the posturing and positioning. America's starved for something. I'm telling you: they're starved for something real. And that's what she brings. She's a real person."

But was he nervous for his wife as she prepared to address the convention? "Not in the least. She's nervous for herself," he allowed, "but she shouldn't be. She's a wonderful speaker, she's got a nice message, and I'm excited for her."

Naturally, Laura was terrified. "*Of course* I'm nervous," she said. "Who wouldn't be? Pretty awesome . . . I get butterflies thinking about it." It didn't help that W. told every rally in every state that she was going to be "wonderful."

"He's *trying* to make me very nervous," said Laura, curled up on the seat next to George as they flew to another rally in Louisville, Kentucky, just two days before the convention. A copy of Katherine Anne Porter's short stories rested in her lap. Peering over his reading glasses at a newspaper, W. pretended to be reading a huge headline: "Bush Makes Wife Nervous!" Laura shook her head in mock exasperation.

Both George and Laura had practiced their convention speeches in front of a TelePrompTer and a dozen family friends—though each was too nervous to do it in the other's presence. The night before she was to deliver her address, Laura slept fitfully, listening to the clock chime 2, 3, 4, and 5 A.M. The next day, she checked out the podium and delivered a few lines to the largely empty convention hall. She even tried out her Miss America wave on the imaginary crowd below. Hours later, standing on stage before rows of children who had been seated at classroom desks, the former school librarian launched into her speech—but not before being greeted by a thunderous ovation. "All right now," she said in her best stern schoolmarm manner, "quiet down." And they did.

A few days before, when the Bushes stood on a stage with the Cheneys for the first time, Laura's drab gray outfit was overshadowed by Lynne Cheney's lime green suit. This time, bound and determined to be the center of attention, Laura wore flashy gold-and-diamond earrings that George had given her—and an eye-popping pistachio green suit of her own.

W., still campaigning in the battleground state of Ohio, beamed as he watched her performance on television with a group of honor students at a Cincinnati high school. "She looks great!" he said as she took the stage.

"You know I am completely objective when I say," she told the delegates and a TV audience of twenty million, "you have made a *great* choice." She went on to point out that Jenna and Barbara, who were on hand to lend their mother moral support, would be leaving home for college in a matter of weeks. "They say parents often have to get out of the house when their kids go off to college because it seems so lonely," she observed. "Everyone deals with it in different ways. But I told George I thought running for president was a little extreme."

Laura went on to pledge that as first lady she would make early childhood development a top priority—alluding to the fact that she had already wrested from her husband a promise to beef up the nation's Head Start program. Then, in a shot at Al Gore, she observed that "George's opponent has been visiting schools lately and sometimes when he does, he spends the night before at the home of a teacher. Well," she added wryly, "George spends *every* night with a teacher."

In another pointed reference to the Clinton Administration, she proclaimed that her husband's "core principles will not change with the winds of polls or politics or fame or fortune or misfortune . . . I sat by his side during some winning and many losing baseball seasons. But George never loses sight of home plate."

Laura, who was interrupted for applause thirty times, was relieved when it was all over. But she was also buoyed by the positive response to her speech, even from jaded members of the political press. Laura struck "a perfect pitch between confidence and humility," wrote *New York*'s Lawrence O'Donnell Jr., "that allowed her to convey the gee-I-never-expected-to-be-standing-here subtext that Hillary Clinton, the determined career politician, never could." Her speech, O'Donnell proclaimed, was "the best ever by a first lady–in–waiting."

Minutes after Laura left the stage, W. was on the phone congratulating her. He only hoped, he told her, that he could do half as well with his acceptance speech. W. had actually spent months honing his own address, sending it back to his speech writers eighteen times before he was finally satisfied. The practice session he had on the eve of Laura's speech was actually only one of more than a dozen rehearsals conducted during the last week in July. When he finally delivered it at the convention on August 2, Laura told him without hesitation that it was the best speech he had ever given. The pundits agreed.

Rave reviews aside, George W. Bush was still fielding questions about his intellect in the days following the convention. "So how do you assure folks you're smart enough to be president?" *Time* magazine Managing Editor Walter Isaacson asked him point-blank.

"I'm confident of my intellect," he answered. "I wouldn't be running if I wasn't. My job will not be to outthink everybody in my administration. My job will be to assemble an administration of capable and bright people." Not that he was looking for people, as Isaacson suggested, to tell him what to do. "No, no, no," W. insisted. "Not tell me what to do. Make recommendations. These people aren't going to decide for me. I'm going to have to decide . . . My job is to get good thinkers and get the best out of them."

W. continued his leisurely campaign pace—only two stops in a day was not unusual—but it was not enough to keep him from being homesick. He told reporters that he missed Spot, his six-toed cat Ernie, his bed, and his feather pillow. He did something about the pillow, bringing one with him wherever he went on the campaign trail. The presumptive Republican presidential candidate longed to be, as he put it, "putting in a little chain saw time" at the ranch— cutting wood, using his John Deere "Gator" tractor to clear brush, and maybe even fishing for bass in his small man-made lake.

For her part, Laura occasionally accompanied her husband aboard

Great Expectations. But she also hied away to the ranch at every available opportunity. As work proceeded on the house, there were still a thousand details to attend to. During the long flights aboard the campaign plane, she flipped through design magazines, then brought her ideas to Ken Blasingame. Among other things, the Fort Worth interior designer had come up with the idea of jazzing up the governor's mansion during the holidays by putting a life-size cowboy Santa on the front porch.

"Her style is very clean, very fresh," Blasingame said of Laura. Opting for comfort over a contrived rustic look, she chose sisal rugs and two camel-colored sofas for the beige-walled living room. A painting of ibis, a species of bird native to the state, was picked to hang over the fireplace. Prescott Bush's desk occupied a place of honor in the living room, while another desk handed down from President George H. W. Bush was moved into W.'s study. Billy Bass, thankfully, was left behind on the wall of their temporary house. No matter. W. had more than a dozen sent by friends who knew he would find the singing fish nothing short of hysterical. On the campaign plane, Bush frequently produced one that belted out "Don't Worry, Be Happy" and insisted that members of the press sing along.

For Laura, overseeing the construction of the ranch house was a godsend. "I love houses," she later said. "It really helped to have that to think about and to daydream about. It was just a great diversion. And there was a nice juxtaposition between running for an office that has a definite end and building something that we'll have the rest of our lives."

Although he missed Laura, W. admired the way she was able to juggle the campaign and the building of the ranch house without becoming rattled. "She has a reassuring calm," he said wistfully. "As a man who goes about a hundred miles an hour, I find that attractive. It is the middle of a presidential campaign, and we're designing and building a house . . . My point is that she is able to live an interesting life that is apart from the political campaign, which I think is very appealing. In other words, politics doesn't totally consume her, and as a result, it doesn't totally consume me."

Laura did not, in fact, appear all that interested in becoming first lady. "If it works out, it works out," she shrugged. "If it doesn't, it doesn't. We'll still have a life."

On weekends, W. tried to join Laura at the ranch. Although she occasionally made a casserole, most of the cooking was left to her husband. "Oh, he's quite the expert at grilling," she said, pointing to the fact that he had expanded his burger-and-steak repertoire to include chicken and vegetables. "He's not much of a vegetable eater," she admitted. "But he does like to eat grilled onions a lot. Then he'll grill other vegetables for us—zucchini and squash."

It fell to Laura to make sure that both Bush daughters were safely ensconced in their new schools. In each case, she helped the girls pick out the linen, lamps, clothing, and personal items they would need in college, then went along to personally check out their dormitories and meet their roommates.

As the children of a presidential candidate, they were not entitled to Secret Service protection—a fact that allowed them to adjust to college life almost like any other freshmen. But they knew that would change if Dad won the election. "They love their father and want the best for him, of course," Laura told friends. But unlike Al and Tipper Gore's children, who took a more active role in their father's campaign, Barbara and Jenna simply declined to participate. Moreover, the children of George and Laura Bush often seemed to show vague disdain and at times outright resentment toward their dad for pursuing an office that would rob them of anything resembling a normal life.

"They kind of sulked around acting as if they had something better to do," a Bush staffer said. "He would have loved it if they had volunteered to give a speech or just showed up at rallies," a key Bush staffer conceded. "After all, the Bushes are like the Kennedys in that sense—it's a one-for-all, all-for-one family. But they didn't volunteer, and the Bushes weren't about to ask them to do something they so clearly had no interest in doing."

W. admitted that his daughters "weren't exactly thrilled" about his running for president just as they entered college, and occasionally remarked that he wished they would "take more pride in what I'm trying to do." More than once, he conceded that he was disappointed that they invariably refused to join him on his campaign stops, even when his schedule took him close to their respective campuses. "It would be nice if they showed up more often, just to see what the Old Man was up to . . . They just aren't particularly interested, I guess." Every time he talked about his daughters' detached attitude, the *New York Times*'s Frank Bruni observed, "there was a hurt look in his eyes."

Laura was more philosophical about the girls' professed indifference to their father's presidential bid. "Actually, they hardly ever think of it," she said. "Like every other teenager, they have their own agenda and their own friends, and that's what they're concerned about." She also said privately that the girls "want the best for their father, but if he didn't become president I think they'd be awfully relieved."

Certainly there was plenty of teenage eye-rolling whenever Dad publicly advocated abstinence as an effective means of birth control. They were not alone. When he spoke to a group of wealthy business owners over lunch at the governor's mansion, W. pointed out that he had urged Texas teenagers to "abstain from sex until you find the partner you want to marry."

"Abstinence?" snickered one of two women seated at the back of the room. "Good luck."

"Abstinence works," he replied. "But it can't work if we don't try it."

Later, W. went to the women's table and asked why they doubted that abstinence was a possible solution to the problem of teen pregnancy. "Well," one said, "were *you* a virgin when you got married?"

He stared at the women for a moment. "No," he said. Oddly, rather than viewing him as a hypocrite, the two women were impressed with W.'s candor. "He's so unlike Clinton," one gushed.

Even before the convention, the specter of the presidential debates planned for October loomed large in the collective mind of Team Bush. Al Gore was by far the more experienced debater, a self-confessed policy wonk with countless statistics at his fingertips. Given W.'s penchant for bloopers, these mano a mano debates were fraught with danger for the Republican candidate.

At the ranch, Laura whipped up a batch of chili in the kitchen of the "governor's house" while her husband's handlers prepped him for the debates. Gradually, she had assumed a more prominent role, campaigning on her own for the ticket in two dozen states. Several times she overruled her husband's advisers on which venues would best suit him, and on at least one occasion nixed a television spot that she felt was too "harsh."

Now she once again took it upon herself to shore up W.'s confidence as he faced the daunting task of besting Al Gore in the debates. He had actually begun rehearsing as far back as June, when Senator Judd Greg of New Hampshire was brought in to play the part of Gore. Often the sessions were conducted past W.'s usual bedtime of 10 P.M., so he would get used to remaining cogent if the debate dragged into the night.

Mastering the issues was one thing; preparing for the possibility that Gore might bring up an embarrassing incident from W.'s past was another. For years Bush's 1976 drunk-driving arrest had been a topic of conversation between W. and one of the passengers in his car, John Newcombe. "You know, George," the tennis star would say, "you better watch out, you're going to run for some important office one day and I might just tell someone about that night in Maine." But Newcombe said Bush always "knew I wasn't going to make anything out of it. We joked about it for years."

Hughes and other key staffers failed to see the humor in W.'s arrest. As far back as 1997, the few Bush staffers who knew about the arrest record suggested that he defuse the issue by simply owning up to it. But W. and Laura flatly refused. Instead, they agreed that this was strictly a private family matter, and that public disclosure would only provide an excuse for Jenna and Barbara to misbehave. "The political advice was all the other way," said one insider. Nor did it help that Dick Cheney had already admitted that he, too, had been arrested for driving under the influence—twice, as a college student.

W. was nonetheless prepped for ways to handle the question of his DUI arrest—just in case it was sprung on him during the debates. Laura, said one eyewitness, grew "visibly nervous" as she watched W. offer a truthful if less-than-forthcoming excuse for covering up the arrest.

Midway through his preparations, W. seized an opportunity to close the "gender gap" that gave the Democrats an edge when it came to women votes. At Laura's urging, he appeared on *Oprah,* greeting Winfrey warmly with a kiss on the cheek and then getting emotional as he recounted Laura's battle against toxemia. "She had that West

Texas determination," he told Oprah. "I'm kind of tearing about it because it was such a . . . powerful statement of motherhood."

Laura, meantime, joined Condi Rice and Barbara Bush on a "W. Stands for Women" bus tour of the Midwest. Also along for the ride was Dick Cheney's outspokenly conservative wife Lynne, controversial chairman of the National Endowment for the Humanities under Ronald Reagan and the author of two racy novels.

Notably absent were the Bush daughters, who once again made it clear that they were not particularly interested in aiding Dad in his quest to become leader of the Free World. Laura was always on hand at each debate to support her husband, who concealed his nervousness by squeezing a small cross he kept in his pants pocket. But Jenna and Barbara declined to attend in person, preferring instead to watch on TV with friends. At one point during the debates, Al Gore announced that all of his children had actually made the effort to come and lend Dad moral support by sitting in the audience.

The point wasn't lost on the Bush twins, who began yelling at their respective TVs, furious at what they correctly perceived to be a not-so-subtle dig at them. From Yale and from the University of Texas, they phoned their mother. "Did you hear what he said about Jenna and me?" Barbara said. "What a . . ."

Both girls went on to ask Mama to convey a message to their father—that they were eagerly following the debates, and that they were rooting for him. When Jenna finally got through to her father, she let him know what she thought of his performance. "Dad," she said, "you did great."

At the other end of the phone, there was only silence. For the first time in recent memory W., tears streaming down his face, was speechless.

As it turned out, W. had shown his emotional side many times during the campaign. Whenever he spoke about Laura or about his father or his children, there was a good chance that he would become, as he liked to say, "teary." One reporter who covered the campaign claimed to have seen him cry on no fewer than a dozen separate occasions.

In the end, W. held his own during all three debates—thanks largely to the fact, as he himself conceded, "everyone's expectations for me were so low." All Bush had to do, observed the *Los Angeles*

Times was "to show the nation he could properly put one word in front of the other. He did that."

Coming into the home stretch, W.'s double-digit lead in the polls had evaporated; Bush and Gore were now in a dead heat. All that could happen at this point was the "October surprise" that Hughes and Rove had been dreading—some last-minute bombshell about W.'s wild past that could conceivably tip the scales in Gore's favor.

Neither George nor Laura were concerned. The press had stopped harping on the drug use rumors, and Laura had managed to deftly field what few questions there were regarding her fatal car crash. Nobody was worried about W.'s 1976 drunk-driving arrest in Kennebunkport. "I'm not worried," W. told Laura. "If nobody's mentioned it by now, they're not gonna. It's too late."

There was no October Surprise, but there was a November Surprise. Just four days before the election, W. was addressing a rally of ten thousand supporters at the College of DuPage in Illinois. After the rally, he was in a conference room conducting interviews with the local press when Hughes came in and whispered the disturbing news. Fox TV was only moments from broadcasting the story of his DUI arrest.

W. told Hughes to get the story out, but it was too late. By this time, Fox was already broadcasting it to the nation. Within minutes W. was on the phone to one daughter and then the next, telling each about the arrest before they saw it on the news. "It's okay, Dad. We all make mistakes. Are you going to be okay?" Again, W. was moved to tears.

W. huddled with his advisers to decide how best to minimize the damage. Laura pressed him to simply tell the truth—that he did not want to set a bad example for his impressionable teenage daughters. After all, the approach had worked so well before, when W. refused to go into detail about his "wild" past for much the same reason.

It scarcely mattered what he did or didn't tell his daughters; only days earlier both Bush girls were getting into alcohol-related troubles of their own. In New Haven, eighteen-year-old Barbara— generally regarded as the more bookish of the Bush twins—was caught using a fake ID at a popular bar called Toad's Place. The security guard, ex-cop Bill Coale, recalled that she was "polite but very argumentative" as she tried to get the ID back. Coale decided not to call police, although he held on to the fake ID, which he framed and hung in his family room. It gave a false Baltimore address, added precisely three years to her age, and identified her as "Barbara Pierce"—her grandmother's maiden name.

Meantime, Jenna was downing potent Long Island iced teas at a University of Texas fraternity party just blocks from the governor's mansion at Austin's Buffalo Club. At one point a clearly inebriated Jenna, cigarette in hand, began dancing with another coed until the two collapsed on the floor laughing. While Jenna and her friend rolled around, the fraternity brothers hooted and cheered. Not long after, she was on the town again—this time partying loudly at another student watering hole, Fat Tuesday.

For the time being, George W. had his hands full trying to explain away his own history with alcohol. At a hastily called press conference, W. acknowledged this arrest in 1976, making it clear that it was something he was not proud of. His mood shifted quickly, however, as he strongly hinted that the eleventh-hour bombshell was nothing more than another political dirty trick.

The day after George's drunk-driving record was made public, the Bushes celebrated Laura's fifty-fourth birthday. On a campaign swing through New Jersey with Republican Governor Christie Todd Whitman, Laura had admired Whitman's Scottie, which had just had a litter. W.'s birthday gift to his wife was one of the puppies, a feisty male they named Barney. But when they got Barney home to the governor's mansion, the Bushes had a change of heart.

"You know, we've lost our minds," Laura told her husband. "Bushie, we don't even know if we're going to be here or in the White House. I just don't think we can handle a puppy right now." But in the end, she conceded, the mischievous Scottie—who bore more than a passing resemblance to FDR's celebrated dog Fala— proved "too darn cute" to be given away. Wherever the Bushes wound up, the family decided, Barney was along for the ride.

Meanwhile, the DUI story fizzled—much to the relief of Team Bush. News organizations were wary of revelations that made it look as if the press was trying to tip the scales at the last minute. W. gave the thumbs-up sign as he boarded his plane, and then told a friend, "See you on Inauguration Day."

On the final flight home to Austin, W. got on the plane's PA system and told reporters that it was their "last chance for malaprops." Then he thanked the press for "the amount of time you've taken away from your families, how hard you've worked . . . Thank you for your hard work for America, and make sure you vote for me. Good-bye." With that, W. gave the signal and all the video screens in the cabin played a blistering *Saturday Night Live* send-up of the Bush-Gore debates.

On November 7, election night, George and Laura, the twins, and the rest of the extended Bush clan were on their way to dinner at Austin's Shoreline Grill on Town Lake when word crackled over the radio that two key states, Michigan and Pennsylvania, were going to Gore. As they slunk from their cars into the restaurant, reporters called out to the candidate and his wife. But this time the normally ebullient George and his perpetually smiling wife looked straight ahead.

They sat grim-faced at their table, trying to concentrate on the food in front of them when, halfway through dinner, it appeared Florida was also lost as CBS's Dan Rather called it for Gore at 7:47 P.M. Eastern Standard Time. Jeb, who had promised the family he would deliver the Sunshine State to his big brother, dissolved in tears. "I'm so sorry," he sobbed as Poppy and Barbara looked on with anguished faces.

At first, W.'s reaction—trapped somewhere between his trademark smirk and pathos—was difficult to gauge. How could this happen? W. wanted to know. Jeb was the *governor* of Florida, for God's sake. But Laura wasted no time reassuring Jeb that no one was blaming him.

Deciding to forgo plans to watch election returns from a suite in the nearby Four Seasons Hotel, a dour W. hastily finished his meal and fled with this family to the governor's mansion. As he got up to leave, he hugged his little brother. "I know you did your best," he told a stricken, tear-streaked Jeb. "It's okay. It's okay."

Upstairs at the governor's mansion, George, Laura, and the senior Bushes sat around a fireplace and watched election night coverage on a television set perched on a bookshelf. On the coffee table in front of them: a biography of one of W.'s heroes, Joe DiMaggio. W. manned the remote, flipping from one network to the other.

Within minutes, W.'s senior staff told him that the outcome in

Florida was anything but clear. At 9:54 P.M. eastern time, the networks abruptly withdrew Florida from the Gore column, and Jeb arrived at the mansion to confirm that Florida was still in play. While Little Brother called Republican precinct captains throughout the state to check on last-minute tallies, Laura sat next to her husband on the living room sofa, rubbing his back and occasionally whispering in his ear.

"Golly," W.'s dad marveled as the evening wore on and tensions mounted, "she sure can calm him down. She's his Rock of Gibraltar."

When a small group of reporters was let into the room, Bush *père* was asked how this evening compared to his own defeat to Bill Clinton in 1992. "Hell of a lot worse," he mumbled.

One journalist asked W. how he was getting through this, given the fact that his whole future was on the line. But W., with Laura virtually pressed to his side, seemed to be holding up quite well. "Actually, my whole future isn't on the line," he said, almost defiantly. "I'm not worried about *me* getting through it," he added, nodding in the direction of his parents.

"Like a prizefighter pulling himself up off the mat," as one observer put it, W. became more and more energized as he racked up one state after another. With each victory, he pumped the air with his right hand as Laura clapped. Finally, at 2:15 A.M. eastern time, the networks declared Bush the winner. In the living room at the mansion, everyone jumped up and cheered. George and Laura embraced, and then it was Poppy's turn. As their wives looked on, ebullient and dry-eyed, father and son wept in each other's arms.

Al Gore called to concede, and Laura sat nearby while her husband graciously accepted. "You're a good man," W. told him, and added that he knew how hard it must be. "Give my best," he concluded, "to Tipper and the children."

But over the next hour, Bush's margin in Florida slipped down to nine hundred, then five hundred, then two hundred. At 3:45 A.M., George took another call from Gore. "As you may have noticed," the Vice President said, "things have changed. Florida is too close to call."

"Let me make sure I understand," W. shot back in disbelief. "You're calling me back to *retract* your concession?"

"Well, there's no reason to get snippy," Gore replied.

Laura sat on the couch just a few inches from her husband as he angrily demanded to know why his rival was no longer willing to concede. This time, she made no effort to calm him down.

"You've got to understand that Laura is totally loyal to the Bushes," said a senior staff member. "It takes a lot to get her angry, but that phone call from Gore did it."

"It's too close to concede," Gore insisted.

"But it's not, we've won the state."

"It's too close to concede," he repeated.

"My brother is right here with the latest numbers off the Florida website, and I'm telling you that is just not the case."

"Let me explain it to you," Gore said. "Your younger brother is not the ultimate authority on this."

"Well, Mr. Vice President," W. said, "you need to do what you have to do."

Bush put down the phone. "I was the mother of a president for thirty minutes," Barbara Bush would quip to a friend, "and I loved it."

For the next "thirty-six days from hell," as Laura's staffers would call it, the nation held its collective breath as the Bush and Gore legal teams battled for supremacy—first in circuit court, then in the Florida State Supreme Court, and ultimately in the United States Supreme Court. At stake were Florida's crucial twenty-five electoral votes, and the presidency—all hinging on chads, both dimpled and hanging.

The tension was "indescribable," Bush Sr. conceded. "I've never been through anything like it." Certainly millions of Americans, who for weeks sat glued to their television sets awaiting the ultimate outcome of the election, shared in that anxiety. "Chaos" screamed the cover of *Newsweek* as the case headed toward the Supreme Court. "Will the War of the Courts Give Us a New President—or a Constitutional Crisis?"

Laura, steely inner core still intact, somehow managed to not show the strain. Just three days after the election, she spoke as planned at the opening of the Texas Book Festival. As her audience marveled at Laura's coolness under unimaginable pressure, she smiled and said, "The unnecessary use of any of the following words—'subliminable,' 'snippy,' or 'recount'—will result in an invitation not to return."

"She's steady as she goes," Poppy said of his daughter-in-law. "I'd say she's a calming influence on all of us. She doesn't get all out of sorts if something isn't just right. The best evidence is the way she conducted herself during those awful days when the election was up in the air . . . It was a savage, horrible period. But she never got rattled, never got vindictive."

George and Laura were not, in fact, along for much of the electoral roller-coaster ride. When he was at the governor's mansion, W. still found time for his daily run and to work out at the University of Texas fitness center. Most of the time, he wasn't even in Austin. Instead, the man who would be president and his would-be first lady escaped to the ranch in Crawford, where there was neither satellite TV nor cable.

After W. dispatched Dick Cheney to Washington to set up a presumptive transition team, George and Laura focused on managing their own stress levels as others decided their fate—and the fate of the nation. "One of the great things about a campaign is that it's supposed to end," he mused. "And we worked our hearts out, and all of a sudden it didn't end. So it's been an interesting period of time that has helped me cope with anxiety and made me a more patient person."

Laura went so far as to claim that the wait "was not really that difficult. I knew George and I would be all right either way. We knew we had worked hard . . . and the wait let us put our lives and even the presidency in perspective."

"At the end," said their friend Charlie Younger, "it was out of their hands. They were at peace with things. Whatever the outcome, both he and Laura were going to be okay with it."

Nevertheless, constant updates from the front kept both George and Laura abreast of unfolding developments. One day, for example, George was at the governor's mansion watching TV coverage of a Florida State Supreme Court ruling that went against him. Less than eighteen hours later, he was at the wheel of a Chevy Suburban when Don Evans called on the cell phone to say the ruling had been stayed by the U.S. Supreme Court.

But for most of the wild ride, W. was described as "calm" or even "serene"—words more frequently used to describe his wife. With good reason. "Laura is his rock," Poppy said. "She changed him in every possible way for the better." He was, said their pal Joe O'Neill, "hell-bent for leather, and she definitely focused him. She mellowed him . . ."

"I'll be at the ranch, so let me know," W. told his advisers as he and Laura headed off for Crawford as his fate and the fate of the nation hung on a few chads. There they donned their favorite garb—jeans, denim shirts, mud-spattered boots—and unwound. While Laura read or smoked a cigarette in blissful solitude, W. "bushwacked" the underbrush with a chain saw, chopped firewood, fished in the man-made pond, or zoomed along the winding dirt roads in his pickup or the Suburban. Each day at sunset, George and Laura hiked the land, sometimes clambering over wet rocks ("Watch it there, Bushie") and trudging through mud until they got to what was arguably the ranch's most scenic spot—a limestone canyon with a waterfall cascading into a blue green pool. The two Bushes had their own name for this enchanted secret place: "The Amphitheater."

Jenna and Barbara viewed the ranch in much the same way they viewed their father's candidacy: with thinly veiled disdain. When her parents excitedly told Jenna that they had bought the sixteen-hundred-acre parcel, Jenna in particular questioned the decision. She contorted her face and offered a one-word reaction: "Why?"

So W. took her to the Amphitheater, and then to "The Cathedral," another cliff-face with a natural vaulted arch of branches and a limestone "staircase" carved by erosion. "The audience will stand there," he told his daughter. "You and I will stand there, and the preacher will stand here . . ." It was then, W. said proudly, that "she got it."

Even at the height of the constitutional crisis, George delighted in taking visitors on extended tours of the ranch, pointing out the different varieties of elm, cottonwood, oak, hackberry, and cedar. Not to mention the Texas Longhorns, the white-tailed deer, and other wildlife that abounded on the property. At one point as he was waxing poetic about the countryside for some guests from New York, a bull decided it was mating time. "Putting on a show," W. huffed.

As he plowed through the cedar underbrush in his John Deere Gator, clearing the way so that Laura would have an unobstructed view from the house, W. admitted that this was his way of coping with reality. "It does just all fall away," he explained. "I could give a damn about the Supreme Court. Well, of course I do care, but you forget."

Not for long. Shortly after 10 P.M. on December 12, George and Laura were in their pajamas at the governor's mansion in Austin, watching CNN's coverage of the historic 5–4 Supreme Court ruling. According to CNN, Gore had won his bid for a recount of the Florida vote. Laura patted W.'s knee reassuringly as he leaned into the TV, shaking his head.

The phone rang. It was Karl Rove, calling from a Virginia hotel not far from the transition office Bush's team had already set up. Rove had been watching MSNBC, which correctly interpreted the complicated ruling in Bush's favor. "This is good news," Rove said.

"No, no this is bad news," W. answered, still believing CNN's incorrect analysis of the court decision. Then, he asked "Turd Blossom" where he was.

Rove told his boss that he was "in the McLean Hilton—standing in my pajamas."

"Well, I'm in my pajamas, too," W. said. Twenty minutes later, Bush was satisfied he had won. He and Laura embraced, and after a few calls to family members and friends, staggered off to bed.

The next afternoon, Laura kept a date with her Austin garden club—much to the astonishment of her friends. "Laura, it's all over!" one said of the five-week power struggle that had so bitterly divided the nation.

"No," said Laura, her voice tinged with melancholy. "It's just beginning."

What I like best is when my husband says, "You look great tonight."

—*Laura*

I'll give this my best shot, and if people decide, heck, if there's someone else they'd rather have as president, I know she'll still love me. And that's more important than winning.

—*George*

I'm concerned about these little girls, I really am.

—*George on daughters Jenna
and Barbara*

If we never saw their pictures in the paper again,
we'd be a lot happier.

—*Laura*

7

⬦

J enna, are you okay, honey?" Laura asked, her tone betraying only the slightest trace of concern. The Bush family had been having Christmas Day lunch at the home of a friend when suddenly the University of Texas coed excused herself from the table.

"It's just a stomachache, Mama," she said, wincing as she pointed to her midsection. "I'll be fine."

The family returned to the governor's mansion, but as the afternoon wore on the stabbing pains in Jenna's abdomen became more intense. Laura grew more and more concerned, and began fidgeting with the diamond on her ring finger—her Christmas present from George. After twenty-three years of marriage, W. had finally given her a proper engagement ring to go with her gold wedding band.

By 5 P.M., Laura took matters into her own hands. With several Secret Service agents in tow, she bundled her daughter into the governor's limousine and sped to nearby St. David's Hospital.

Once there, Jenna was rushed to a second-floor operating room where doctors sedated the President-elect's daughter and performed an emergency appendectomy. Had they waited even an hour longer, there was the life-threatening possibility that Jenna's appendix might have burst. "Thank God," W. said when doctors informed him that the surgery had been successful. "Thank God."

That Christmas night—her last before becoming America's First Lady—Laura slept alongside her daughter Jenna on a sleeper sofa in room 5903 at the hospital. The nurses understood completely. "Mrs. Bush is a mom," one said matter-of-factly, "and that's what moms do."

The President-elect, meanwhile, left as planned the next day for a vacation with the rest of the Bush clan in exclusive Boca Grande, Florida. He joked that if Jenna wasn't well enough to join him in Florida, she could just stay home and "clean out her room."

For Laura, it was not the first health scare of the holiday season. Just a few days earlier Laura's mother, who had been staying at the governor's mansion, was rushed to Austin's Brackenridge Hospital complaining of dizziness. Following a battery of tests, doctors could find nothing wrong with the eighty-one-year-old widow. Much to Laura's relief, she was released the next day.

These episodes helped put other, lesser crises in perspective. Exactly one week before Jenna's appendicitis attack, Hillary Clinton stood on the White House steps waiting for Secret Service agents to pry Laura out of her limousine—the car door had literally frozen shut. Outgoing first ladies traditionally gave their successors an introductory guided tour of the executive mansion, but in this case that seemed superfluous. "I feel like I sort of know it," said Laura, who had been a frequent guest of her in-laws. "I've slept in the Lincoln Bedroom and the Queen's Bedroom."

But Laura, who wore a purple plaid suit for her White House visit with Hillary, was not prepared for the next day's catty remarks in the press. "Look," said the President-elect when asked about the brouhaha over his wife's fashion sense, "she's going to be a fabulous first lady. All the wagging tongues—I personally am going to completely ignore them, and I think most Americans will as well."

He would get no argument from the folks back home in Midland. On January 17, he donned a white cowboy hat and with Laura at his side bade a symbolic farewell to their hometown. "Our deepest values in life often come from our earliest years," he told the thousands of supporters who came to see him off. "It is here in Midland and in West Texas where I learned what it means to be a good neighbor . . . It is here in West Texas where I learned to trust in God." In a swipe at Bill Clinton, who was now charging that W. had not fairly won the election, Bush promised that his administration "will never forget the dignity and duty the White House represents to millions of Americans."

He also had little use for the folks "up East . . . In a way, Laura and I will never quite settle in Washington because, while the honor is great, the work is temporary." Laura smiled and did her well-rehearsed Miss America wave, then followed George up the gangway into the Air Force Boeing 757 the Clinton Administration had dispatched to take them to Washington. "All we're bringing," Laura said, "is our family photographs, our clothes, and our pets."

And their daughters, who were foremost on Daddy's mind as he prepared to be sworn in as the forty-third President of the United States. "I am going to be angry at people mistreating my girls in the public arena," he stated flatly. "I'm going to let people know if they do, too. I'm fair game. And, uh, Laura's semifair game . . . But the girls, the girls aren't. And I mean that."

Meantime, the girls were more than willing to show up at the preinaugural concert starring, among others, Destiny's Child and Ricky Martin. Not surprisingly, they were visibly mortified when Dad got up onstage with Martin and mimicked some of the Latin heartthrob's hip-swiveling moves.

It was not the twins but Laura who caused a stir the next day when she revealed on national television that she and her husband disagreed on the dicey issue of abortion. When asked on Inauguration Eve about *Roe v. Wade* during a *Today* show interview, she stated flatly, "I don't think it should be overturned." She went on to add that "we should do what we can to limit the number of abortions, and that's by talking about responsibility with girls and boys, by teaching abstinence, having abstinence classes everywhere in schools, in churches, in Sunday Schools. There are a lot of ways we could reduce the number of abortions, and I agree with my husband on that issue."

Instantly, the President-elect's advisers were deluged with calls from leaders of the right-to-life backers wanting to know if W. had softened his position. They were reassured that he had not—though Attorney General–designate John Ashcroft also pointed out that overturning *Roe vs. Wade* was "not on the agenda."

When they met up later that day at a "Salute to America's Authors" she was hosting, Laura apologized to her husband for her "making a mess." She later said she wouldn't do it again. "I'll be perfectly frank," she said. "I was not elected and George was. And I would never want to undermine him in any way."

If he felt "undermined" by his wife's candor, W. did not show it. Introducing her to the crowd at the Salute to America's Authors, he said, "Her love for books is real, her love for children is real, and my love for her is real." As Laura stepped up to the podium, they hugged, and George gave her an affectionate pat on the behind.

In the midst of all the euphoria, a friend from Midland asked George if he wasn't really dreading the burden he was about to undertake. "Are you nervous, worried, anxious?" he asked.

"No," George W. replied. "I'm very much at peace."

Laura was equally cool, which came as no surprise to her mother. "She is just eager to please—always has been," Jenna Welch said. "She will do whatever is asked of her, and she'll do it without complaint."

The next day, January 20, both Georges were fighting hard to control their emotions as W. rose to take the oath of office. Laura, by comparison, was all business. Only moments before the swearing-in, she motioned to United Methodist minister and Bush family confidant Kirbyjon Caldwell, who was about to deliver the benediction. Laura wanted George to place his hand on a specific piece of scripture, and she was having a hard time finding it herself. When the moment came, Laura held the historic Washington Bible—the Bible used by George Washington and several presidents thereafter, including W.'s father. Barbara and Jenna—both wearing stiletto-heeled Jimmy Choo snakeskin pumps their mother eyed warily—stood smiling beside their parents as Dad raised his right hand. Charlene Gnagy, Laura's beloved second grade teacher, watched it all from her seat in the VIP section.

"George is star-crossed," said Joe O'Neill, another Midland pal in the VIP section that day. "Always has been. I've told him that a thousand times. Standing up there, I counted the faces of no fewer than fifteen people who wanted to be president. Most of them had worked their whole lives for it. And there was George, who hadn't even *been* in politics seven years before, taking the oath of office."

Following the inaugural parade ("I hope the girls don't plan to walk too far in those shoes," Laura muttered), the new First Couple was whisked by motorcade to the White House, where they dressed for that evening's nine inaugural balls. Unlike Jackie Kennedy, Laura ("We're Mr. and Mrs. Punctual") did not keep her husband waiting that first evening in the executive mansion. She quickly changed out of the size eight peacock blue suit she wore to the swearing-in ceremony—she had had Dallas designer Michael Faircloth add brown saddle-stitching ("We had to have a little bit of Texas")—and into her gown.

"Bushie, you look beautiful!" the President said when she emerged wearing a figure-hugging, lipstick-red Chantilly lace design embroidered with Swarovski ruby crystal beads. "Just beautiful!"

Laura had had her doubts about the gown. It wasn't just the fact that the color had been co-opted by Nancy Reagan. For the girl from Midland, scarlet just seemed so—showy. "Oh, red," she said when designer Michael Faircloth first showed her the sketches. "I'll get so much attention."

Faircloth gave her a puzzled look. "All the world's going to be looking at you anyway!" he said.

With Dick and Lynne Cheney in tow, the Bushes made the rounds of all nine balls. Describing himself as a "cumbersome" dancer, the President nonetheless whisked his First Lady across the stage at each event—though not for long. Dancing for less than thirty seconds at the first ball and fifty seconds at the last, W. actually subjected Laura to his halting box step for only about six and a half minutes throughout the entire evening. They returned to the second-floor family quarters at 11:39 P.M.—eighty minutes ahead of schedule but still more than an hour past their customary bedtime.

The White House they woke up to the next morning already bore the stamp of its new occupants—a style that in many ways reflected that of another first couple, Jack and Jackie Kennedy. Rather than use his father's desk in the Oval Office, George installed an artifact that Jackie had exhumed from storage four decades earlier: a mammoth desk carved from the British warship HMS *Resolute,* a gift from Queen Victoria to President Rutherford B. Hayes in 1878. Woodrow Wilson had used it, and FDR sat behind the desk as he delivered his famous "Fireside Chats" on the radio. It was also the desk that JFK Jr. ("John-John") loved to hide beneath as a child. President Kennedy was often locked in serious conversation with cabinet members or even heads of state when a hinged door swung open and out popped John Jr., who would proceed to laugh and whoop as he careened around the room.

An unabashed admirer of Jackie Kennedy ("She had the most marvelous taste"), Laura yanked down the heavy print curtains the Clintons had hung in the upstairs yellow living room and retrieved Jackie's favorite velvet-upholstered chairs from the basement. She had wanted to restore the room, the focal point of first family life at the White House, so that it was "just the way Jackie left it."

The only furnishings Laura brought with her to the White House were a chest of drawers and a portrait of the twins that had just been painted. No matter. Like first ladies before her, she soon discovered that she enjoyed repainting walls, replacing portraits, shuffling antiques from room to room, and discovering hidden treasures locked away in storage. Aside from the *Resolute* desk, George had only one other request—that Ulysses S. Grant's furniture be moved into his upstairs office. "I'm not crazy about Victorian," she shrugged, "but if it's what he really wants . . ."

Now that they were entrusted with some of the nation's most prized period pieces, the Bushes made the painful decision not to bring Ernie along. The six-toed, orange-and-white "outdoor" cat still had his claws, and there was genuine concern that he might rip the furniture—not to mention the draperies—to shreds. (Ernie had been living in Los Angeles with investment banker and Bush family friend Brad Freeman for five months when, inexplicably, he vanished. Much to the relief of the President, Ernie was found three weeks and five miles later, wandering up Century City's Avenue of the Stars.)

Back at the White House, Laura was busy returning things to the way they had been before the Clintons took office. Although the residential and ceremonial East Wing had always been considered the First Lady's territory, Hillary had demanded and gotten a West Wing office next door to the office of the White House counsel.

"In a lot of ways," Bush media adviser Mark McKinnon said of the Clintons, "it was sort of like a copresidency. There was a sense that what drove the Clintons, not just professionally but personally, was politics." One also was left with the impression, McKinnon said, "that it never got turned off."

It was not an impression Laura, who moved the First Lady's offices back to the East Wing, wanted to convey. She continued to insist that the President and his wife "don't sit around and talk politics . . . we get a lot of solace with being with each other and maybe not talking about the tough issues at those moments. It gives us a little bit of relief."

Yet there were other times when she let down her guard and admitted that she did offer political advice—and that her husband often took it. "Do we talk about issues? Sure. But not all the time," Laura said coyly. "I've looked at speeches some. I might say something like, 'Oh, I don't think you ought to say that.' "

"She's got a great sense of how the President is perceived," said Mark McKinnon. "She looks out for that. She has a good sense of when his message is not being communicated well and received the way it should be."

W. trusted his wife's judgment just as much when it came to sizing up people. Continuing to downplay her role as trusted adviser, Laura nonetheless conceded that she was consulted by her husband as he picked his White House team. "To some extent," she allowed, adding quickly, "a lot of the team I already knew."

White House Chief of Staff Andy Card, "High Prophet" Karen Hughes, Condi Rice, and domestic policy adviser Margaret La Montagne were just a few top aides Laura talked to regularly. "She doesn't go over there [to the West Wing] and attend meetings," explained Laura's press secretary, Noelia Rodriguez. "But she feels very comfortable picking up the phone if she's got an idea or a question. It's natural for her to interact with them, especially with the folks who came from Texas, because they have been together all these years."

But Laura's influence extended well beyond this tight circle of Texans. W. asked his wife to weigh in on every senior White House appointment and on every prospective cabinet appointee. "Laura has great instincts about people," said a senior member of Bush's political team, "and she has a kind of sixth sense when it comes to people who might end up causing problems for the President. It rarely happened, but if Laura had any serious qualms about a person—and this includes people being considered for the cabinet—they didn't get the job."

More frequently, the opposite occurred. Laura was an enthusiastic early backer of many who wound up with key posts in the new Bush Administration. "I'm proud that a lot of women are at the table over there," she said, pointing to the eight women among her husband's eighteen top White House staffers.

"Laura and George have always been very close," Jenna Welch said. "He does like to use her as a sounding board, definitely. But that's nothing new. Laura is a very smart woman—of course, this is her mother talking—and to the President's credit he's always appreciated that."

No first couple in history had traveled quite so rocky a road to the White House. So it struck the Washington press corps as odd that, just two weeks after her husband's inauguration, Laura left. She wound up spending half of her husband's first month in office back at the ranch in Texas—a seemingly bizarre absence that spawned rumors of a marital rift. "Either that," gossiped one Washington socialite, "or a face-lift."

For those who were familiar with Laura's nest-building ways, it was only logical that she would return to put the finishing touches on the ranch house in Crawford. In addition to kitchenware, bedding, sheets, and toiletries, Laura and her friend Regan Gammon did some last-minute furniture shopping. "We looked all over old furniture stores in Austin for a piece she needed for a certain spot," Gammon recalled.

When Laura apologized to her Secret Service agents for "dragging them all over the place," Gammon told her friend, "I'm sorry about them, but we can't let you become a prisoner."

Over time, Laura would become accustomed to the well-dressed men with earpieces who shadowed her virtually around the clock. "She's nice to the agents," Nancy Weiss said, "although they know for her sanity she really has to ignore them. Laura has the ability to just put the whole Secret Service thing out of her mind."

Laura's low profile was in sharp contrast to W., who presented both his education plan and his promised tax cut to Congress, met with the leadership of both the House and Senate, and announced that there would be a regular Sunday T-ball game for local children on the South Lawn—all during his first week as president. Through it all, he maintained a studied air of informality. At first he refrained from having "Hail to the Chief" played when he entered a room; he felt vaguely uneasy amid the pomp and ceremony of the office.

Despite the grueling weeks that led up to the Supreme Court decision and the lingering resentment that followed in some quarters, W. was determined not to take himself too seriously. The first week of his administration, all eighteen members of the senior staff were meeting when the President peeked into he room.

"Mr. President," Andy Card said, and everyone stood.

W. motioned for everyone to sit down. "Just checking," he said.

Two minutes later, he popped his head in again—and again the chairs slid back as everyone snapped to attention.

"I just wanted to see you do that again," he said with a smile.

W. also insisted on sticking to the schedule he had maintained as governor and on the campaign trail. He always found time in the early morning hours to run three or four miles on an indoor treadmill or outdoor track—"sweating down" (cooling down) afterward in a small garden area outside the Oval Office. Determined to remain fit ("Inside me there's a fat person trying to get out"), Bush also made time for his midmorning workout—first bench-pressing 155 pounds, then picking up barbells to do three sets of curls, ten repetitions each. (The President did not interrupt his exercise regimen even when he was airborne; during long flights he often burned calories on the treadmill installed aboard Air Force One.)

The Bush presidency was scarcely three weeks old when a mentally deranged man was shot and wounded by Secret Service agents after opening fire on the White House. At the time, Vice President Cheney was working at his desk in the West Wing. The President was pumping iron in the East Wing gym, unaware of what had happened until breathless Secret Service agents rushed in to tell him.

It was just as well, W. figured, that Laura was still in Crawford, ostensibly getting the ranch house ready for his imminent arrival. The President had slyly engineered his first presidential trip abroad to begin on a Friday, so that he could swing by the ranch on the way home and spend a full weekend there. "There are very few places," he explained, "where a president can get kind of lost." The ranch, he added, "helps me keep perspective . . . and a president must have perspective."

Jenna and Barbara, meanwhile, were still nowhere to be seen. "The hardest part for me," Laura said, "is that the children don't think of Washington as home. I have tried to get them to come here for spring break—one of them has two weeks—but they don't want to come here. They want to go to Austin. I hope they realize," she said sighing, "how much their mother misses them."

Did their father miss them? "Not really," shrugged the President, now resigned to the fact that they still showed little interest in what he and Laura were trying to accomplish. "They'll be around. Trust me. I love them, but I'm really thrilled they're out on their own." He now talked to them on the phone once a week, while Laura managed to catch up with them every two or three days. "We spend as much time with our girls," she said with an air of resignation, "as they'll spend with us."

Returning to Washington in late February, George and Laura plunged into the D.C. social whirl by attending a dinner party at the Georgetown home of legendary former *Washington Post* publisher Katharine Graham. They joined a decidedly bipartisan group that included Microsoft founder Bill Gates, financier Warren Buffett, Secretary of State Colin Powell, Federal Reserve Chairman Alan Greenspan, Diane Sawyer, Barbara Walters, and such influential Democrats as Vernon Jordan and Daniel Patrick Moynihan. After dining on caviar, shrimp, lamb, and a fruit glacé, Graham stood up to thank the new president for being "awfully nice in every way to reach out to Washington." (While vacationing in Idaho less than five months later, Katharine Graham died from injuries she suffered in a fall. She was eighty-four.)

The day after making her Washington social debut as first lady, Laura kicked off her first solo event since the inauguration with an appearance at an inner-city school. Now she referred to Washington—the same city her husband often called "a snake pit"—as "our new home town," and pledged the administration's support for public education. "To me there's something almost sacred about teaching," Laura said. "Watching a child's eyes brighten with under-standing is an experience that defies description, but it's something that every teacher can understand." Her husband was, she added wryly, "partial to teachers."

W. had so much confidence in Laura's expertise as an educator that he essentially gave her carte blanche to fashion her own agenda. "Look," he said, "Laura can set her own policy. She's doing her own thing. And she's going to make a difference in people's lives."

The First Lady wasted no time staking her claim as the administration's most high-profile advocate for early education, reading initiatives, and teacher recruitment. She urged corporate executives to take a year off to teach in urban schools, and military retirees to take up teaching as a second career. She convinced her husband to set aside thirty million dollars for the Troops-to-Teachers program—ten times the amount allocated by the Clinton Administration. She also got behind Teach for America, a group that recruited recent college graduates to commit two years to teaching in public schools, and—as advertised—persuaded the President to boost the budget for Head Start to a whopping $6.5 billion.

Her own obsession with reading continued unabated. She devoured the writings of Willa Cather and Pearl Buck, started reading the collected works of Edith Wharton a second time—and still found time to polish off modern fiction like *Henry and Clara* and *Two Moons* by Thomas Mallon and Tracy Chevalier's bestselling historical novel on the life of the painter Jan Vermeer, *The Girl with the Pearl Earring*. The President, meantime, was reading up on the lives of John Adams and his son John Quincy—prodded by the fact that Poppy was now calling his son "Quincy."

Unfortunately for her early-rising husband, the First Lady did much of her reading in bed, and well into the night. She would tell friends that nearly every night, the President's final words to his wife were "Laura, for God's sake, turn off the light!"

He would need his rest, if for no other reason than to handle the crises—both foreign and domestic—that confronted him in the coming months. Twenty-four American servicemen and servicewomen were held by Beijing after a U.S. Navy spy plane collided with a Chinese jet fighter over the South China Sea on April 1. After a tense standoff between the two nations, the Americans were released eleven days later. A month later, W. ignited a storm of protest by announcing that the United States intended to violate the 1972 Antiballistic Missile Treaty by proceeding with plans to build a shield against intercontinental ballistic missiles. On the home front, the Bush Administration was dealt an unexpected blow in June when Republican Senator Jim Jeffords of Vermont formally abandoned his party to become an independent—effectively turning control of the Senate over to the Democrats.

Yet none of these events seemed to capture the public's imagination more—or cause George and Laura more personal anguish—than the trials and tribulations of Barbara and Jenna Bush. At first, the press had heeded the President's warning concerning his daughters. W.'s stern words were enough to persuade skittish producers at the Comedy Central cable TV network to abandon plans to depict the girls as lesbians on its new sitcom *That's My Bush*. The First Family spoof would stagger along for a single season before being canceled.

It was not long, however, before the girls' own antics made ignoring them all but impossible. Just days after the President and First Lady dined with Katharine Graham, Jenna narrowly escaped being arrested at another wild frat party—this one near Texas Christian University in Fort Worth. While four Secret Service agents waited outside in a black Chevy Suburban, Jenna was inside downing glass after glass of homemade rum punch with boyfriend William Ashe Bridges.

Responding to complaints from neighbors, police raided the party at 12:30 A.M., sending students climbing out windows and vaulting over fences. While police slapped handcuffs on Bridges, who had known both Bush girls in high school, and hauled him away to jail, Secret Service agents managed to spirit Jenna away.

Screaming that he was "Jenna Bush's boyfriend," Bridges used his cell phone to call Jenna. A few minutes later, according to Fort Worth Sheriff Dee Anderson, Secret Service agents arrived to pick Bridges up. Jenna, Anderson was told, was waiting outside in the black Suburban.

A few days later, it was Barbara's turn. Jenna's sister and several of her Yale buddies got into trouble when they attended Texas rocker Robert Earl Keene's show at the Bowery Ballroom on New York's Lower East Side. While Secret Service agents tried to be unobtrusive, the Yalies became so rowdy that bouncers had to eject at least one member of Barbara's group. "You guys have been great," an angry Keene told his audience, "ninety-nine percent of you, at least."

Not long after, Barbara spent part of her spring break at the Mexican resort of Playa del Carmen, knocking back tequila shots with her friends as Secret Service agents watched from behind palm trees and beach umbrellas. That March Barbara drove into New York with friends to watch a World Wrestling Federation match at Madison Square Garden, her Secret Service detail trailing behind in a separate car. When they reached the Triboro Bridge leading into Manhattan, the Secret Service agents stopped to pay the toll. But the Lexus SUV in which Barbara was a passenger zoomed ahead, through an automated E-Z Pass express lane and down the FDR Drive. Realizing they had lost sight of the President's daughter, the agents put on their sirens and floored the accelerator. Reaching speeds reportedly in excess of seventy miles per hour on rain-slicked FDR Drive, agents finally caught up to the runaway Lexus.

George was miffed that Barbara had momentarily given her protectors the slip, but chuckled at the image of Secret Service agents waiting at a toll booth while his daughter and her friends sped through the express lane. Laura, on the other hand, failed to see the humor in any high-speed chase; given her own tragic experience, she had long feared one of her daughters might be injured or worse in an auto accident. "It's something every parent worries about," a Midland friend said. "But when you've been through something like that the way Laura had, you worry that much more."

In a stern phone call to Barbara, Laura laid down the law. "The agents had to speed to catch up with you," Laura said. "You put other people's lives in danger when you do something like that. Don't ever do it again."

Not to be outdone, Jenna was busted again that April—this time after cops spotted her drinking a beer at Cheers Shot Bar in Austin's Sixth Street nightclub district. Two weeks later, she appeared in court wearing a sleeveless black blouse, pink Capri pants, black sandals, and a toe ring on her right foot. "This poor girl, I feel so sorry for her," said the prosecutor in the case, John Wall. "She's getting all this media attention for something as commonplace as alcohol possession in a college town."

After a visibly agitated Jenna complained to the court that photographers were taking her picture through a courtroom window, she pleaded no contest to possession of alcohol and was sentenced to perform eight hours of community service, attend a six-hour alcohol awareness class, and pay $51.25 in court costs. Once she had passed sentence, Judge Elisabeth Earle looked up and smiled. "Good luck to you, Miss Bush," she said.

Back in Washington, Laura took her mother and a group of friends from around the country to visit the Holocaust Museum on Holocaust Remembrance Day. Laura had not been informed that during the ceremony an American flag would be presented to each of the U.S. Army units that had liberated concentration camps. Harold Welch's outfit, the 104th Infantry, had liberated Nordhausen. When the flag bearing the timber wolf—the emblem of her dad's division—was announced, Laura and Jenna Welch broke down. "I was so glad," Laura said of her mother, "she was there for that."

Although her husband had yet to set foot in New York as President, Laura traveled there the following week to attend the opening of "Jacqueline Kennedy: The White House Years," a lavish exhibition of Jackie's trendsetting Camelot-era fashions at New York's Metropolitan Museum. Unaware that Laura had long idolized her mother, Caroline Kennedy Schlossberg virtually ignored the new First Lady, perfunctorily thanking Mrs. Bush "for coming tonight." But Jackie's daughter went out of her way to heap praise on Hillary Clinton, who deigned to arrive only after Laura had departed, as the woman who "interpreted the role of First Lady for our times."

Just one week after being snubbed at the Jackie exhibit, Laura was chosen as one of *People* magazine's "50 Most Beautiful People"— along with the likes of Julia Roberts, Catherine Zeta-Jones, George Clooney, and Halle Berry. "She just seems fresh and warm and really lovely," proclaimed *People*'s Elizabeth Sporkin. It was an honor the magazine had not seen fit to bestow on Hillary Clinton during her entire eight-year tenure as First Lady.

"I am glad that Americans are getting a chance to find out something I've known for twenty-three years," the President said. "Laura Bush is a beautiful person, inside and out." In typically self-effacing fashion, Laura deflected the compliment. "I don't know that I'm trying to say anything with my appearance," she commented. "I hope I'm saying something with my actions."

Privately, Laura, who had just ordered up a pricey new wardrobe from New York couturier Arnold Scaasi, was not about to let this opportunity pass by. "Gee, Bushie," she cracked, flipping through the magazine, "I don't see *your* face in here . . ."

Laura's new designer look—and what it cost to maintain that look—prompted some good-natured ribbing from her husband. The notoriously tightfisted George could now appreciate why JFK had railed against what he considered to be Jackie's spendthrift ways. No sooner did Laura return from a clothes-buying trip to New York than the President confronted her. "So," he said with a smirk, "any money left in the Treasury?"

These were just the latest in a series of tongue-in-cheek skirmishes that were the hallmark of the Bush marriage. "From the very beginning they have loved to needle each other," Joe O'Neill said. "He might tease her for being prim and proper and studious, and she'd needle him right back for mangling the English language—again."

The same month Laura landed in *People*'s "Most Beautiful People" issue, Yale bestowed an honorary degree on George. Coming just five months into his presidency, the honor seemed to many to be undeserved. Former Yale graduate Gerald Ford was out of office by the time he was similarly honored, and W.'s dad had to wait until the last year of his presidency. Yale Law School graduate Bill Clinton had yet to receive an honorary degree from Yale.

Dozens of professors boycotted the commencement ceremonies, and hundreds of protesters showed up to boo and wave placards. But the President was not about to have anyone spoil the moment for him. "To those of you who received honors, awards, and distinctions," Bush told the graduating seniors, "I say, 'Well done.' And to the C students, I say, 'You, too, can be President of the United States.' "

W. also joked about napping on the leather couches in the library and partying until dawn. "If you're like me, you won't remember everything you did here. That," he said with a laugh, "can be a good thing."

Back then, of course, Bush did not have to contend with Secret Service agents or the national media when he went out drinking with his fraternity brothers. On May 29, 2001, the manager of Chuy's, a Tex-Mex restaurant in Austin, called 911 to report that an underage student was trying to buy alcohol with a false ID. Police arrived to find Secret Service agents, all wearing Hawaiian shirts, getting ready to escort two men and three women—including Barbara and Jenna—out of the restaurant.

Barbara was charged with consuming a margarita, Jenna with trying to buy liquor using a friend's driver's license—both class C misdemeanors. The bar owner's motives for calling 911 notwithstanding, it was inconceivable that the daughters of the President of the United States actually believed they could buy drinks using someone else's ID. It was no less mind-boggling that Secret Service agents would stand by and watch this all happen—on several occasions.

Even though they were law enforcement officers, Secret Service agents did not feel it was their job to protect the girls from themselves. "The Secret Service mission is to protect the lives of their protectees," White House Press Secretary Ari Fleischer said, "and that is their job and they're doing it."

In fairness, the Secret Service agents protecting both girls had warned them repeatedly not to go to bars and try to buy drinks— regardless of the fact that "everybody does it." One agent told Jenna: "You're putting yourselves in real danger of being arrested, and your family is going to be very embarrassed. Think of your mom and dad."

But Jenna so resented the agents who dogged her every move that she was, in the words of a classmate, "not about to listen to them. She's always saying how she never asked for any of this, that she wants her old life back. You can't blame them, the agents, because it's their job. But you can't blame her for hating it, either."

Jenna had no trouble making her feelings known. Most of the time, according to another University of Texas student, "she just sort of sulks. She's always shooting the agents one of those looks, you know? Sort of like that sneer her dad uses when he's angry about something. She's a sweet girl, but she's under a lot of pressure."

More than once, however, Jenna snapped. "Get away from me,"

she screamed at two agents who were keeping an eye on her at one off-campus party. "Leave me alone. *You're ruining my life!*"

Understandably, the press—not to mention comics and late-night talk-show hosts—had a field day with the misadventures of the Bush children. "Double Trouble" screamed the headline in the *New York Post,* while the cover story in *People* magazine proclaimed "Oops! They Did It Again." CBS's David Letterman called the twins J&B, while on NBC Jay Leno dubbed them Bartles & Jaymes, with an "Anheuser" Bush chaser. "Jenna & Tonic" trumpeted the headline in London's *Daily Mail.*

Don Imus made no apologies for repeatedly parodying the girls on his national radio show. "You can't go to the most popular bar in Austin, surrounded by Secret Service agents in Hawaiian shirts, and pull out a fake ID," Imus said. "Being a recovering alcoholic myself, it doesn't sound like alcoholic behavior, it sounds like idiotic behavior." Echoing the sentiments of many comics, *Politically Incorrect*'s Bill Maher said he held off on making fun of Bush's daughters until, by their own actions, it "seemed like they absolutely insisted."

At the White House, George and Laura angrily demanded to know why their daughters, among the 90 percent of college students who confess to drinking, were being singled out for such harsh treatment. "Who's making these 911 calls?" a Bush family friend asked. "You do get the feeling people are out to get these young girls."

Still, the President and First Lady were not about to let their daughters off the hook. Just three days after they were cited for violating Texas state liquor laws, Jenna and Barbara were at Camp David, the wooded retreat in Maryland's Catoctin Mountains, for a long-planned reunion with Mama and Dad. "It wasn't a Kodak moment," said a senior White House staffer. "The parents are disappointed and concerned."

Concerned in part because of George's own history with alcohol. Laura, in particular, was aware of a genetic predisposition to alcohol abuse; she had read up on the topic years earlier when she tried to figure out what to do about her husband's drinking problem.

The Bushes had actually begun worrying about Jenna's behavior years earlier. Although it had gone unreported because she was a minor, Texas Alcoholic Beverage Commission records allegedly showed that when Jenna was only sixteen she was cited for an alcohol-related offense on New Year's Eve 1997. Jenna's nickname, which was even referred to in her high school yearbook, spoke volumes. To her friends, Jenna was known as "Gin."

Now, with tabloid photographs showing Jenna sprawled on a barroom floor and two new brushes with the law, George and Laura were worried that their daughter might be sowing the seeds of a more serious drinking problem. "We've got to do something about this, George," Laura told her husband, "before it really gets out of hand."

But they disagreed over what that "something" should be. Laura, who had undergone counseling after the death of her friend Mike Douglas, believed the girls—Jenna in particular—would benefit from professional help. "She was very concerned about the pressures these girls were being subjected to," a Texas acquaintance said. "She thought they might need someone to unburden themselves to—a psychologist or a minister, just as long as it was someone with some expertise in the field."

Dad, however, resisted the idea. He had quit drinking cold turkey, and was convinced that what the girls were going through was "just a phase."

"They're fierce about their love for their girls," Regan Gammon said, noting that they always present a united front when dealing with the twins. "They'd talk it out, and if they disagreed, they'd compromise."

W. agreed that if things did not improve, he would join Laura in pressing to have the girls seek counseling. For the time being, however, George and Laura would only sit the girls down and give them a stern talking-to. "I'm sorry if there are things other kids can get away with that you can't," W. allegedly told them. "But what you do reflects on this office and on your family, and that's just the way it is."

There was an added warning for Jenna. Having committed two alcohol-related offenses in one year, she faced mandatory jail time if she violated Texas's tough "zero-tolerance" underage drinking laws a third time. W. was all too familiar with the consequences: He signed the stiff three-strikes rule into law when he was governor. (As a result of the Chuy's incident, Jenna was fined six hundred dollars and had her driver's license suspended for thirty days. She was also ordered to attend a meeting where relatives of victims tell about the devastating effects of drunk driving on families. Barbara was fined one hundred dollars and sentenced to three months probation and eight hours of community service.)

Duly chastised, the twins promised that they would stay away from bars until they turned twenty-one. They also pledged not to use fake IDs.

Publicly, the President would only say "I love them a lot. I love them and will love them." By way of damage control, Barbara Bush Sr. was hauled out by the White House to put a funny spin on her granddaughters' shenanigans. She marveled that the President was the same person she used to nag to clean up his room, then added, "Now he is getting back some of his own."

Laura, as always, provided her embattled daughters with an emotional safe harbor. "She's very nonjudgmental. She's always going to stand by you," Regan Gammon said. "I think she just sort of has an attitude that would say, 'Well, we can get through this.' It's kind of living in the moment. You deal with it right then. You can handle anything, because you know it's all part of life. There's no way any one of us can make it through some perfect way. You have to deal with whatever you have to deal with and go on."

To preserve her own sanity, Laura often fled back to Texas. In Austin, with her Secret Service detail trailing at a discreet distance, the First Lady paid a visit to her dentist, then dropped in on her friend Gammon. The two women walked to the local hardware store, then went shopping for place mats and plants that Laura would be taking to the ranch. On their leisurely stroll back, they talked about old times. "We sit around in my backyard, talk to my neighbors, look at their babies—normal stuff, like anyone," Gammon said of her pal. Laura, she went on, had not changed at all.

Being First Lady, Gammon said, hadn't altered Laura's "style or her personality, or made her go faster or speed up, be hyper. She continues to be calm and collected. She doesn't worry about what happened yesterday or what will happen tomorrow. I think that's why she's so full of grace when she meets people—she's right there. She's not trying to get rid of you or trying to impress you or anything—she's just being *with* you."

That quality came though when she accompanied George on his first official trip to Europe in June 2001. While thousands of protesters filled the streets to protest her husband's policies, Laura managed to steer clear of the mayhem by doing what first ladies traditionally do. Instead of talking about women's rights the way Hillary Clinton did, Laura visited museums, schools, gardens, and libraries.

In a Brussels candy store, she picked out sixty-six pieces of chocolate while W. begged her to keep the calorie count "under twenty thousand." At a preschool in Warsaw, the children greeted her by singing "Deep in the Heart of Texas," and in Madrid she was visibly moved when passersby burst into an impromptu rendition of "God Bless America." In Sweden, where police battled back anti-Bush demonstrators, Laura visited a botanical garden and told her aides that she was impressed with "the friendly people and the peaceful countryside."

Notwithstanding the obvious differences between them, Laura and her predecessor had one thing in common: a desire to be taken seriously when it came to the issues they most cared about. As soon as she arrived back in Washington in late July, Laura held a summit of 350 scientists, educators, and children's advocates aimed at improving preschool education.

"Before President Bush and I married we had a couple of theories on raising kids," she said. "Now we have a couple of kids and no theories." When it came to the uncertainty of parenthood, she added, "George and I are perfect examples. We have these two premature babies, and we bring them home, and we didn't know what to do with those little babies . . ."

At the time babies—unborn babies—were very much on the mind of both George and Laura. For months, W. had struggled with one of the most profound and complex questions of the age: Should society, via genetic research, manipulate the building blocks of human life? Embryonic stem cells held great promise for curing Parkinson's, diabetes, Alzheimer's, and many other devastating conditions. But the issue had proven bitterly divisive, pitting the religious right against those who felt that the frozen, early-stage embryos needed for stem-cell research did not in fact constitute life. There were plenty of conservatives, in fact, who advocated allow-

ing research on stem cells from frozen embryos that would otherwise be discarded. Senator Orrin Hatch supported such research, as
did Nancy Reagan, whose husband suffered from Alzheimer's. But
the issue remained fraught with political peril for the President, who
had pledged during the campaign to oppose federal funding for
research on stem cells obtained by "destroying living human
embryos."

George immersed himself in the topic, consulting everyone from
the president of Notre Dame to geneticists, theologians, and bioethi-
cists. Yet no one would hold more sway with the President than his
First Lady. Laura argued strongly on behalf of stem-cell research,
urging him to continue the policy of the Clinton Administration.

George had a compromise in mind. Several scientists believed
that there were enough existing embryonic cell lines to satisfy
research needs. What if we limited research only to them? Laura,
however, had done research of her own. By limiting research only to
existing stem cell lines, finding cures to diseases like Parkinson's and
diabetes would take much longer. According to White House insid-
ers, Laura pressed her husband not to tie the hands of researchers.
"These embryos will be destroyed anyway, George," she said. "This
is about the right to life. Just think about all the lives that could be
saved by stem-cell research."

Still, it was the President's decision to make. "After having been
married as long as we have, we understand each other's viewpoints,"
Laura explained on CNN. "And I know that he is the President. I'm
not. And so I certainly, in private, might say some things to him."

In the end, W. decided to allow research only on existing stem cell
lines—a Solomonic verdict he explained to the American people in
a nationally televised prime-time address originating from the ranch
in Crawford. Publicly Laura stood firmly behind her husband's decision. But away from reporters, Laura told friends she was disappointed by the compromise.

George and Laura would hole up at the ranch for the rest of
August—a thirty-day vacation that, according to a *USA Today/
CNN*/Gallup Poll had 55 percent of all Americans complaining
that the President was taking too much time off. Not so, insisted
George, who once again complained of life in the "bubble. I under-
stand the bubble. I recognize the President is in a bubble. But I like

to—to the extent that I can—kind of expand the diameter of the bubble. The ranch is a good place to do so."

Besides, this was nothing if not a working vacation. "The amazing thing about this job," George said, "is that the job seems to follow you around."

By now the Bushes settled into a leisurely routine at the ranch, albeit always under the watchful eyes of the Secret Service. In addition, a military aide, a communications technician, a staff physician, and a nurse were always on hand. So was a White House chef. "I like to read cookbooks," Laura said, "but I'm not really much of a cook." On Sunday nights, however, the President could be counted on to make chopped eggs à la George—hard-boiled egg sandwiches.

Without the aid of an alarm clock, the President awoke every day before 5:45 A.M. and shuffled into the kitchen to make coffee. Then, with his coffee cup in one hand and a small flashlight in the other, he took Barney outside to chase the armadillos out of Laura's flower bed. That done, he brought coffee and the newspapers— always the *New York Times,* the *Washington Times,* and the *Washington Post*—back to read in bed with Laura.

Heading off on his own, George would run four miles and walk another mile before returning shortly before 8 A.M. for his daily national security briefing. At nine, while Laura began working in the garden, the President would start working the phones. There were calls to Colin Powell and Defense Secretary Donald Rumsfeld and—more than any other adviser—to Condi Rice. In preparation for the state visit of Mexican President Vicente Fox in September 2001, W. was mulling over ways to loosen up immigration rules for Mexicans living in the United States illegally.

George also spoke with Israeli Prime Minister Ariel Sharon, but he felt powerless to do anything about tensions between Palestinians and Israelis. "There's nothing we can do to keep those people from killing each other," he told Laura. "Nothing."

By late morning George, who seemed to thrive in the sweltering one-hundred-plus-degree summer heat, invariably headed out with his chain saw to work on clearing another trail. Then he shared a light lunch with Laura before retiring to his study with a book around 1:45 P.M. He had just finished Nathaniel Philbrick's *In the*

Heart of the Sea: The Tragedy of the Whaleship Essex and was starting *Founding Brothers* by Joseph Ellis.

By 4 P.M., George was dashing off e-mails—despite his affinity for them, Laura shied away from the computer—and poring over memos and reports. An hour later, he might go fly-fishing for bass in his small lake—always throwing them back—or just as often pile into the pickup with Laura and drive around the ranch.

After dinner on the porch—they dined with friends virtually every night—the Bushes might, in the President's words, "kind of lounge" in the "whining" pool. He insisted that outdoor speakers be installed "so we can crank up a little music"—Laura's favorite, Van Morrison, as well as Aaron Neville, Bonnie Raitt, George Jones, and Willie Nelson. By 9:15 P.M., the Bushes were in bed—she reading herself to sleep while he watched baseball on TV.

It was a far cry from the life Jenna was enjoying as a summer intern at Brillstein Grey Entertainment, one of Hollywood's most powerful management production companies. Founded by famed Hollywood hell-raiser Bernie Brillstein, the firm produced NBC's *Just Shoot Me* and HBO's *The Sopranos* and numbered among its clients Brad Pitt and Jennifer Aniston. Another Brillstein Grey client, John Belushi, died of a drug overdose in 1982. The *New York Times* called Bernie Brillstein a "vintage swell who loved the 'big life' (degenerate gambling, broads with great legs); he was catnip to a doomed party animal like Belushi."

Not surprisingly, Jenna did not bother to tell her parents about the internship until it was a fait accompli. "They were both very worried," said a longtime Bush supporter, "that it wasn't exactly the right atmosphere for a girl like Jenna."

They were right. Although she stayed with Brad Freeman, the family friend who adopted Ernie the cat, chain-smoking Jenna wasted no time hitting the Los Angeles party circuit. At the popular nightclub Deep, she was photographed cavorting with other girls around a table stacked with drinks. Jenna also showed up at a booze-fueled Beverly Hills party complete with strippers, and was later seen knocking back Bloody Marys with friends poolside at the Grande Colonial hotel in the California coastal town of La Jolla.

Five days later, Jenna brought her sister Barbara along to another celebrity-packed Beverly Hills party. After rapper Snoop Doggy Dogg got up to sing, a fight broke out and Secret Service agents descended on the twins, hustling them to safety. "The girls got out unhurt," said eyewitness Raul Roa, "but shaken."

To further complicate matters, Jenna was now dating former model Brandon Davis, twenty-year-old grandson of billionaire Marvin Davis. A recovering alcoholic, Brandon warned Jenna that her drinking was out of control and begged her to stop. Instead, it was Brandon who wound up back in rehab after mixing vodka, beer, margaritas, and cocaine at a party in Hugh Hefner's Playboy mansion. Jenna was not with him at the time.

"I certainly went out with a bang," said Davis, who was flown in the family's private jet to Minnesota's renowned Hazeldon clinic. "It was a wild night." But, he said in reply to those who suggested Jenna had been a bad influence, "I'm not blaming Jenna for this situation." Her internship over, Jenna returned to Austin and began her second year at the University of Texas.

Now that George and Laura were back in Washington the first week in September, it was duly noted in the press that the President had spent two of his first six months in office at the ranch, as well as a long weekend in Kennebunkport and fourteen weekends at Camp David. It was time well-spent, W. said, "with real people in the heartland."

Those "real people" might have sympathized with Laura's dilemma as she prepared her first state dinner, for Mexican President Vicente Fox. "It's just like a party at your own house," the First Lady said, "where at the last minute, you're washing the windows, wiping the fingerprints off the doors, setting the table."

And where the slightest faux pas could trigger an international incident. When W.'s dad was hosting Mexico's then-president Carlos Salinas, White House pastry chef Roland Mesnier decorated his ice cream cake with a charming scene of a Mexican boy in sombrero snoozing against his adobe hut. A White House aide, realizing this would be seen as an insult, swiped the boy off the cake just as it was being carried with great fanfare into the State Dining Room. Barbara Bush then finished the job, flattening the hut with a spoon.

This time, Mesnier's dessert was still spectacular if politically correct—a dome of mango ice cream festooned with spun sugar hummingbirds and hibiscus flowers. It followed a meal of Maryland crab and chorizo pozole and pumpkin seed–encrusted bison with whipped potatoes and fava bean ragout.

Laura, wearing a hot pink and red Arnold Scaasi gown, beamed beside tablemate Clint Eastwood as her husband rose to give the toast. The Bushes were still serving hard liquor and wine at the White House—"only some of us won't drink it," the President allowed. W., wearing cowboy boots with his tuxedo, raised a glass of 7UP and welcomed his guest of honor to the "Casa Blanca." Fox, in turn, praised his friend "Jorge" and spoke of their shared love of all things western. Laura, meanwhile, drank champagne, and sipped each of the four wines served with dinner.

"For those of you who like to stay up late," the President said, "you are welcome to dance. For those of us who like to go to bed early"—George looked over to see his wife glaring at him—"I guess I'll be here for one dance."

When an elaborate fireworks display lit up the skies over the South Lawn at 11 P.M., the White House switchboard lit up. With panic in their voices, many of the callers asked the same question:

Was America, they wanted to know, under attack?

This is our call to tell you, number one, we love you, and number two, we love you.

—*Since 9/11, the phone message George and Laura leave their daughters every day*

It's not the life she would have chosen, but the truth is Laura loves being First Lady almost as much as George loves being President.

—*Joe O'Neill*

You see them together, and it's like they're reading each other's minds.

—*A family friend*

Since September 11 I've had the opportunity, maybe I should say the responsibility, to be steady for our country—and for my husband.

—*Laura*

8

September 12, 2001
5:30 A.M.

L ike millions of Americans, Laura stirred awake the next
morning wondering if it had really happened. Maybe, she
devoutly prayed, it was just a terrible dream—the worst
nightmare imaginable. But as she lifted herself up and looked at the
newspapers George had spread out on the bed, the inescapable reality hit her full force.

"It really happened," she said softly.

"It really happened," the President replied.

The next few weeks and months would define both George and
Laura as they rose to confront a challenge unlike any America had
ever faced before. Yet like any parents, their first thoughts were for
the safety of their children. It would be easier to protect the twins,
the Secret Service had advised the President and First Lady, if they
remained at their respective campuses. As much as they wanted to
see their daughters, George and Laura both knew that in the coming
weeks they would have little time to spend with them. Laura reluctantly agreed that not seeing the kids was "for the best," but told

anyone who would listen that being away from her children was "hard. It's very hard."

That first morning after the attacks, their thoughts were also not far from those victims they had known personally. Washington lawyer Ted Olson had argued the Republicans' case before the Supreme Court during the election recount battle, and was rewarded by George with an appointment as solicitor general. His forty-five-year-old wife Barbara, the conservative writer and commentator, had been aboard the plane that crashed into the Pentagon. Laura had watched with her hand to her mouth as it was reported on the Fox News Channel that Barbara Olson had placed a cell phone call from the plane to her husband in the final moments before the crash. "How horrible," Laura said, shaking her head. "Poor Ted." George placed a call to the stunned Olson, barely controlling the emotion in his voice as he expressed his condolences. Then, steadying himself, he went back to work.

Laura also burned up the phone lines, calling the girlfriends in Texas who for all intents and purposes had been her surrogate sisters over the years. "Are you okay?" she asked Jan O'Neill, Regan Gammon, Nancy Weiss, and the others. "Yes, I'm okay . . . We'll get through this . . ."

"She had the urge to speak to the people she loved," Weiss said. "You could hear it in her voice—the same shock and disbelief we all felt."

At 10:30 A.M., W. presided over a Security Council meeting and over the next few hours telephoned a series of world leaders to line up support. Among them: British Prime Minister Tony Blair, French President Jacques Chirac, Canadian Prime Minister Jean Chretien, German Chancellor Gerhard Schroeder, and Chinese President Jiang Zemin. He would speak twice with Russian President Vladimir Putin. For the first time ever, NATO invoked its mutual defense provision stating that an armed attack against any member would be treated as an attack against all. Calling the attacks "acts of war," Bush asked for and got forty billion dollars in emergency funding. He also met with the congressional leadership. Two days later, both houses would overwhelmingly vote to authorize President Bush to use all "necessary and appropriate force" needed against those responsible.

While her husband moved to assess the threat and decide what to do about it, Laura met with her staff. "Many of them had been at the White House and were told to run for their lives," Laura recalled. "They didn't sign on for this. They felt very vulnerable. I wanted them to think about ways they could be constructive."

Donating blood and visiting hospitals were the first things that came to Laura's mind, and at three that afternoon she visited White House staffers who had volunteered to give blood. At the same time, the President and Secretary of Defense Rumsfeld inspected the spot where American flight 77 slammed into the west wall of the Pentagon, killing 189.

Two days after the attacks, which in the end would claim the lives of nearly three thousand people, Colin Powell identified Saudi expatriot Osama bin Laden and his Al Qaeda terrorist network as the prime suspects. George was not surprised. A month before the attacks, the President had been warned that bin Laden, who was being shielded by Afghanistan's Taliban regime, had been planning multiple hijackings in the United States. Later, a date for the attacks had even been pinpointed: September 11. "The President was provided information about bin Laden wanting to engage in hijacking in the traditional pre-9/11 sense," White House press secretary Ari Fleischer said, "not for the use of suicide bombing, not for the use of an airplane as a missile."

Eventually, it would be learned that the President had actually asked his advisers to draw up a plan that would destroy Al Qaeda once and for all. "I feel like I'm swatting at flics," he had told Condoleezza Rice and CIA director George Tenet. "I want a way to take the network down." But the CIA plan had not arrived on his desk in time for action. There would also be allegations that, in what surely constituted the greatest intelligence failure in U.S. history, the CIA, the FBI, and other government agencies had missed important clues that might have led to the prevention of the attacks.

At the time, the nation was in shock—and unaware that the President had been warned, albeit without enough specific information to act. But within earshot of two White House aides, W. did say to Laura that he wondered if there wasn't something that might have been done—some action he should have taken—to prevent the tragedy. "Bushie," Laura said reassuringly, "there wasn't anything you or anyone could have done to stop this."

For the time being, he was forced to deal with criticism that, instead of returning to Washington immediately on 9/11, W. zigzagged from one base to another aboard Air Force One. "You have to remember, I'm scrambling," he explained. "I want to go back to Washington. There is strong advice that I not, primarily from the Vice President." Laura, though undeniably angry over the implication that her husband had behaved in a less than heroic fashion, had two words of advice for W.: "Ignore them."

Two days after the attack, the President phoned New York Mayor Rudy Giuliani and New York Governor George Pataki from the Oval Office to pledge his support. Then he spoke to reporters. "I wish I could comfort every single family whose lives have been affected," he said. "But make no mistake about it; my resolve is steady and strong about winning this war."

At one point, a reporter asked if he had said a prayer for himself. "Well, I don't think of myself right now," he said, choking back tears. "I think about the families, the children. I am a loving guy, and I am also someone, however, who has got a job to do and I intend to do it. And this is a terrible moment. But this country will not relent until we have saved ourselves, and others, from the terrible tragedy that came upon America."

That afternoon, the President would again be overcome with emotion—and Laura along with him—when they visited victims of the Pentagon attack being treated in the Washington Hospital Center's burn unit. "It was really tough," she told a friend from Midland. "It was so sad seeing these guys wrapped up like mummies, trying to salute the Commander-in-Chief."

It would not get any easier. Laura sat down at the desk in her White House office and wrote open letters to schoolchildren—one for elementary school students and another for older children—to be distributed by district superintendents around the country. "When sad or frightening things happen," Laura wrote, "all of us have an opportunity to become better people by thinking about others."

Then Laura turned her attention to planning a memorial service at Washington's National Cathedral the next day—a job delegated to her by her husband. At the emotionally charged service, Poppy reached over Laura to grasp his son's hand. Both men brushed away tears as their wives looked on. Hours later, the President was standing at Ground Zero, talking to rescue workers over a bullhorn.

"This nation," the President said, "stands with the good people of New York and New Jersey and Connecticut as we mourn the loss of thousands of our citizens . . ." Then someone in the crowd yelled "I can't hear you!"

"I can hear you," W. replied instantly. "The rest of the world hears you. And the people who knocked these buildings down will hear all of us soon!" With that, the crowd burst into chants of "USA! USA!"

As they did nearly every weekend, George and Laura helicoptered aboard Marine One to Camp David. The President's top advisers were there, brainstorming over what action to take. After dinner, everyone gathered around the piano. Attorney General John Ashcroft played while Condi Rice sang patriotic American songs and hymns. Recalled Laura: "It was really comforting and relaxing to listen to them."

The following morning the President took Barney and Spot for their usual 5 A.M. walk. At 10:30, he addressed the nation. "We will smoke them out of their holes," he said. "We will get them running and we'll bring them to justice. They have stirred up the might of the American people, and we're going to get them, no matter what it takes. This message is for everyone who wears the uniform: Get ready."

Over dinner that first dismal weekend at Camp David, everyone joined hands and prayed. The local minister had selected the prayer well before the attacks, but it was eerily appropriate: "Though a host shall encamp against me, my heart shall not fear," read Psalm 27. "Though war shall rise against me, in this I will be confident." Laura was so impressed by the message that she had the White House Christmas cards redesigned to include it.

Soon Laura was being dubbed "Comforter in Chief" and "First Mother" in the press. With good reason. As her husband prepared the nation for war, she offered soothing words of sympathy and reassurance. At a memorial service in Pennsylvania for victims of Flight 93, she recited lines from Kahlil Gibran that gave poetic meaning to the cell-phone calls placed by passengers before they overwhelmed their hijackers. "Love," she read, "knows not its own depths until the hour of parting."

Then the First Lady spoke directly to the families. "You are the ones they thought of in the last moments of life," she said. "You are the ones they called and prayed to see again. You are the ones they loved. And I want each of you to know today that you are not alone. We cannot ease the pain, but this country stands by you."

She went on the morning television shows to tell parents to make their children feel secure. "They need their parents to give them lots of hugs," she said. Appearing on *Oprah* one week after the attacks, she held host Oprah Winfrey's hand throughout most of the hour-long interview as she urged adults not to forget the impact of 9/11 on children. "It's very reassuring for children to hear their parents' voices," she said. "Of course, we can't explain terrorism, you know, we really can't. It's just a horrible, evil thing."

Although clearly not as demonstrative as her husband, the First Lady also experienced her own moments of profound despair. Laura was determinedly upbeat when she visited children in Manhattan whose school had been closed by the attacks, but "crashed" afterward, said friends. And, later, at a memorial service for the victims of the Pentagon attack, she broke down crying. "I'm not usually teary," she said, laughing it off. "That's a Bush family characteristic. I married that." She was not alone that day; after "Taps" was played and a chorus sang "The Battle Hymn of the Republic," weeping family members stood waving tiny American flags. "It was," she said, "so moving."

To cope with mounting anxiety, Laura once again turned to the written word. "Reading is certainly a way I've handled stress," she said. "As well as loneliness, as well as boredom, as well as any other thing during my life that I've had to deal with." In the days following the attacks, she tore through mystery writer Sue Grafton's *P Is for Peril*—"an unlikely choice," she agreed. "But I've always loved mysteries . . ."

Laura also followed her husband's lead and began exercising—seriously. She walked three miles a day on the treadmill, and had a personal trainer into the White House every other day.

It was more important than ever for Laura to maintain her stamina—and her equilibrium. Unbeknownst to the public—and despite her own statements to the contrary—she had always been one of her husband's most trusted advisers on affairs domestic and foreign. When George told the nation he wanted Osama bin Laden "dead or alive," Laura winced at his macho talk and Marlboro Man delivery. Sidling up to George afterward, she gently teased, "Bushie, you gonna git 'em?" Later, she told him she disapproved of his Wild West act. "Not very statesmanlike, Bushie," she complained.

"She didn't like my choice of words," he said. "She didn't want to see me become too bellicose, react with bloodlust."

Indeed, over the coming weeks Laura repeatedly cautioned her husband not to "do anything rash" and urged him never to act "out of revenge." She also told George how pleased she was that there had been no "immediate retaliation" to the September 11 attacks—that she was glad he was taking his time building an international coalition as he weighed his options. "I knew the President was going to do the right thing," she said, "but like a lot of women, I was hoping that was going to be nothing."

Laura had also urged her husband to speak out after there were reports of violence directed at Arab-Americans and those thought to be Arab-American. The day after a Sikh man was shot to death in Arizona simply because he happened to be wearing a turban, the President visited a mosque at the Islamic Center in Washington. "Muslims make an incredibly valuable contribution to our country," he declared, "and they need to be treated with respect."

The First Lady also continued to "discuss personalities" with her husband—Tony Blair was a particular favorite, Israeli Prime Minister Ariel Sharon was not—and shared her thoughts on the Middle East. Unlike Hillary Clinton, whose outspoken support of an independent Palestinian state had long-lasting repercussions for her husband's administration, Laura was determined never to undermine her husband's credibility. But she felt strongly that the Palestinian people deserved a nation of their own, and told W. so. On October 3, he announced he was backing the creation of a Palestinian state.

Three days before he authorized the bombing of Afghanistan as part of Operation Enduring Freedom, George told Laura of his decision to launch the attacks. The First Couple kept with their original plans to have a few Midland friends at Camp David that weekend, along with Condi Rice, the Cheneys, and the rest of the national security team. As usual, they ate chicken-fried steak, took long walks in the woods, and worked on a jigsaw puzzle of the White House—the President's favorite.

Laura had always been intensely protective of her husband and her family, and never more so than after the attacks. While the President now relied on the news summaries provided for him each morning, Laura scoured the newspapers to make certain they were treating George fairly. When a *Washington Post* photograph made it appear as if the President had horns, she told Karen Hughes to "check into it."

She took particular offense at published reports that, as an oilman back in Texas, George had actually done business with the bin Laden family. One of those Texans who invested in Bush's Arbusto Energy drilling company, Houston businessman James R. Bath, had at one time actually represented several Saudi investors. Among them: Sheik Salem M. bin Laden, Osama's eldest brother. Salem and several other bin Laden brothers—not Osama—had extensive business interests in Texas, including the Texas-based air charter company Binladen Aviation. But there were no direct ties between the Bush and bin Laden families. (In an odd twist of fate, Salem bin Laden was killed in 1988 when the British Aerospace BAC 1-11 ultralight plane he was piloting crashed into power lines at an air park north of San Antonio.)

George and Laura were determined not to disrupt their daily routine at the White House. Trying to resume a "life as normal" stance, the Bushes went out with two friends to a suburban Tex-Mex restaurant for enchiladas and—in W.'s case—nonalcoholic beer. "We want to encourage Americans," Laura said, "to go about their lives in a normal way."

But Laura's life—and her role—had changed dramatically. Increasingly, she was being called on to act as her husband's surrogate. She appeared on *60 Minutes* and CNN's *Larry King Live* and spoke at the National Press Club. There, she revealed that her new exercise regimen had trimmed inches off her hourglass figure. "I'm working out," she said. "Can y'all tell?" She also joked that she might write a book like Hillary Clinton ("if I can get that eight-million-dollar advance or whatever it is—only kidding"), that she didn't think the strain of the war was taking a toll on George's appearance ("I don't think his hair is really grayer—I'll have to look again"), and that she would not be preparing this year's Thanksgiving turkey. When several members of the audience began to chuckle, she snapped, "Why are you laughing? I haven't had to cook for a few years. It's been a great relief for my family."

On November 17, Laura became the first First Lady ever to deliver the President's Saturday radio address, seizing the opportunity to decry the plight of Afghan women and children under the harsh Taliban regime. The next week, she met with eleven exiled Afghan women in the White House and argued that the rights of women must be safeguarded in a post-Taliban government.

George was depending on Laura in other ways, as well. Now W. always told Laura whenever the Secret Service informed him of threats on his life. "My attitude about threats," he said, "is, if it's the Lord's will . . ."

It helped that Laura, unlike other first ladies who became unglued by the thought, shrugged off such matters. "I really am not that afraid," she said. "I mean, you know, if something happens, it happens. I think both of us have a little bit of an attitude that, you know, this is our life right now and we can deal with it. We can handle it."

Her cool-headed response to such threats, said one White House staffer, "always calms his nerves." In public, he might reach for her hand without even looking to see where she was, knowing she would grab it and hold on tightly. At other times when he seemed anxious or upset, Laura would touch his arm or the back of his neck reassuringly.

Then there were those unspoken moments, when George and Laura's eyes locked and, said a friend, they seemed to be "reading each other's minds. Those of us who have known them over the years can look at them and see they are communicating, even when they aren't talking."

George conceded that, at this time of crisis, he needed Laura "more than ever. You know, this is a moment of high drama, needless to say," he mused. "And she [Laura] couldn't have been more calm and resolved, almost placid, which was a very reassuring thing to me. I can't imagine what it would be like had Laura been hysterical, highly emotional . . . never did she say, 'Get me out of here, what have you done this for, why are we here, it's a miserable experience . . . It's your war, see you later.' "

For the first time in seven years, the Bushes would not be spending Thanksgiving at the Austin home of Billy and Regan Gammon. Instead, they gathered with the rest of the family at Camp David for roast turkey with cornbread sage dressing ("Every time my mother made stuffing, my dad would say, 'Be sure to put in plenty of sage' or 'Do you think you put in enough sage?'" Laura recalled), mashed sweet potatoes, green beans, pumpkin pie, and pecan pie.

"All of us are much more aware of the things we took for granted: our family members, our loved ones, our freedoms, our incredible life that all Americans are lucky to have," Laura said of the first post-9/11 Thanksgiving. "For that reason, it will be a particularly special holiday, but also, I think, slightly bittersweet . . . there will be a lot of families who will have an empty seat at the table."

The lesson was not lost on Jenna and Barbara, who now promptly returned all their parents' phone calls. "Like every other American family, we are talking to them more now," Laura said. "And it's not just us calling them, they are calling in more now." The girls were also making a concerted effort to spend more time with Mama and Dad at the White House and Camp David—even at the Crawford ranch.

Like everything else, Christmas at the White House had been drastically altered by the events of September 11. The screens that used to shield the First Family from hordes of tourists were no longer needed; for obvious security reasons, the public had been barred from the White House since the attacks. "We have to err on the side of caution," she said, "but it gets pretty lonely around here."

Still, a forest of forty-nine glistening snow-covered evergreens spread across the main floor, wreaths tied with red ribbon hung in the windows and the Truman Balcony was draped with pine garlands. There was a nine-foot tree by the door in the Oval Office, and eighteen miniature reproductions of past presidents' homes were placed on fireplace mantels throughout the ceremonial rooms. In the State Dining Room: a 130-pound gingerbread, chocolate, and marzipan house depicting the White House in 1800.

Just opposite the elevator in the family's second-floor residence was a Mexican nativity scene fashioned in clay that they brought with them from Texas. In the Yellow Oval Room, which Laura had restored to its Kennedy-era elegance, there was a tree bedecked with family ornaments.

Decorating the White House had not been easy. Laura's "Home for the Holidays" Christmas theme, chosen the previous July, now took on added poignancy. As she helped volunteers trim the eighteen-foot White House Christmas tree in the Blue Room, Laura "thought about the single mother or the single dad who are trying to decorate a tree right now and trying to make their child or their children have a . . . happy holiday . . ."

Yet Laura continued to embrace her new role as the nation's chief nurturer. When New York kicked off the holiday season with the lighting of the Rockefeller Center Christmas tree, it was Laura who threw the switch. "As we remember the loved ones lost and reflect on the spirit and courage that New Yorkers have shown in abundance," she said, "let us be thankful for our family, our friends, and our great country. America loves New York!"

The morning after Christmas, George and Laura flew to Crawford. No longer were the guardians of his image worried that the President was spending too much time at the ranch and away from Washington; since September 11, his approval rating had soared to 86 percent—the highest of any sitting President. What's more, 39 percent of all Americans said George W. Bush was the man they admired most—the highest any single person has received since Gallup began the survey in 1948.

Where he chose to spend his time scarcely mattered, now that an elaborate videoconferencing system had been set up at the ranch to enable him to conduct business as usual. Nor was there any doubt, given his conduct of America's ongoing war on terrorism, that he was very much the man in charge.

Going to the ranch, the President explained, simply gave him the opportunity to spend "a little quality time with the First Lady"—as well as fish in his pond and plant an oak tree the White House staff had given him. W. was not about to agree to the notion that terrorists had in any way changed his attitude toward the ranch, or made his trips there that much more indispensable. "I liked coming to the ranch before September 11," he said, "and I like coming to the ranch after September 11."

He also still liked to watch football on television. On January 13,

2002, the President was on a couch in the White House family quarters watching the Baltimore Ravens–Miami Dolphins playoff game when a pretzel lodged in his throat. He pitched forward, striking his left cheek and lip on a coffee table. He was wearing his glasses at the time, and on impact they raked his cheek, cutting into his face.

"I hit the deck," he said, "and woke up, and there was Barney and Spot showing a lot of concern." Because they had not moved, W. figured that he could have only been unconscious a few seconds.

"Laura! Help!" The First Lady, on the phone in the next room, came running. Within two or three minutes, White House nurse, Cindy Wright, was taking the President's blood pressure. Doctors would determine that pressure from the pretzel stimulated W.'s vagus nerve, which in turn lowered his blood pressure and caused him to faint.

The pretzel episode made headlines abroad, sparking speculation that the President was seriously ill—or had gone back to drinking. George and Laura laughed it off. The next day, he sent a bag of pretzels to the reporters aboard Air Force One. W. had scrawled on the bag: "From POTUS [President of the United States]. Chew slowly."

With Jenna and Barbara now keeping a low profile at their colleges, Barney and Spot were playing a larger role than ever in George and Laura's lives. Once when she was kept waiting outside the Oval Office with a group of friends while her husband held a meeting, Laura tied a note to Barney's collar and sent him inside. They waited until they heard George burst out laughing—he had found the note. "Isn't he adorable?" Laura frequently said of Barney. "He's everybody's favorite."

"They have a sense of duty," their friend Robert McCleskey said. "They know they have an awesome responsibility on their shoulders. At the same time, there is no doubt that they are both enjoying every minute of it." Added Doug Hannah: "Hell, they're having the time of their lives."

From the White House pastry chef's elaborate creations to the private shower aboard Air Force One, the President delighted in all the perks—large and small—that come with the office. "They don't let the job overwhelm them," Jenna Welch said. "They deal with what they have to deal with, but they also make time for fun."

As comfortable as they had become there, the Bushes never lost their reverence for the White House. In a radical departure from his predecessor, the President decreed that no one be allowed to enter the Oval Office without being properly dressed—for men, that meant a coat and tie. "One evening we were watching a movie in the White House theater," Joe O'Neill said, "and the President, who was wearing a sweater, went to fetch something from the Oval Office. It's just sort of down the hall, and he should only have taken a couple of minutes. But after about a half hour went by I asked what had happened to the President. 'Oh,' his aide told me, 'he went upstairs to change into a suit and tie.' He doesn't believe any-one, including the President, should set foot in the Oval Office without correct attire. To him, it's hallowed ground."

Still, the steady stream of overnight guests from Texas were made to feel as "comfortable as if they were back home," said pal Nancy Weiss. "When you drive up to the White House, you are in total awe. But the minute you step inside, it's like it's Laura's house. She just has that warm and welcoming way about her—she wants you to feel at ease."

Even when there were no visitors from back home, George and Laura kept in constant touch on the phone. Laura spoke with Nancy Weiss, for example, perhaps three times a week; she talked to her mother nearly every day. "They both want to know what people are up to—George will ask about how certain people are doing in the oil business, Laura wants to know about how their wives and their kids are doing," Joe O'Neill said. "They don't want to talk about national politics or foreign affairs—that's what they're trying to get away from."

Weiss agrees. "They both have a knack for compartmentalizing their lives," she said. "They try not to let things spill over from one area into another—that's how they stay sane in the midst of all the activity swirling around them."

By the spring of 2002, the Bush Administration was still waging its war on terrorism while at the same time coping with the collapse of Enron, a plethora of corporate scandals, and a worsening econ-omy. In describing how Enron's hapless shareholders had been duped by management, the President pointed to the fact that his mother-in-law had lost about eight thousand dollars by investing in the firm. "That's the last time," Jenna Welch said as she headed for a meeting of her ladies' investment group in Midland, "I tell him any-thing about the stocks I'm buying."

For all the issues confronting him, the President still found time to talk about the First Family dogs. Spot and Barney had, in fact, become part of his standard political patter around the country. W. talked about walking them each morning, and how he sometimes took a racket and whacked tennis balls from the top of the driveway onto the South Lawn for them to fetch.

At a political fund-raiser in Kansas City, Missouri, George called Barney "a fabulous little guy," and "the son I never had." He told a crowd in Little Rock, Arkansas, that "the family's doing well. Bar-ney the dog is in great shape. Spot . . . is getting a little up in the years, but she's doing well, too. She's used to the confines of the South Lawn. And I invite her every morning into the Oval Office to start my day. Spot makes herself comfortable on the new carpet. That's why," he added with a wink, "Barney's not invited in the morning."

George admitted that when he was visiting Latin America that spring, he worried not about his girls, but how the dogs were faring back at the White House. "I thought a couple of times during the trip about the pets," he admitted. "I wanted to make sure they were happy and didn't miss us."

"Jenna and Barbara are never mentioned," observed the *New York Times*'s Elisabeth Bumiller, "but Spot and Barney get whole para-graphs of reverie. Recent listeners to Mr. Bush might be excused for thinking the President had no daughters at all, only dogs."

Meantime Laura's in-laws were still very much a part of the fam-ily dynamic, keeping Georgie grounded. When he visited "forty-one" and his mother at Kennebunkport for the July 4th weekend—and to celebrate his fifty-sixth birthday two days later—"forty-three" slept upstairs in a small guest bedroom the same size as his brother Marvin's.

Rising as always before 6 A.M., W. padded downstairs in his slip-pers, grabbed a cup of coffee, plopped down on the sofa opposite his parents, and put his feet up.

"Put your feet down!" Mother commanded.

"For God's sake, Barbara," forty-one said, "he's the President of the United States."

"I don't care," she snapped. "I don't want his feet on my table."
George promptly obeyed, and his wife had no trouble under-
standing why. When someone asked Laura what Barbara Bush
thought about her daughter-in-law surpassing her in the polls,
Laura's eyes widened. "Please don't tell her," she pleaded.

Appearances notwithstanding, George's wife never was, as he had
said before, some "shrinking violet." When an American bombing
raid in southern Afghanistan accidentally killed more than forty
civilians, Laura pressed the President to phone the country's new
American-backed president, Hamid Karzai, and apologize. On July
5, George called Karzai from Kennebunkport to express his sympathy to the families of those who lost their lives.

In the wake of 9/11, the President and his team of advisers
increasingly came to view the First Lady as an important weapon in
his political arsenal. She continued to be the White House point
person on literacy and education, but as the fall 2002 elections
approached Laura was also dispatched to various parts of the country to speak on behalf of Republican candidates.

She also took her husband's message abroad. Traveling solo to
Eastern Europe, Laura delivered a thirteen-minute radio address in
Prague about the continuing plight of Afghan women. The speech
was translated into both Dari and Pashto and beamed into
Afghanistan. During a stopover in Budapest, she was informed by
"High Prophet" Karen Hughes that the President was being criticized back home for allegedly ignoring warnings prior to September 11 that a terrorist attack was imminent. Incensed, Laura spoke
out in defense of her husband—something she would never have
done prior to 9/11.

"I think it is very sad that people would play upon the victims'
families' emotions, or all Americans' emotions," Laura said. "I know
my husband, and all Americans know how he has acted in
Afghanistan and in the war with terror. I think, really, we need to
put this in perspective, and I think it's sad to play upon the emotions
of people as if there were something we could have done to stop it,
because that's just not the case."

In July 2002, Karen Hughes returned to Texas to spend more time
with her husband and teenage son. The surprise decision left a
power vacuum at the White House, and made Laura even more

indispensable as both sounding board and surrogate. White House Chief of Staff Andy Card bemoaned the fact that Hughes would no longer be there to balance the more stridently conservative Karl Rove. "Now Laura speaks up where she knew Karen would have," said one White House staffer. "The President listens to strong women . . . and that makes the First Lady a much more powerful voice in the administration than people realize."

And that much more prone to outrage on her husband's behalf. That summer, as financial markets reeled after it was disclosed several top corporate officers had falsified their firms' earnings statements, W. once again came under fire for his sale of Harken stock in 1990. At the time, the Securities and Exchange Commission had investigated the sale—which occurred shortly before Harken's stock tumbled—and the fact that he had failed to file the proper paperwork. The S.E.C. decided no action was warranted.

"Why do they keep bringing this up?" said an irritated Laura. Her advice to W. this time: Let Press Secretary Ari Fleischer handle it.

That July, W. made one of those requisite stops in the farm belt—this time at the Iowa State Fairgrounds in Des Moines. "Unfortunately, my wife didn't come with me," the President said, pausing as the audience groaned in response. "Yes, I agree with you. You know, I'm really proud of her. The country has gotten to know Laura like I have gotten to know her. People now understand why I asked her to marry me. A lot of people are still confused as to why she said yes. But she has been a great comfort to our nation, and the great love of my life."

The President paused, eyes glistening. And the audience, as it always did, cheered.

From the beginning, George's most daunting task was already cut out for him—or so he thought. Less than half the country had voted for W., yet a controversial Supreme Court handed him the presidency. His job, he vowed as he took the oath of office, was to win the trust of the American people—and to restore their confidence in government.

But like Franklin Roosevelt, who began his presidency believing his biggest challenge was to end the Great Depression, George W. Bush would be called upon to take on the greatest responsibility of all—leading his nation in time of war. Neither man would do it alone: FDR had Eleanor, George turned to Laura.

Both rooted in the same small Texas town, George and Laura nevertheless grew into two very different people: he the boisterous, backslapping prankster with a sentimental, weepy streak; she the softspoken bookworm with a tight rein on her own emotions and an uncanny knack for soothing the troubled souls of others.

They did have one important thing in common. Scarred by death early in their lives, they found a healing balm in the act of helping others. Laura became a teacher, George the self-appointed purveyor of mirth. Still, it hardly seemed conceivable—even to George and Laura—that so much would ultimately be demanded of them. "You never know where life is going to take you," George said. "Being President of the United States was never part of the plan."

Unlike Jack and Jackie and Bill and Hillary or even Franklin and Eleanor—all of whom begged the question—it hardly seems worth asking if George and Laura love each other. They always have, and no one could ever suggest otherwise.

They are part of a political dynasty unique in American history. Yet the President and his First Lady seem anything but regal. They grappled with alcoholism; he found in her the motivation—and the strength—to quit drinking. They have fretted about infertility and faced a life-threatening pregnancy. They have delighted in their daughters as children, and worried about them as teenagers. They have bolstered each other—and their 250 million countrymen—at a time when the world was turned upside down.

In their very ordinariness, George and Laura have proven themselves to be extraordinary—as man and woman, as husband and wife, as father and mother. Theirs is, in every way, an American marriage.

ACKNOWLEDGMENTS

Like millions of other Americans, my wife Valerie and I happened to be watching live coverage of the fire caused by an airliner mysteriously crashing into the north tower of the World Trade Center when a second plane struck the south tower. And like millions of our fellow New Yorkers, we were instantly on the phone to friends and family in the city, checking to make sure they were out of harm's way. When I drew parallels between the events of 9/11 and that other day that would live in infamy, my father, a career naval aviator who had flown bombing missions off carriers in the Pacific during World War II, corrected me. "It's worse than Pearl Harbor," he said, "because they struck at the heart of our country—and the targets were civilians."

Even before 9/11, I was intrigued by George and Laura. My books about Jack and Jackie Kennedy, Katharine Hepburn and Spencer Tracy, Bill and Hillary Clinton, and Princess Diana explored the strange forces that attract people to one another and hold them together in the face of seemingly overwhelming odds. Like *Jack and Jackie, George and Laura* is the biography of a sometimes poignant, often inspiring, always riveting relationship—a marriage that has stood both the test of time and the time of tests, both political and personal. Stronger and more resilient than any of us might have expected, the couple known as George and Laura would turn out to be far more than the sum of its parts.

For the eighth time, I have the great good fortune of working with my consummately professional friends at William Morrow. I am particularly grateful to my editor Maureen O'Brien, both for her editorial skill and her passionate commitment to seeing that the full story of George and Laura Bush be told. Once again, I must also extend my thanks to the entire William Morrow/HarperCollins publishing family, especially Jane Friedman, Cathy Hemming, Michael Morrison, Laurie Rippon, Lisa Gallagher, Beth Silfin, James Fox, Chris Goff, Kyran Cassidy, Richard Aquan, Brad Foltz, Katie Hellmuth, Michelle Corallo, Kim Lewis, Betty Lew, Christine Tanigawa, Debbie Stier, Rome Quezada, and Camille McDuffie, Grace McQuade, Brooke Fitzsimmons, Simone Cooper, and Lynn Goldberg of Goldberg-McDuffie Communications.

Virtually every year for the past two decades, I have thanked Ellen Levine for being a wonderful agent and an equally wonderful friend. Twenty years and twenty books—there are few author-agent partnerships that have flourished as long as ours has, and for that I remain eternally grateful. Ellen surrounds herself with the best of the best, and once again I owe a debt of thanks to her gifted associates Diana Finch and Louise Quayle.

My daughters Kate and Kelly, two distinctly different yet completely captivating personalities, are a source of inspiration and comic relief. I am also grateful to their grandparents, Edward and Jeanette Andersen, for their wisdom and the perspective only time and experience can bring. Of course, no one is more deserving of my gratitude (not to mention my love) than Valerie, my wife, partner, and best friend for thirty years—five years longer than George and Laura.

Laura's mother, Jenna Welch, was most helpful, and I thank her for her cooperation and her kind words of support and encouragement. Additional thanks to Joe O'Neill, Jan O'Neill, Dr. Charles Younger, Doug Hannah, Nancy Weiss, Cathryn Wolfman Young, Robert McCleskey, Brad Freeman, Mike Proctor, Mike Conaway, Don Jones, Donald Etra, Kent Hance, Ralph Way, Earle Craig, George Strake, Parker Ladd, John Bizilo, Teel Bivens, Ernie Angelo,

Polly Davis, Robert Reisner, Michael Weiss, Tana Sherman, Bradford Lee, Bobby Burns, Nicholas Redman, Todd Houck, Morris Burns, Oleg Cassini, Mary Higgins Clark, Greg Strake, Ruth Quattlebaum, Mark Harris, Bonnie Burlbaw, James Cruz, Amy Hooker, William Simon, Betsy Sullivan, Tom Freeman, Morris Williams, David Garrido, Susan Greene, Rosemary McClure, Kathy Way, Sharon Britton, Donna Johnson, Jane Inskeep, Linda Steel, Yvette Reyes, David Plotkin, Rosa DiSalvo, Dudley Freeman, Kenneth P. Norwick, Andrew Nurnberg, Gary Gunderson, Susan Rhyne, Paula Dranov, Michelle Lapautre, Farris L. Rookstool III, Nicole Vivona, Betsy Loth, Norman Currie, Jeanette Peterson, Jean Chapin, Valerie Wimmer, Ray Whelan Jr., the late William Colby, Pamela Redmer, Janet Lizop, Barry Schenck, Hazel Southam, Betty Beale, Charles Furneaux, the George Bush Presidential Library and Museum, the Permian Basin Petroleum Museum, the Midland Chamber of Commerce, the Midland Country Club, the Railroad Commission of Texas, the Texas Alcoholic Beverage Commission, the Hockaday School, Phillips Academy at Andover, Yale University, Harvard University, the University of Texas, Southern Methodist University, the Midland, Dallas, Austin, and Houston public libraries, the Lyndon Baines Johnson Library, the New York Public Library, the Gunn Memorial Library, the Greenwich Library, the New Milford Library, the Silas Bronson Library, AP Wide World, Getty Images, Globe Photos, Reuters, the Associated Press, the *Houston Chronicle,* the *Midland Reporter-Telegram, Texas Monthly,* the *Dallas Morning News,* Design to Printing, and Graphictype.

SOURCE NOTES

The following chapter notes are designed to give a general view of the sources drawn upon in preparing *George and Laura*, but they are by no means intended to be all-inclusive. The author has respected the wishes of many interviewed sources—including government officials still serving in Washington as well as longtime Bush family friends in Texas, Connecticut, Maine, and Washington—to remain anonymous and accordingly has not listed them either here or elsewhere in the text. The archives and oral history collections of, among other institutions, the George Bush Presidential Library, the Lyndon Baines Johnson Library, the John F. Kennedy Library, the Permian Basin Petroleum Museum Library and Hall of Fame, and the libraries of Yale, Columbia, Harvard, and Southern Methodist universities yielded a wealth of information. There have also been thousands of news reports and articles concerning the Bush family over the decades—including George W.'s rise to political prominence, his campaigns for governor of Texas and for the White House, the cliffhanger presidential election of 2000 and the constitutional crisis it precipitated, and of course the terrorist attacks on September 11, 2001, and their aftermath. These reports were broadcast on all major television and radio networks, and appeared in such publications as the *New York Times,* the *Washington Post, Time, Newsweek,* the *Wall Street Journal, Vanity Fair, U.S. News & World Report,* the *New York Post,* the New York *Daily News, Dallas Morning News,* the *Houston Chronicle,* the *Chicago Tribune,* the *Los Angeles Times,* the *Boston Globe, Texas Monthly Life,* and *The New Yorker,* and were carried over the AP, UPI, Knight–Ridder, Gannett, and Reuters wires.

Chapters 1 and 2
Interview subjects included Jenna Welch, Joe O'Neill, Doug Hannah, Dr. Charles Younger, Cathryn Wolfman Young, Robert McCleskey, Mike Proctor, Earle Craig, Robert Reisner, John Bizilo, Ralph Way, Don Jones, Bob Holton, Todd Houck, Morris Barns, Bradford Lee, Donna Johnson. Published sources included Nicholas Lemann, "The Options," *The New Yorker,* October 1, 2001; Howard Fineman and Martha Brant, "This Is Our Life Now," *Newsweek,* December 3, 2001; James Carney and John F. Dickerson, "Inside the War Room," *Time,* December 31, 2001; Mark Silva, "Bush Reading to Children as Siege Begins," *Orlando Sentinel,* September 11, 2001; Vickie Chachere, "Bush Hears News in Sarasota," Associated Press, September 11, 2001; Kathy Gambrell, "Journalists Detail Hours After Bush Told About Attack," United Press International, September 11, 2001; Nicholas D. Kristof, "Earning A's in People Skills at Andover," *New York Times,* June 10, 2000; Pamela Colloff, "The Son Rises," and Helen Thorpe, "Go East, Young Man," *Texas Monthly,* June 1999; George W. Bush, "Defends DKE," Letter to Editor, *Yale Daily News,* November 7, 1967; "Branding Rite Laid to Fraternity," *New York Times,* November 8, 1967; Bill Minutaglio, *First Son: George W. Bush and the Bush Family Dynasty* (New York: Three Rivers Press, 2001); Nicholas D. Kristof, "Ally of an Older Generation Amid the Tumult of the 60s," *New York Times,* June 19, 2000; Donnie Radcliffe, *Simply Barbara Bush* (New York: Warner Books, 1989); Barbara Bush, *Barbara Bush: A Memoir* (Lisa Drew Books/Charles Scribner's Sons, 1994); transcript of interview with Prescott Bush Jr., Oral History Project, Greenwich Library; David Maraniss, "The Bush Bunch," *Washington Post,* January 22, 1989; Jo Thomas, "After Yale, Bush Ambled Amiably into His Future," *New York Times,* July 22, 2000; Herbert S. Parmet, *George Bush: The Life of a Lone Star Yankee*

(New Brunswick, N.J.: Transaction Publishers, 2001); "Understanding What the National Guard Is All About: An Interview with Governor George W. Bush, *National Guard Review*, Winter 1998; George Bush, *A Charge to Keep* (New York: William Morrow, 2000); John Solomon, "Bush, Harvard Business School and the Makings of a President," *New York Times*, June 18, 2000.

Chapters 3 and 4

For these chapters, the author drew on conversations with Jenna Welch, Joe O'Neill, Nancy Weiss, Robert McCleskey, Dr. Charles Younger, Jan O'Neill, Michael Weiss, Doug Hannah, Ralph Way, George Strake, Polly Davis, Kent Hance, Oleg Cassini, Bobby Burns, Ernie Angelo, James Cruz. Among the published sources consulted: "Lee High School Senior Dies in Traffic Mishap," Midland *Reporter-Telegram*, November 7, 1963; Claudia Feldman, "First Lady," *Houston Chronicle*, July 20, 1997; Kathryn Casey, "The Other Mrs. Bush," *Ladies' Home Journal*, September 1999; "Miss Welch, Bush Wed in Methodist Rites," Midland *Reporter-Telegram*, November 6, 1977; Antonia Felix, *Laura* (Avon, Mass.: Adams Media, 2002); Nicholas D. Kristoff, "How Bush Came to Tame His Inner Scamp," *New York Times*, July 29, 2000; Georgia Temple, "Childhood Friends Say Laura Bush Loved Books, Scouting," Midland *Reporter-Telegram*, July 2000; Paul Burka, "The W. Nobody Knows," *Texas Monthly*, June 1999; Susan Schindehette, "The First Lady Next Door," *People*, January 29, 2001; Elizabeth Mitchell, *W: Revenge of the Bush Dynasty* (New York: Hyperion, 2000); Richard Behar, "The Wackiest Rig in Texas," *Time*, October 28, 1991; Richard V. Allen, "The Accidental Vice-President," *The New York Times Magazine*, July 30, 2000; Liz Steven, "Laura Bush Draws Praise, Respect for Poise," *Fort Worth Star-Telegram*, January 28, 2001; John Paul Pitts, "Bush Pays His Dues as West Texas Oilman," Midland *Reporter-Telegram*, July 2000; Beth Whitehouse, "Avoiding the Spotlight," *Newsday*, January 3, 2001; Lois Romano, "Laura Bush: A Twist on Traditional," *Washington Post*, May 14, 2000.

Chapters 5 to 8

Information for these chapters was based in part on conversations with Brad Freeman, Jenna Welch, Ernie Angelo, Nancy Weiss, Robert McCleskey, Joe O'Neill, Mike Conaway, Don Jones, Donald

Etra, Calvin Bridges, George Strake, Kent Hance, Mike Proctor, Teel Bivens, Dr. Charles Younger, Paul Sadler, Kathy Way, Morris Williams, David Garrido. Published sources included Laurence I. Barrett, "Junior Is His Own Man Now," *Time,* July 31, 1989; "George W. Bush: An Operative for His Father," *Houston Chronicle,* May 8, 1994; "The Bush Inaugural," *Houston Chronicle,* January 18, 1995; Michael Barone, "Best Little Governor in Texas," *U.S. News & World Report,* December 25, 1995; Skip Hollandsworth, "Reading Laura Bush," *Texas Monthly,* November 1996; Tucker Carlson, "Devil May Care," *Talk,* September 1999; Gail Sheehy, "The Accidental Candidate," *Vanity Fair,* October 2000; "Shadow and Substance," *Washington Times,* August 13, 1990; Howard Fineman, "The Bush Family Franchise," *Newsweek,* July 4, 1994; Bud Kennedy, "The Strange Death of Bin Laden's Brother in Texas," *Fort Worth Star-Telegram,* September 27, 2001; Julia Reed, "Lone Star Stars," *Vogue,* February 1999; Nicholas D. Kristoff, "For Bush, Thrill Was in Father's Chase," *New York Times,* August 29, 2000; Jeffrey H. Birnbaum, "The Man Who Could Be President," *Fortune,* March 29, 1999; Paul Burka, "Laura Bush Is Her Husband's Secret Weapon," *Texas Monthly,* April 2001; Sam Howe Verhovek, "Is There Room on a Republican Ticket for Another Bush?" *The New York Times Magazine,* September 13, 1998; "Here Comes the Son," New York *Daily News,* July 30, 2000; Brian Blomquist and Vincent Morris, "Laura Shines in the GOP Spotlight," *New York Post,* August 1, 2000; Steve Brodner, "Dubya!" *Esquire,* October 1998; Eric Pooley, "How George Got His Groove," *Time,* June 21, 1999; Patricia Kilday Hart, "Austin Power," *Redbook,* August 1999; "What Laura Wants," *Austin American-Statesman,* April 18, 1999; Nina Burleigh, "A New Life for Laura Bush," *Us Weekly,* October 15, 2001; Andrew Phillips, "The Bush Bandwagon," *Maclean's,* July 12, 1999; Julia Reed, "First in Command," *Vogue,* June 2001; Michael Duffy and Nancy Gibbs, "The Quiet Dynasty," *Time,* August 2000; Glenna Whitley, "George & Laura, Love & Marriage," *Ladies' Home Journal,* February 2002; Lloyd Grove, "Mrs. Bush Goes to Washington," *Harper's Bazaar,* June 2001; Ed Todd, "President? Young George W. Bush Just Wanted to Play Baseball," Midland *Reporter-Telegram,* July 2000; Sandra Sobieraj, "Bush Says Bye to Hometown," *USA Today,* January 18, 2001; James Barnes, "The Un-Hillary," *National Journal,* April 28,

2001; "From Party Boy to Party Leader," *Fort Worth Star-Telegram,* November 29, 1998; Julia Reed, "The Calm Amid the Storm," *Newsweek,* November 22, 1999; Ellen Levine, "We're Going to Be Okay," *Good Housekeeping,* January 2002; "The Teaching of Laura Bush," *Readers Digest,* January 2002; Frank Bruni, *Ambling into History* (New York: HarperCollins, 2002); Laurence McQuillan and Judy Keen, "Texas White House a Refuge from Stress," *USA Today,* April 13, 2001; Pete Slover, "I Was Young and Irresponsible," *Dallas Morning News,* November 15, 1998; Samantha Miller, "What a Difference a Year Makes," *People,* January 21, 2002; Marjorie Miller, "World Press Tries to Unknot Tale of Bush and the Pretzel," *Los Angeles Times,* January 16, 2002; Elisabeth Bumiller, "Out of Lamb Chop Pan and into Fire," *New York Times,* June 10, 2002; Ann Gerhart, "Learning to Read Laura Bush," *Washington Post,* March 22, 2001; David Jackson, "Life After Attacks Is 'More Precious,' First Lady Says," *Dallas Morning News,* November 11, 2001; Christopher Buckley, "War and Destiny: The White House in Wartime," *Vanity Fair,* February 2002.

BIBLIOGRAPHY

Brady, John. *Bad Boy: The Life and Politics of Lee Atwater.* New York: Addison-Wesley, 1997.

Bruni, Frank. *Ambling into History.* New York: HarperCollins, 2002.

Bush, Barbara. *Barbara Bush: A Memoir.* New York: Lisa Drew Books/ Charles Scribner's Sons, 1994.

Bush, George, with Victor Gold. *Looking Forward: An Autobiography.* New York: Bantam, 1988.

———. *A Charge to Keep.* New York: William Morrow, 2001.

———, with Doug Wead. *Man of Integrity.* Eugene, Ore.: Harvest House, 1988.

———. *Our Mission and Our Moment: President George W. Bush's Address to the Nation Before a Joint Session of Congress September 20, 2001.* New York: Newmarket Press, 2001.

Cassini, Oleg. *In My Own Fashion: An Autobiography.* New York: Simon & Schuster, 1987.

Cramer, Richard Ben. *What It Takes.* New York: Vintage, 1993.

Felix, Antonia. *Laura: America's First Lady, First Mother.* Avon, Mass.: Adams Media, 2002.

Germond, Jack W., and Jules Witcover. *Mad as Hell: Revolt at the Ballot Box, 1992.* New York: Warner Books, 1993.

Gitlin, Todd. *The Sixties: Years of Hope, Days of Rage.* New York: Bantam, 1987.

Goldman, Peter, and Tom Mathews. *Quest for the Presidency.* New York: Touchstone, 1989.

Green, Fitzhugh. *George Bush: An Intimate Portrait.* New York: Hippocrene, 1989.

Grimes, Ann. *Running Mates: The Making of a First Lady.* New York: William Morrow, 1990.

Hatfield, J. H. *Fortunate Son: George Bush and the Making of an American President.* New York: Soft Skull Press, 2001.

Helgesen, Sally. *Wildcatters: A Story of Texans, Oil, and Money.* New York: Doubleday, 1981.

Hyams, Joe. *Flight of the Avenger: George Bush at War.* New York: Harcourt, 1991.

Ivins, Molly, and Lou Dubose. *Shrub.* New York: Vintage, 2000.

Matalin, Mary, and James Carville. *All's Fair.* New York: Random House and Simon & Schuster, 1994.

Minutaglio, Bill. *First Son: George W. Bush and the Bush Family Dynasty.* New York: Three Rivers Press, 2001.

Parmet, Herbert. *George Bush: The Life of a Lone Star Yankee.* New York: Scribner's, 1997.

Radcliffe, Donnie. *Simply Barbara Bush.* New York: Warner Books, 1989.

Tierney, Gene, with Mickey Herskowitz. *Self-Portrait.* New York: Simon & Schuster, 1979.

Woodward, Bob. *Shadow: Five Presidents and the Legacy of Watergate.* New York: Simon & Schuster, 1999.

INDEX